Praise for *Philosophy of the United States*

"With unusual scope and clarity, Anderson explores key moments in the development of Western civilization and the distinctively American qualities it presently embodies. With penetrating insight and constructive criticism, the book charts a course that the United States is well advised to follow if it is to live out the best meanings of its creed."
—John K. Roth, Edward J. Sexton Professor of Philosophy and Director, The Center for the Study of the Holocaust, Genocide, and Human Rights, Claremont McKenna College

"...an informative and challenging book on the relationship between religion, philosophy, and government that discusses all the right issues about which we should think and debate."
—Morton A. Kaplan, Distinguished Professor of Political Science Emeritus, University of Chicago and publisher of *The World & I*

"…a most timely call for the reassessment and streamlining of the workings of America's system of justice, which has been increasingly questioned and maligned in recent times. As former counsel to the U.S. Senate Judiciary Committee, a constitutional and criminal lawyer, and an advisor to the Haitian, Philippine, South African and several other constitutional drafters, I have found few concise analyses and explications of this country's legal and constitutional machinery to share with those seeking to draw inspiration from the United States experience. Anderson's book clearly presents and outlines the fundamental questions that must be addressed by any constitutional democracy in the twenty-first century. If democracy is not only to survive but is to flourish it is incumbent upon citizens of all nations to understand the issues which Anderson articulates and advances so very well."
— Nicholas N. Kittrie, University Professor, Washington College of Law and author, *The Future of Peace in the Twenty-First Century*

"…provides a clear understanding of the legitimate use of political power. As a former military commander, political advisor, and professor of United States history, I am impressed with the way Anderson discusses our founding fathers' understanding of human nature. This is important in developing a US foreign pol

D1205714

world leadership. It is imperative that contemporary Americans grapple with the issues he discusses. Any citizen who wants to vote with a broad view of the challenges we face should read this book. It is a call for action"

—Col. Buford Johnson (ret.), professor of political history, and senior policy advisor to the Independence Party of Minnesota

"Students, scholars, and lay readers will come away with a new understanding of historical parallels and of the relevance of considering the past for shaping our future. Given the events of September 11, 2001 and the political, economic, and military responses to those events by the government of the United States, I think this is a very important book."

—Bryan Hilliard, Department of Philosophy, New England College and author of *The United States Supreme Court and Medical Ethics*

"Perhaps the most valuable features are the comparative analyses of Babylon, Rome and the United States, and the useful incorporation of many relevant historical details into its narrative..."

—Patrick Hayden, Lecturer in Political Theory, Victoria University, Wellington, New Zealand

"Americans in general are lost in terms of where this country came from and what it is about. I was particularly interested in the sections on financial power and globalization which show that Americans have often viewed corporations naively, with critics underestimating their potential for good and supporters ignoring their potential for harm, and often misrepresenting the philosophy of Adam Smith. Anderson provides a non-partisan and balanced framework for understanding the issues the United States faces."

—Kenneth R. Gray, Associate Professor of International Management, Florida A&M University

"...answers a newly recognized need to understand the role of the United States in the modern world. America must discover a new recognition of itself, as its old self-image disappears. Oceans are no longer enough to keep the world's violent problems from our doors. The world we live in today cries for a reassessment of our founding principles. *The Philosophy of the United States* does this."

—Frederick Sontag, Department of Philosophy, Pomona College, and author of *The American Religious Experience: The Roots, Trends and Future of Theology*

PARAGON ISSUES IN PHILOSOPHY

PARAGON ISSUES IN PHILOSOPHY

THE PARAGON ISSUES
IN PHILOSOPHY SERIES

A t colleges and universities, interest in the traditional areas of philosophy remains strong. Many new currents flow within them, too, but until recently many of these—the rise of cognitive science, for example, or feminist philosophy— went largely unnoticed in undergraduate philosophy courses. The Paragon Issues in Philosophy Series responds to both perennial and newly influential concerns by bringing together a team of able philosophers to address the fundamental issues in philosophy today and to outline the state of contemporary discussion about them.

More than twenty volumes are scheduled; they are organized into three major categories. The first covers the standard topics—metaphysics, theory of knowledge, ethics, and political philosophy—stressing innovative developments in those disciplines. The second focuses on more specialized but still vital concerns in the philosophies of science, religion, history, sport, and other areas. The third category explores new work that relates philosophy to fields such as feminist criticism, medicine, economics, technology, and literature.

The level of writing is aimed at undergraduate students who have little previous experience studying philosophy. The books provide brief but accurate introductions that appraise the state of the art in their fields and show how the history of thought about their topics has developed. Each volume is complete in itself but also complements others in the series.

Traumatic change characterized the twentieth century and the twenty-first will be no different in that regard. All of its pivotal issues will involve philosophical questions. As the editors at Paragon House continue to work with us, we hope that this series will help to encourage the understanding needed in a new millennium whose times will be as complicated and problematic as they are promising.

John K. Roth   Frederick Sontag
Claremont McKenna College   Pomona College

GORDON L. ANDERSON

PHILOSOPHY
OF THE
UNITED STATES

Life, Liberty, and the
Pursuit of Happiness

PARAGON HOUSE ✦ ST. PAUL

First Edition 2004

Published in the United States by
Paragon House
2285 University Avenue West
St. Paul, MN 55114

Library of Congress Cataloging-in-Publication Data

Anderson, Gordon L. (Gordon Louis), 1947-
  Philosophy of the United States : life, liberty, and the pursuit of happiness / Gordon L. Anderson.
    p. cm.
  Includes bibliographical references and index.
  ISBN 1-55778-844-8 (pbk. : alk. paper)
  1. United States--Politics and government--Philosophy. 2. Legitimacy of governments--United States. 3. Political culture--United States. 4. Social values--United States. I. Title.

JK31.A535 2004
320.973'01--dc22
                              2004009352

The paper used in this publication meets the minimum requirements of American National Standard for Information Sciences—Permanence of Paper for Printed Library Materials, ANSIZ39.48-1984.

Manufactured in the United States of America
10 9 8 7 6 5 4 3 2 1

For current information about all releases from Paragon House,
visit the web site at http://www.paragonhouse.com

For Mary Jane
Tami, Jayna, Greta, and Evan

Acknowledgements

This book is a reflection of my thoughts on the United States as a citizen and a philosopher. However, this could not have taken place without the assistance of a number of people with whom I have discussed these subjects, and who have made it possible to discuss these subjects. I wish to thank the United States government and the Unification Theological Seminary, whose scholarships made it possible to study philosophy of religion, ethics, and politics at Union Theological Seminary in New York and the Claremont Graduate University in California. Friends and colleagues who inspired me with intelligent discussion and debate on issues as I prepared this book, particularly members of the Professors World Peace Academy, the Minnesota Independent Scholars Forum, and the Association of Private Enterprise Education. Thanks are due the series editors, John K. Roth and Frederick Sontag for their guidance and support. Thanks to those who proofread the manuscript and made valuable suggestions, including Morton A. Kaplan, Bryan Hilliard, Patrick Hayden, John White, Kenneth Gray, Eunice Anderson, Buford Johnson, Walter Klaus, and Fred Stitt. Thanks also to Cynthia McLoughlin for copyediting the manuscript and preparing an index, to Rosemary Yokoi at Paragon House, who steered the book through the editorial process to completion. Finally, a special thanks goes to my wife, Mary Jane, and my children, who endured my hours of commitment to this project.

Contents

Introduction

1158 B.C., 410 A.D., September 11, 2001

The United States was shocked on September 11, 2001, when terrorists flew commercial airliners, filled with innocent passengers going about their business, into the towers of the World Trade Center in New York and the Pentagon in Arlington, Virginia. For most people it was an unexpected violation of the freedom and security they had grown to expect. It was an invasion of the world's sole superpower, aimed at the heart of its national symbols. How could this take place?

How could this take place? That was the question asked by Babylonians in 1158 B.C. when a massive invasion of Babylon by Elamite troops under the leadership of Shutruk-Nahhunte I destroyed the great Babylonian cities and plundered them, taking statues of the Babylonian gods and the stele with Hammurabi's Law Code.[1] It was also the question asked by Romans when, in 410 A.D., Alaric, king of the Visigoths, marched into Rome with his Army and pillaged for three days, leaving behind a mass of corpses and ruins.

To many Romans, the otherworldliness of the Christian religion, which had become the official religion of the Empire, was to blame. When asked how he could still profess Christianity after the sack of Rome, Augustine, the influential Bishop of Hippo, replied unexpectedly that the pagan Romans had already preached the same virtues for which Christians were being blamed. It was not Christianity that brought ruin to the Empire, but vices within the Empire itself. Christianity, he argued, had two goals: to save human society and to build up a society that would be divine. By pursuing the second goal, Christianity would automatically achieve the first.[2] Augustine set about to correct all of the blasphemies, rumors, and errors spreading through the Empire in 413 A.D. by writing his book, *The City of God.*

His book turned out to be more than a defense of Christianity, it was his history of the work of God in the world and a political and social philosophy. Augustine accepted the Roman notion that justice was the foundation of human society, and he affirmed Cicero's idea that the true Rome had ceased to exist when its justice ceased. He argued that the traditional virtues and justice of Rome were the basis of an authentic temporal society, but that a true society, one of lasting peace, had to be infused with the love of God. Augustine wrote about two types of love, love of God and love of the world, or put another way, love of higher goals or pursuit of selfish interests.[3]

The sack of Rome was a wake-up call. It was a time to reflect on what had made the Empire successful, how it had drifted off course, and how it could be guided toward a peaceful and prosperous future. September 11, 2001 was a wake-up call for the United States. The first reaction of most Americans was to blame the terrorists who had orchestrated the strike. Americans also expressed great patriotism and love for the United States. However, we should ask, as Augustine did, whether there was something that had changed in the United States that had allowed or encouraged such a strike to take place.

In his *New York Times* bestseller, *Breakdown: The Failure of American Intelligence to Defeat Global Terror,* Bill Gertz argued that, if the people in the United States government had been doing their jobs well, the September 11 attacks would probably have been thwarted.[4] He argued that cumbersome bureaucracy, departmental infighting, selfishness, incompetence, and general malaise characterized intelligence institutions that had been much sharper during the cold war period. Such widespread problems in government agencies are a symptom of a wider failure within the entire society.

The United States was founded on principles of justice that, like those of ancient Rome, enjoyed wide respect before their decline. Is there a parallel to Rome in the United States? Is there an inconsistency in foreign policy and hypocrisy between the rhetoric and the reality of the uses to which United States power is put? Is there any truth to the claim by critics that the United States is morally degenerate and a bad influence on other cultures?

Today Americans, like the Romans of Augustine's day, need to reflect on the purpose of their nation and the changes it has undergone since it was founded. This book is an attempt to reflect on the political philosophy of the nation—its strengths and weaknesses—and to consider whether that philosophy can be reclaimed and reshaped to guide us into a promising future.

Challenges to the Foundation of the United States

The United States of America owes its prosperity to a unique set of historical circumstances. These include: (a) inheriting the values of Western civilization and the Protestant Reformation; (b) a large amount of land available for a low price or free to homesteaders; (c) a unique system of government set up by its founding fathers; and (d) a population of strong, self-sufficient immigrants who saw the United States as a land of opportunity.

These foundation stones of the United States have changed or eroded greatly since 1789. Other social conditions have been introduced that strain or create new challenges to the American experiment. The founding fathers did not anticipate all of the developments of the last two hundred years, or institute necessary legal principles to address them. Since their day, new forms of unchecked power have arisen. Further, many of the principles that they put in place have been eroded by time, ignorance, and selfishness. If the United States continues on its present course it will decline and collapse. There are many parallels between the United States and other empires from which lessons can be drawn.

The inherited values of Western civilization have been challenged by cultural pluralism, especially with the immigration of large groups of immigrants from non-Western societies. Advances by science have called into question the worldview of the eighteenth century. Modern secularists believe that the religious symbols of the United States should be ejected. Hedonists, and those who earn a healthy profit from selling the vices that traditional society has condemned, mock traditional values. And large numbers of people, who never learned these values from their parents, churches, or schools make up the voting population.

Most early Americans were farmers or could homestead land and make a living if they had no other business. But farmland has not been available for homesteading since the 1920s. Today if one owns a farm, a life like the subsistence farming of the nineteenth century is neither desired nor possible. Whereas early settlers were happy with the fruits of the land and homemade clothing and crafts, today people want goods and services like cars, televisions, and computers. Large industrial farms have made it impossible for family farmers to compete in the marketplace. Much of the land is taxed at a rate that a farmer cannot afford to pay out of the small profits he might make.

The system of government set up by our founders assumed that most citizens would either be farmers or run family shops in small towns. They did not anticipate large-scale industry, corporate political lobbies, or economic globalization. They did not anticipate cars, television, computers or airplanes. They assumed citizens would be able to educate their children to be good citizens without the help of the government. They did not expect the federal government would be involved in social welfare. They established checks and balances on power, some of which have been undermined by the institutions they created. Other developments have led to new concentrations of power they did not expect.

The original population of strong, self-sufficient immigrants has been diluted with descendants that have never known hardship and immigrants from cultural backgrounds that did not promote an ethic of achievement.

The general unity of "one nation under God" despite religious affiliation has been broken apart by "culture wars." There is a growing movement among secularists and the courts to remove the word "God" from money, from public statements, and from public displays. There are people who seek a strong welfare state rather than self-reliant citizens.

Many of the challenges faced by the United States—and the world—stem from science and technology that enables people to travel quickly, communicate quickly, and live longer. Much of this technology was developed in the United States and is a byproduct of the freedom that the founders established. Political and economic freedom, coupled with economic competition and the general desire of citizens to improve their lives, stimulated great technological development and massive accumulations of capital in the last two hundred years. While these developments provided great opportunities for a more comfortable life and a more efficient operation of the nation-state, they also have led to new issues stemming from the growth of large multi-national corporations that were unexpected by the founders of the United States.

Globalization, expanded by technological development and multinational institutions, has changed the position of the United States in the world. The United States is no longer a remote nation, accessible only by a long dangerous ocean voyage. It is no longer a nation whose economy is self-contained, without economic interests in other nations.

The United States no longer ventures to war only when it feels a military invasion is imminent but, as the world's sole superpower, it feels compelled to use that power to keep the rest of the world from war. It feels a moral obligation to help those less fortunate. But there is also a temptation to use the vast power of the United States for less than noble goals: to acquire resources for American corporations, to exact revenge against real or imagined enemies, or to use as a club to extort something from others.

The system of justice in the United States, designed to treat all people as equals, to defend the rights of the poor and the innocent, and to provide the freedom to pursue one's own livelihood without the interference of evil or unscrupulous people, is increasingly believed to protect the interests of the rich and powerful. The system of laws, originally thought to be a reflection of higher laws of the universe, is often derisively viewed as a human creation designed by the collusion of lawmakers and interest groups to redistribute resources from hard-working taxpayers to social dependents and thieves in high places. The legitimacy of the law is being severely tested.

Today, neither Republicans nor Democrats are addressing these issues in a coherent way, based on a sound political philosophy. When the parties were formed, Democrats were more agrarian and populist, Republicans were more industrial and preferred a representative form of government. Both parties represented responsible and achievement-oriented people who were actively pursuing their dreams and neither party sought a welfare state. As agriculture was replaced by industry, Democrats came to represent laborers and unions, then other minority and disenfranchised groups. As the Democrats advocated social welfare, business owners, producers, and many wage earners lined up on the Republican side.

Today the political parties are more about money than philosophy. The majority of Democratic voters have an interest in the redistribution of wealth from the rich to the poor, many are on government payrolls or recipients of welfare. Republicans tend to be defenders of the producers of goods and services, arguing that redistribution destroys the economy. However, many of the profits they defend are obtained as a result of noncompetitive practices and governmental favoritism. When politics degenerates to a fight over money and is no longer addressing the major issues which the country faces based on sound and coherent philosophy, the society is rudderless. The nation is like a ship carrying gold; all the crew members are so busy fighting over the cargo that no one is steering the ship or even looking to see where it is headed.

These are some of the changes that challenge the long-term viability of the United States and its influence in the world at large. Many people feel politics in the United States has become too corrupt to give honest people a place. The political parties and the legal system, they say, are controlled by a few elites that have the economic and legal resources to control everyone else's destiny. Many people feel that, despite corruption in the system, it will continue to carry us forward the next two hundred years as it did the last. This is not the case.

The brief outline of changes listed above should be cause enough for the reader to understand the system will not continue forward uninterrupted without a guiding light at the helm and a steady hand on the rudder. An understanding of the rise and fall of other mighty nations and empires, as is discussed in Part I, should further drive this point home.

The Need for Reflection and Leadership

One purpose of this book is to provide a general understanding of the philosophical underpinnings of the design for the government of the United States of America. This will not be done by presenting detailed studies of the entire philosophies of our predecessors, but by focusing and elaborating on those points essential for the working and continuation of the American experiment. Each of the political philosophers that contributed to the collective thought of Western civilization was stimulated by challenges that arose in his own day.

Human civilization is an evolving process that, to advance, must heed the lessons learned in the past as well as develop solutions to pressing issues of the present. Good leadership involves knowledge of the past, the ability to accurately identify the issues of the present, to find solutions, and to execute them. Good leadership is required to keep social evolution moving forward. Good leaders require a climate in which they are able to acquire positions in government without being squelched by dominating elites. In a democracy, citizens need enough knowledge about basic political principles to vote for policies that will improve society rather than tear it apart.

The United States today stands in a position in the world similar to that of Rome at the height of its expansion. The early Roman Republic, based on laws respected by rich and poor alike, found that nations around it capitulated willingly, because doing so provided them a better and more just society than what they had experienced under the arbitrary whims of kings and dictators. However, the legitimacy of the laws of the Roman Empire was gradually undermined by changing social conditions and an accumulated body of contradictory decrees by regional governors and the Emperor.

Caesar Augustus spoke of a "natural" limit to the Roman Empire based on geography—that England and the Germanic areas were beyond a natural affinity to the Roman way of life. However, it is more likely that the limits were not set by cultural geography, but by the fact that, by the time the boundaries of Rome had reached that distance, the benefits of joining the Empire were less attractive. Arbitrary use of force, unjust taxation, and large disparities of wealth overshadowed the justice known in earlier times.

Likewise, the so-called "clash of civilizations" that Western civilization faces in the Middle East today is not so much an inevitable clash between Christian and Islamic faiths as is it an expression of inconsistency between the principles upon which the United States was founded and professes, and the policies it actually pursues—including apparently arbitrary expressions of power, inconsistent foreign policy, and hypocrisy. In recent times, the United States has been unable to articulate a unified and consistent political philosophy that legitimizes its legal system and its foreign policy.

Outline of the Book

Part I of this book "A Tale of Two Empires" looks at the rise and fall of two empires that gave birth to our present world, Babylon and Rome. Features of these societies that allowed them to grow and prosper are examined. What systems of justice were viewed as legitimate by their inhabitants, rich and poor? What conditions allowed people to freely pursue their economic and cultural activities? Why was very little police power required to keep order? In its early stages, each commanded the respect and admiration of other peoples and nations. As each empire aged, abuse of the law and corruption of power led to a decline in the legitimacy of the government, rising discontent, and increased need for police to keep social order. In the later stages, each became feared for its arbitrary use of power.

The decline of each empire led to the rise of reform movements aimed at rescuing the basic civilization by purifying the moral behavior of the citizens and the laws of the society. Judaism and Christianity represent spiritual impulses aimed at reform of Babylonian and Roman civilizations respectively.

The last chapter of Part I looks at developments in political theory and culture in the West after the collapse of the Roman Empire and how these developments set the stage for the political philosophy of the founders of the United States. This section concludes with some reflection on the relationship of love, power, and justice to prepare the reader for better understanding of the unique relation between religion and society in early America and the concerns with power that preoccupied the minds of the founders.

The founding fathers knew much more about the history, philosophy, and governments of Western civilization than we can outline here. But today, Americans graduate from high school and college with little understanding of that history, and therefore little understanding of the reasons the United States Constitution was written as it was. As Cicero told the ancient Romans, and as the philosopher Santyana has said more recently, "He who does not understand history is doomed to repeat it."

In Part II, the founding of the United States is discussed. Chapter 4 is on the relationship of God, religion and the state, a relationship that people today seldom understand the way the founders did. The United States, to the extent that its government is legitimized by reference to God, is more like the Babylonian Empire than the social contracts at the foundation of the Roman Empire. It is important for people today to understand that the founding fathers spoke of "general religion" and "particular religion." General religion corresponds to the "self-evident truths" referred to in the Declaration of Independence, not to "established religion." There was a clear distinction in the minds of Benjamin Franklin and Thomas Jefferson between those transcendent truths that could be grasped by reason and those opinions about God that could only be held by faith.

Chapter 5 discusses the formation of the government of the United States of America itself, the Constitutional Convention, the Bill of Rights, and the general political philosophy of the founders.

Part III is devoted to issues that have arisen to challenge the United States because they were either not addressed by the Constitution or changing social conditions and opinions of the American people have brought about changes in the government, some in the form of amendments to the Constitution, others in the form of legislation, others in the outlook of the general culture.

Chapter 6 examines checks and balances on power and areas in which the checks and balances designed by the founders have been circumvented or abused. Chapter 7 is a look at the issue of financial power, especially that of banks and corporations. The founding fathers did not believe in corporations as they exist today, yet in 1886 a Supreme Court ruling gave them the status of "persons" protected by the Bill of Rights. How did such a dramatic change take place?

Chapter 8 looks at the area of education, something mostly done by parents and private tutors at the time the United States was founded. How did we end up with the federal government, an entity designed as an umbrella government for the states, getting involved in public education? Why did education shift its focus from the development of character to the development of technical skills and how has this affected our political life?

Social welfare is the subject of chapter 9. It looks at the history of the federal government's involvement with social welfare, a concept foreign to the founders' idea of the nation. The chapter looks at the extent to which the United States government should act as a safety net for people who are not self-sufficient.

If "life" is as important as "liberty" and "happiness," then the government itself should be subjected to a test, like medical doctors, about how well they adhere to the Hippocratic oath. At the time of the founding, there was no place for government in health care. However, mandatory and uniform public education and medical care compromise the ability of citizens to pursue life, train and care for themselves. How can government provide a safety net without compromising the freedom and pursuit of happiness it is also supposed to foster?

Chapter 10 addresses issues related to globalization and the United States' power in the world. The founding fathers established the United States almost as an island separated from the rest of the world. Today New York and Washington can be viewed as the center of the world. This chapter points out economic challenges to the United States as a result of this development and addresses problems of foreign policy that derive from the type of government that the founders created.

Charting a Course

All these issues should be on the minds of responsible American politicians when they pass legislation and on the minds of voters when they go to the polls. These are issues the Supreme Court should more clearly understand and articulate in its decisions. And they are issues that the President, as leader of the nation and Commander-in-Chief of the armed forces, needs to show he/she understands in speech as well as action.

The media and news reporters should show they understand these issues as they frame issues for the news. The media has a role as a watchdog, not just to expose abuses of power, but to alert citizens when the nation is on a collision course or pursuing a dead end. The role of the media is not just to expose two sides of an issue if both positions would take the nation off course.

Listening to the rhetoric of politicians, public debate, and reading reports in the media today clearly sounds the alarm that there is no one at the helm; the ship has been hijacked by pirates fighting over the loot. It is floating aimlessly on a turbulent sea, easily sunk by a violent storm or pushed into rocks by a change in the wind.

It is time to turn to our analysis and map the waters in which the ship called the United States is floating so that the reader can better take part in charting a course for its future.

Part I
A Tale of Two Empires

1

The Rise of Empires on a Foundation of Justice

ANCIENT BABYLON, THE ANCIENT ROMAN REPUBLIC, and the United States of America all adopted codes of justice that were viewed as fair and worthy of respect by those they were designed to govern. These were the Code of Hammurabi (c. 1792 B.C.), the Twelve Tables (c. 455 B.C.), and the Constitution of the United States (1789 A.D.). On their respective foundations of justice, each of these societies prospered and expanded. During their expansion, each of these societies enjoyed the respect of people in neighboring countries. As a result, influence and annexation were relatively easy because inhabitants envied the life of a citizen of the empire. Living freely under the rule of law was preferred to an unpredictable life under kings, tyrants, and dictators who ruled as they wished with arbitrary force.

It is relatively easy to maintain order when a society's laws are accepted as legitimate by nearly all the citizens. They police themselves by reminding their own family members and neighbors what is right. In such societies there is no popular basis for mass unrest, revolution, or guerilla warfare. Under these regimes, citizens who obey the law and pay taxes they feel are just, are free to the farm their land and sell their goods and services in an environment that is secure. These are conditions of peace and stability that allowed the citizens of these three societies to generate and accumulate great prosperity and wealth as a result of their own labor.

A brief overview of the foundations of justice in Babylonia and Rome will help set the stage for the discussion of the philosophy of the United States.

Babylon

> The great gods have called me. I am the salvation-bearing shepherd, whose staff is straight, the good shadow that is spread over my city. On my breast I cherish the inhabitants of the land of Sumer and Akkad. In my shelter I have let them repose in peace. In my deep wisdom have I enclosed them. That the strong might not injure the weak, in order to protect the widows and orphans, I have in Babylon the city where Anu and Bel raise high their head, in E-Sagil, the Temple, whose foundations stand firm as heaven and earth, in order to bespeak justice in the land, to settle all disputes, and heal all injuries, set up these my precious words, written upon my memorial stone, before the image of me, as king of righteousness.
>
> —Hammurabi, Epilogue to the Hammurabi Code

The Code of Hammurabi

Hammurabi is the first known ruler to implement a highly successful Code of Law. His reign is usually put from c. 1792-1750 B.C. Hammurabi incorporated elements of the laws of the Sumerians, Akkadians, and Semites who preceded him. While the city of Babylon was founded several generations before him, the Babylonian civilization was raised to a high point during the reigns of Hammurabi and his son Samsu-iluna (c. 1750-1712 B.C.). It endured, with ups and downs, for about 1250 years until Cyrus of Persia absorbed it into the Persian Empire in 539 B.C.

H m mu bi's Code has been preserved on an eight-foot-high stone monolith that was uncovered in Susa in the Persian mountains by French archeologists in 1901. It is thought that it was carted off as a prize by the Elamites in their sack of Babylon in 1158 B.C. Today the monolith stands in the Louvre in Paris.

There are four significant concepts contained in the code:

1. Equal legal protection to all citizens, peasants as well as nobles. This includes protection of the person as well as property.

2. That the state, not some other delegated group, was responsible for enforcement of the law.

3. That justice is for all people. It defends the oppressed and specifically mentions widows and orphans that cannot provide for themselves.

4. The basic principle was equal justice—"an eye for an eye."

While Hammurabi was an able military commander and political administrator, he did not take credit for the Code. The source of the legitimacy of the Code he attributed to the supernatural Lord Marduk, son of Ea, the God of Righteousness.[1] On the stone, Hammurabi explains that he was called, because he feared God,

> to bring about the rule of righteousness in the land, to destroy the wicked and the evil-doers; so that the strong should not harm the weak; so that I should rule over the black-headed people like Shamash, and enlighten the land, to further the well-being of mankind.

Although Hammurabi claimed a supernatural basis for the legitimacy of his Code and his righteous rule, in addition, he apparently obeyed his code and saw to just enforcement of it for rich and poor. He led by example. He demanded strict compliance from others who governed. The upper classes and those in responsible positions were often more severely punished than the common freeman. It was a code of behavior that the people could memorize. The 282 sections of the code covered murder, adultery, agriculture, business, and nearly any other activity that could lead to disputes and violence. Hammurabi called himself a "salvation-bearing shepherd" who cherished the inhabitants of the land.

Many elements of the Code of Hammurabi would seem harsh or unacceptable to cultural standards of today. However, it was equal justice. And there was a greater emphasis on the rights of the poor and the care of the helpless than had existed in preceding societies. Property rights and contracts were vigorously enforced. Capital punishment was common and was a strong deterrent to crime. Slavery existed, and women and children could be sold into slavery by husbands to pay debt. However, they still had a claim on the inheritance of the man at his death. When a woman slave had children by a master, she was free upon his death. Monogamy was a legal rule. Children could lose their hand for striking their father. Slaves were treated liberally by standards at the time and were frequently emancipated. It was indeed a different culture from the United States today.

Social Organization

The family was the primary social institution, and the success of a family, by its very nature, is determined by its ability to train the children to become responsible adults. The family, with its intimate relations rooted in love, has the ability to surpass mere rational justice or equality and to look after the actual needs and nourish the unique skills of each of its members, potentially creating productive citizens.

In ancient Babylon, the families and communities were the source of love. The Babylonian "religion" referred to those activities and beliefs related to the cycles and powers of nature—the forces behind human existence. It was not a separate institution of culture. The word religion did not exist. What we call religion was their cultural worldview and activities related to it. The term *religion* was to be coined later by the Romans. Festivals were associated with planting and harvest and various "gods" or supernatural beings were thought to assist the fertility of the soil. Each family and clan developed its own practices. Family deities were important. Each family patriarch entered into a covenant with the family's personal deity or god. While families could be fiercely loyal to their gods, their gods descended from the father of gods, El,[2] the father sky God, too distant for communication with mortals.

There were community and city gods as well. Every community had a temple, and larger communities had major and minor temples. These temples served some of the functions of today's city halls. They were not only places for public ceremonies, but provided a form of social security. They owned fields on which displaced people, often in families, could work for food and shelter. Temples also sheltered the handicapped. After a blessing from the priest, people who had no food were allowed to share the food that came from the table set for the god of the temple.[3]

These religious practices were not generally considered a threat to political society, but an integral part of it. The pantheon of gods above reflected the components of society below. The gods were a reminder to human beings that they lived for a higher purpose. One's duty to the gods fostered a consciousness of public purpose and provided a philosophical framework for citizens to orient their life activities.

Hammurabi's Leadership

Hammurabi was intimately involved in his administration. He paid attention to minor details. He did not oppress or unduly tax citizens. He rebuilt temples that were destroyed by fighting as his military subdued surrounding territories, earning him the loyal support of priests. He made sure people that had been uprooted or lost their jobs were cared for and re-employed.[4] Taxes were used to build irrigation systems and infrastructure. Babylon was a center of engineering feats and the development of ancient mathematics and building trades. Craftsmen were organized into guilds.[5] Citizens could feel protected under his rule as long as they obeyed the laws. They could invest themselves in their work and know that the fruit of their labors would be safe.

The ancient Babylonians did not mint coins, but weighed gold and silver ingots and other objects, such as rings, and even barley and other perishables, as payment for labor. There were accumulations of capital among businessmen who loaned "money" for interest—often at rates of 20 to 30 percent. This capital was put to work in building and other enterprises. Dyed cloth, copper pots for cooking, and luxury furniture were among their exports. Excavations of the homes of businessmen and professionals of Old Babylon reveal a life much like that of the middle classes of today. They reveal internal courtyards and bitumen-lined, terracotta-paved toilets and bathrooms.[6]

Over the next several hundred years, Babylon suffered many ups and downs as various armies vied for control of the Fertile Crescent. However, Marduk remained the god of Babylon and the Code of Hammurabi had made a lasting impact on the civilization. Nebuchadrezzar I (1125-1103 B.C.) and Nebuchadrezzar II the Great (605-562 B.C.) were both known for great periods of building and claimed Hammurabi as their founder. Most famous is the artificial mountain known as the ziggurat. The ziggurat in Babylon was called é-temen-an-ki (House of the foundation of Heaven and Earth). It was built several centuries after Hammurabi. It was a terraced and brick-covered temple tower with outside steps; it was solid inside, with no rooms. It was surrounded by massive walls with strong towers and gates guarded by statues of giant human-headed bulls.[7] Priests would ascend to the top to be closer to the gods when they performed sacred ceremonies. Ziggurats were built in central areas surrounded by commercial activity.

There is a passage in the book of Genesis about the building taking place in the middle Babylonian empire:

> And the LORD came down to see the city and the tower, which the children of men builded.

> And the LORD said, Behold, the people [is] one, and they have all one language; and this they begin to do: and now nothing will be restrained from them, which they have imagined to do. [8]

A nomadic goat-herder or simple farmer must have looked upon the wealth and the technological achievements of ancient Babylon with wonder. Most Babylonians were undoubtedly proud of their accomplishments, but like the machine-wrecking Luddites of the nineteenth century, who feared machines were taking human jobs, this biblical writer was afraid that traditional life in Mesopotamia was being destroyed by the Babylonians. By contrast, the Greek historian Herodotus described the hanging gardens of ancient Babylon as one of the wonders of the ancient world. The stone masons of the Middle Ages and the Freemasons of our time trace their early roots to the construction guilds of ancient Babylon.

Ancient Babylon is a cradle of civilization that cross-fertilized and influenced the ancient Greeks and Romans who learned from them. The Babylonians learned and taught principles of political philosophy that allowed large numbers of people to live together peacefully, basically pursuing their own livelihood under the protection of a system of justice and a political regime that had the well-being of the entire society at heart. It was a prescription for prosperity in the ancient world.

Ancient Rome

> If a man were called to fix the period in the history of the
> world during which the condition of the human race was
> most happy and prosperous, he would, without hesitation,
> name that time which elapsed from the death of Domitian
> to the accession of Commodus. (96–180 A.D.)
>
> —Historian Edward Gibbon, 1776

The Roman Empire, like the Babylonian Empire, arose on the
foundation of its system of justice. The history of Rome begins
with legends of Romulus, the first of seven kings, who settled on
Palatine Mount, one of the Rome's seven hills, in 753 B.C. Legends refer to the god Mars as his father, and to his murder of his
twin brother, Remus, who mocked his building of a walled fortress. Archeology of the ancient site dates the most ancient walls
to the same time period as the legends recounted by the Roman
historian Titus Livius (Livy) in his *History of Rome*,[9] a classical text
which has been required reading for nobles, aristocrats, and politicians in the West ever since. Another version of Rome's founding
is contained in a fragment of writing by Stesichorus, a Graeco-
Sicilian poet (638-555 B.C.) that suggests Rome was named after
a Trojan woman called Roma,[10] who, with her Trojan fleet, fled
the war-torn city of Troy and found a beautiful place to stay.

Regardless of its original founding, the famed Roman system
of justice developed later. Livy describes how, in 510 B.C., the
wife of a Roman nobleman was raped by Sextus, the son of king
Tarquinius Superbus.[11] This led to a revolt against the kings by
the aristocracy, or *patricians,* and the beginning of the Roman
Republic, headed by two praetors, later called consuls.

A Social Contract

The power of the Republic originally lay with about fifty noble-
men from a few prominent families. In 501 B.C. they appointed

a dictator. As the largest and most powerful city in the region (*Latium*), they became feared and warred with the forces of the other cities in the Latin League. Much of the fighting was done by non-nobles, or *plebeians*. Some of these plebeians were wealthy landowners, but most were peasants who felt the pain of economic oppression and believed they were being treated unjustly by the patricians. The plebeians organized themselves like a union to bargain with the patricians; this was called the "Conflict of Orders." In 494 B.C., upset that they were not receiving their rightful share for the work they did, the plebeians seceded from Rome in an action similar to a modern labor strike; they refused to cooperate with the patricians unless they were treated more fairly. This became an ongoing tactic used to get concessions from the patricians. In 471 B.C., the patricians recognized the legitimate plebeian right to organize and elect their officers, who were known as tribunes. However, they still had no direct part in the rule of the Republic.

The plebeians, who suffered variously under the arbitrary rule of the nobles, demanded that the rules of justice be written down in a law code which could be an objective basis for justice. In 451 B.C. the constitution of the Republic was suspended and a commission of ten patricians, the *decemviri,* was established to create a simple code of laws. According to some stories, a few of the decemviri traveled to Greece to study their laws.

After a year the decemviri produced ten tables listing laws that should govern Rome. The plebians did not think it was adequate and asked for revisions and additional laws. Some say another ten men were appointed, this time consisting of five patricians and five plebeians. Others say that the same ten men remained for two years. In either case, the second group produced two more tables of law, forming the famous Twelve Tables, which was adopted by both patricians and plebeians.

The Twelve Tables were engraved in copper and permanently displayed to public view. While by modern standards they would still be seen as biased towards the patricians, they were accepted as a legitimate code of justice by the plebeians. Many crimes were punished by the harsh sentence of death. However, arbitrary death sentences, for example declared by lenders against debtors who had not paid, were no longer allowed. Death sentences had to be issued by law courts and an appeal process was established. For murder, the law distinguished between intentional and accidental death. Public demonstration for a cause was allowed, but demonstration against a person was forbidden. Levels of punishment were harshest for slaves, milder for plebeians, and mildest for patricians.

New Roman Citizens Under Common Law

The legal alliance of patricians and plebeians led to a unified foreign policy of the Romans, and they fought side by side to expand their territory. Intermarriage began to occur. The wars led to a decrease in the number of patricians, who were commanders in battle. However, the plebeians, who did much of the fighting as soldiers, expected a share of the conquered lands and became disgruntled when they did not receive it. Wealthier plebeians had an eye on political power. In 367 B.C. these demands were accommodated with the passing of the "Licinian Rogations" which further blurred the distinctions between the two classes. The final disappearance of the legal inequity of the plebeians was legalized in the "Hortensian Law" of 287 B.C., which recognized the plebeian assembly as a constitutional legislative body (a lower house).[12]

Whereas the Babylonian system of justice had been promulgated by a wise ruler, the rise of Roman justice was accompanied by the continual devolution of power from nobles to commoners. And, whereas Babylonian law had been justified by its divine origin, Roman law evolved more as a social compact, a secular law. However, in both cases the law was viewed as legitimate by all citizens and a sense of security was felt under the protection of that justice. It was the basis for peace and prosperity.

The expansion of Rome continued. In 264 B.C. Rome controlled the entire Italian peninsula except the Po valley, which was contested by the Gauls. By 146 B.C., Rome had defeated the Gauls and the Carthigians, who controlled Greece and held Egypt as a protectorate. This expansion was aided by people who desired to be freed from the rule of Carthage or Gaul.

However, the spoils of war led some Roman armies to acquire a taste for the riches and the taxes which came with a conquest. Rome's part-time farmer soldiers were replaced by full-time soldiers who stayed in foreign territories for several years at a time, supported by "tributes" paid by the local authorities. Little police force was required to keep domestic order.[13] In most cases the citizens of "conquered lands" were happy to be rid of their dictators and proud to become citizens of the Roman republic.

The body of law that grew up around the Twelve Tables was known as *jus civile*, or civil law. The respect that earlier Roman citizens had for these laws can be grasped in the writings of Cicero (106-43 B.C.), as he nostalgically looked back to the time when they governed Rome:

> Though all the world exclaim against me, I will say what I think: that single little book of the Twelve Tables, if anyone look to the fountains and sources of laws, seems to me, assuredly, to surpass the libraries of all the philosophers, both in weight of authority, and in plenitude of utility.[14]

As the Roman republic expanded and included peoples not involved in the original legal pact between the patricians and plebeians that led to the Twelve Tables, the Romans were forced to work out a new system for administering justice in the foreign territories and for the treatment of foreigners in Rome. The laws for non-Romans developed from the edicts of the territory's praetor, or magistrate, who interpreted the laws and settled disputes. Originally, decisions were guided by the intentions of the inherited civil law, with which the magistrates had grown up, but new situations and individual differences led to many new laws being promulgated. This body of law came to be known as the *jus gentium.*

Over time, trade, intermarriage, and migration from outlying regions to Rome led to a blending of the general population. The *jus gentium* was gradually adopted for all Roman citizens. Respect for the Roman system of law was high.[15] Domestic peace and unity were high and obedience was voluntary throughout the empire. In this state of general security, leisure, and opulence developed.[16]

In its height, life in the Roman Empire was prosperous and happy, at least for those who gained the status of citizenship. Its jurisdiction had a breadth of 3,000 miles from the Atlantic Ocean to Persia and from England to the Sahara desert. The ruins of Pompey contain ruts in the stone roads several inches deep where thousands of carts driven by citizens and merchants carrying out business and personal travel testify to a vibrant daily life in a bustling city. Hundreds of houses and shops with indoor plumbing and sewage disposal created a level of civilization without parallel in the ancient world.

Pompey was only one of many flourishing cities of ancient Rome, which enabled over 120 million inhabitants to live in its territory. But, while Pompey succumbed to the natural force of the volcanic eruption of Mount Vesuvius, the rest of the Roman Empire was to succumb to human forces far different from those that gave it birth.

Every human society, regardless of how good its founding, has struggled to perpetuate itself. The continual struggle with the forces of invading armies from without and usurpation of power and justice from within have required constant vigilance and ongoing reform. No generation has been able to sit idly by and expect prosperity for all to increase. The next chapter describes the ups and downs of the Babylonian and Roman Empires.

Questions for Reflection

1. How did legitimization of the governments of Babylon and Rome differ?

2. Can you think of other ways that governments could be legitimated?

3. Apart from a code of justice, what else is necessary for a nation or empire to become prosperous?

4. Are there any lessons to be learned from the rise of the Babylonian and Roman Empires that could be applied to the United States to improve it today?

2

Maintaining the Empires of Babylon and Rome

All empires and kingdoms are predestined to fall. We do
not know how or when it will happen, whether by inte-
rior or exterior forces, yet the likelihood inspires many
thoughts....

—Aleksis Rannit, Curator, Russian and East European Studies,
Yale University, 1960-1983

IN 1776, THE YEAR THE UNITED STATES DECLARED INDEPENDENCE
from the British, Edward Gibbon also published his book, *The
Decline and Fall of the Roman Empire.* Rome did not collapse in
a day. It declined and rose again several times before it finally
disappeared. Alaric had brought the citizens of Rome to their
knees in 410 A.D., but the Empire reorganized. Gibbon marked
the end of the Roman Empire as 1453 A.D., when Mahomet II
captured Constantinople, bringing to an end the Eastern half of
the Empire. However, in the West, remnants of the defunct Western Empire were reorganized under Charlemagne as the Holy
Roman Empire in 800 A.D. This political system persisted in Aus-
tria and Germany until 1866 when Otto von Bismarck organized
the remaining non-nationalized principalities into the German
state. Today, Roman law still serves as the basis of much of the
law in continental Europe.

When discussing the decline or collapse of an empire or a political state, a distinction must be made between the collapse of the physical regime and the collapse of the philosophy, system of justice, and civilization that supported the regime. For example, even though Hammurabi's dynasty lost political control of ancient Babylon to the Kassites, the culture remained relatively unchanged. At other times, regime changes brought new philosophies.

The histories of the Babylonian and Roman empires contain lessons that can help establish a framework for the study of issues important to a philosophy of the United States. Babylonian and Roman civilizations also provide a direct line from ancient times to the founding of the United States. Greece also contributed to the development of Western civilization as an intermediary between the ancient Babylonians and the Romans. The founders of the United States knew the writings of Greece and Rome well, and quoted them to one another as they developed the United States' Constitution. They did not know much about Babylon other than what was written in the Bible and by the Greek historian, Herodotus. Today that history has been rediscovered on ancient tablets uncovered in the last two centuries.

The Babylonian Empire

Ur

No civilization has arisen in a vacuum. Civilizations and empires are defined by and against the societies that preceded them. Babylon is no exception. Artifacts of early civilizations in Mesopotamia show that farming, irrigation canals, pottery, and metallurgy existed as far back as 3200 B.C. It is thought that writing was invented in the region about 3000 B.C. and wheeled transport introduced about 2600 B.C.

The ancient city of Ur, on the Persian gulf, became a center of civilization under Sargon of Akkad (c. 2334 B.C.) who, through military prowess, founded the Akkadian dynasty over Mesopotamia and Elam (part of modern Iran). Ur became a center of civilization and its kings developed a centralized system of government with the king's representatives on city councils; they also expanded food production with a system of irrigation. The third dynasty of the kings of Ur (UrIII)(c. 2200-2047 B.C.) ruled over an extensive empire that included lands to the north of Babylon. This dynasty built the first temple, or ziggurat, at Ur. UrIII had a flourishing textile industry and a more efficient system of taxation than its predecessors. However, the rising population, overuse of the land, increased salinity of the land, and neglect of maintenance on waterways and irrigation canals eventually led to political instability and food shortages.

This empire collapsed when the Amorites, "barbarians" from the southwest, moved into Mesopotamia. The collapse was aided by Ishbi-Erra, a senior official in Middle Babylonia, who had once been governor of Mari. He conspired with the Amorites and strategically delayed shipments of grain to Ur, leading to starvation and capitulation. Ishbi-Erra founded a new dynasty centered at Isin in the South and the Amorites occupied northern Mesopotamia. Ur was sacked and destroyed by Elamites from the hills to the northeast in 2007 B.C. Since then the delta has expanded in the Persian gulf, leaving the ruins of Ur buried in the middle of a desert.

Old Babylonian Empire

Babylon was in the middle of Mesopotamia on the Euphrates river. An Amorite, Sumu-abum, conquered the city in 1894 B.C. and made it his petty kingdom. Hammurabi, the sixth king in his dynasty, proved to be a very able ruler. When he took the throne, his kingdom consisted of Babylon and the old cities of Kish, Sippar, and Borsippa. Through patience, strategic alliances, and opportunistic attacks on neighbors Hammurabi took control of all of Mesopotamia over a thirty-year period. He earned the favor of priests and farmers alike by rebuilding temples and waterways. He cared for and resettled refugees from devastated areas, among them intellectuals. He encouraged scribal centers. Thus he won the loyalty of virtually everyone except the old rulers, viewed as oppressors by comparison with his regime.

Records show that Hammurabi made a concerted effort to be available to his people and that he was actively involved in minute details of administration. Numerous letters survive that record his correspondence with senior officials. He elevated the status of Marduk, a little-known deity, to one who bestows kingship, and by the end of his rule (his 39th year) had fashioned the Law Code as it exists on the stele, which is now in the Louvre.[1]

Most of the expansion and development under Hammurabi is credited to his hard work, skill and dedication. The empire was larger than most rulers, including Hammurabi's successors, could personally administer. During the reign of his son, Samsu-iluna, encroachments were made on the perimeter of the empire. A group known as the Kassites, steppe people skilled with horses, moved into the Northern part of Babylonia. The Sealand dynasty arose in the fertile marshes near the gulf in the south, A new Amorite kingdom asserted its independence around Terqa. Nevertheless, Hammurabi's successors faithfully continued his polices in the territories they controlled. They supported the scribal centers, rebuilt sanctuaries, and were determined to uphold the Law Code and be fair arbiters of justice.

This period, known as the Old Babylonian Empire, has been characterized as one in which people lived in small towns and cities in relative middle-class comfort and security. There is a written record of increased royal acts of justice at the end of the Old Babylonian Empire that hints at growing debt burdens, high interest rates, and food shortages in the South as the infrastructure and waterways gradually fell into disrepair.

The final demise of the Old Babylonian Empire came as a result of an outside attack from Anatolia, where the Hittites had formed a powerful expansionist state. Around 1595 B.C.,

King Mursili I, emboldened by other military successes, raided Babylon for its treasures. His armies marched right through the Kassite territory in the north without resistance. Samsu-ditana, the last King of the Old Empire, lost his throne and recorded history seems to have stopped. There is a gap of more than 100 years in current knowledge of this ancient civilization that has been called a period of "dark ages."

The Middle Empire

About 1475 B.C. the Sealand king Gulkishar seized northern Babylonia and the Kassites residing there rose up under the leadership of Ulam-Buriash, who established a new Babylonian kingdom and stabilized the area under a new political center at Aqar Quf, west of modern Baghdad. The Kassite dynasty ruled for several hundred years, until 1158 B.C.

It is important to note that the Kassites did not impose any foreign names, gods, or customs on the people of Babylonia. The city of Babylon remained the religious and cultural center, and the government restored other temples and helped build new ones, keeping the old forms of legitimization intact. The Kassites maintained the waterways and a centralized infrastructure. The country was rich in resources and encompassed central trade-routes.

The Kassites felt no need for expansionism or aggressive foreign policy. Babylonian writing continued and became the diplomatic language of the entire Near East. Its scribes were in use in foreign courts and Mesopotamian literature, which included the *Gilgamesh Epic*, were used for training scribes in other lands. It was even used by Egyptian diplomats. This cultural supremacy and adoption of language occurred during a period of diplomacy, not political expansion. One could conclude that not forcible conquest but practical utility was the reason for its use as with other technologies that are adopted across political boundaries.

The Kassite dynasty later accommodated to, and was, for a while, a puppet of its powerful neighbor, Assyria. Around 1235-1210 B.C., Assyria's enemies the Elamites attacked, destroyed Der, and replaced the ruler of one province with their own. Then in about 1158 B.C. the Elamites raided Babylon and other great cities and plundered them. Ancient monuments, including statues of Marduk and the stele with Hammurabi's Law Code, were taken. The demoralized Babylonians tried to throw off the oppressor, but their king was killed about 1155 B.C., ending the Kassite dynasty.

What remained of Babylonia was reorganized further South in the city of Isin. One of these Isin kings, Nebachadnezzar I (1125-1104 B.C.), was able to attack and defeat the Elamite King and return the statues of Marduk and his consort Sarpanitum to Babylon, greatly reinvigorating the pride of the Babylonians. Numerous ceremonies and songs involving Marduk and the annual recitation of the creation epic were elaborated, if not invented, during this period.

Nebachadnezzar I became revered as a great liberator in the same manner of Hammurabi. He tried to revive a standard of good kingship and Old Babylonian culture. He was a builder. But his successors could not continue his work. Their reigns were racked with internal strife and tribal warfare and overburdened with large-scale immigration from other regions where people had been displaced. The next five hundred years were a period of turmoil, save for two or three rulers who lasted for twenty-thirty years.

The Neo Babylonian Empire

Assyria had become the main power in the region and was frequently in control of Babylonia. By 615 B.C., the Medes in Persia had arisen and exerted influence in the region. The Babylonian Nabopolassar made an alliance with the Median King, Cyaxares. Their combined forces defeated the Assyrian capital of Nineveh.

The Babylonians were able to take their share of the spoils to Babylon and establish a new Babylonian dynasty there. Nabopolassar's son Nebuchadnezzar II (604-562 B.C.) became an illustrious soldier and ruler.

The Neo-Babylonian Empire lasted from 626 to 539 B.C. It was a period of grandios building in Babylon, some of which is recounted by the Greek historian Herodotus (c. 490-425 B.C.), who wrote of the city after the period of the Greek and Persian wars. It had impressive double-thick walls, the Ishtar Gate, the ziggurat Etemenanki and temple to Marduk, the Processional Way, and the Hanging Gardens. The myths and glories of Old Babylon and Nebuchadnezzar I were used to legitimate the forty-three year reign of Nebuchadnezzar II. After the defeat of the Assyrians, Babylonian expansion reached the Mediterranean and included Israel. To solidify their control of the region, the Babylonians captured the intellectuals and ruling class in the region and relocated them in Babylonia (the Jewish captivity), where they lived in relative freedom, unable to provide any political destabilization in Canaan.

The Fall of the Babylonian Empire

Nebuchadnezzar II's dynasty was lost five years after his death through palace assassinations and intrigues. Nabonidus (555-539 B.C.), who had no connection to the royal family, took power with the help of his son, Bel-shar-usur (Belshazzar in the Bible). Nabodius' dreams of further expansion and his promotion of the moon god Sin led to increased hatred against him by both Babylonian taxpayers and the priestly class. The Persians entered Babylon unopposed in 539 B.C. This was the end of the Babylonian Empire. The Persians held the area until defeated by Alexander the Great in about 323 B.C. It is rumored that Alexander wanted to make Babylon his capital, but he died in 321 B.C. before that was possible.

When the Roman Empire expanded and included Syria in

its outermost grasp, Babylon became a remote and forgotten corner of the world. Its canals and irrigation forgotten, the entire area became depopulated and was finally buried in the blowing sands.

Israel Is a Remnant of Babylonian Civilization

Babylonian civilization gave birth to Israel, both by cultivating Abraham, the Father of Faith, in the Old Babylonian Empire,[2] and by forging the faith of a new unified Israel during the Babylonian captivity.[3] The creation story of the Old Testament is a variation on the older Babylonian creation stories, and the Code of Hammurabi laid the foundation for much of Moses' secular law. Israel was, for the most part, a land of poor farmers and pastoralists that had suffered variously under the Egyptians to the South, the Assyrians to the North, and other powers in the region.

Before the Babylonian captivity, Israel was divided. Judah, the kingdom in the South, proclaimed loyalty to Yahweh, the God of Moses. It was closer to Egypt and drew its faith from stories of liberation from Egypt. The larger northern kingdom of Samaria in Canaan related to the culture of the ancient Canaanites. Elohim was the high God, similar to Babylonian theology.

Following the collapse of the Old Babylonian Empire, some descendants of Abraham ended up in Egypt. After their liberation by Moses and wandering in the wilderness (c. 1280-1250 B.C.) they became monotheistic, eliminating all family gods and claiming obedience to Yahweh, the God of Moses. The Hebrews had settled in Canaan by 1200 B.C. and established the rule of twelve judges.

The ancient kingdom of Israel was unified under Saul, David, and Solomon from about 1020 B.C. to 922 B.C. The Deuteronomist later wrote that, near the end of his reign, Solomon became furious about a prophecy that Jeroboam, an Ephrathite, would become king. Evading Solomon's assassins, Jeroboam escaped to

Egypt where he met a powerful ally, King Shishak the Pharaoh. Upon King Solomon's death, with Egyptian backing, Jeroboam claimed leadership over the ten northern tribes (Samaria), dividing the nation. Solomon's son, Rehoboam, remained king over the two large southern tribes (Judea).

The Israelites remained as two kingdoms until the Assyrians conquered the north in 722 B.C. The prophet Isaiah blamed this conquest on the failure of the northern tribes to remain true to the God of Israel. Judea remained centered on Jerusalem, but fell to Nebuchadrezzar II in 597 B.C. The prophet Jeremiah saw this as a reprisal for a failure of faith in God by the Israelites. Unable to contain rebellion under their puppet regime, the Babylonians brought the Hebrew people to Babylon in captivity.

When the New Babylonian Empire fell to Persia in 539 B.C., the exiles returned to Jerusalem to rebuild the temple. It was not a rebuilding of the earlier wooden temple of the pastoral tribes, but a strong stone temple conceived by exiles living in the glorious city of Babylon. The theology blurred the distinctions between Elohim, the sky God of the northern tribes, and Yahweh, Moses' Lord of Hosts. The Old Testament refers to both gods somewhat interchangeably. The Greeks translated El as "God" and Yahweh as "Lord."

The New Temple in Israel was built by priests, intellectuals, and masons who had learned building and commerce in Babylon.[5] The Temple was not built by a political leader who had consolidated power from great military conquests, but by intellectuals and priests who managed to obtain social control during a military power vacuum. It was a theocratic society based on the rule of the Mosaic Law and a transcendent, omniscient, and all-powerful creator God. There was no room for worship of lesser deities. God was One—God of the state, God of the city, and God of the individual family. God was the Lord of Creation, Lord of Righteousness, and the Lord of Love. God was the Creator of Adam and Eve, the God of Noah, the God of Abraham, the God of Moses and the God of David. This conception of

God in the Old Testament came from the confluence of Yahweh, Elohim, Deuteronomic and Priestly traditions of Israel's sacred history. These sources merged into the Pentateuch during the Babylonian exile as Israelites in Babylon sought to preserve their collective heritage and faith in a foreign land. This merger represents the victory of monotheism over pantheism in the ancient Near East.

The Fall of Israel

However, the united Israel was unable to withstand the power of the empires of the world. Jerusalem fell to the Greeks under Alexander the Great in 332 B.C. and to the Romans in 63 B.C. In 66 A.D., when the Jews (and this includes Jewish Christians and other sects) rebelled against the Romans, they retaliated by destroying the temple in Jerusalem (70 A.D).

This monotheistic culture, built on legal and cultural foundations going back to Abraham and Hammurabi, was a spiritual and philosophical faith capable of transcending political and military empires of the world and sustaining individuals, families, and communities in a diaspora throughout the world. It was a faith that provided believers with a legitimate foundation for true justice and an unchanging national moral and ethical code, as opposed to the varied and arbitrary secular pronouncements of the kings and empires.

This was also the faith that would give birth to Christianity and to theocratic political rule in New England, in America, sometimes called "God's New Israel." The Puritan colonies based their laws on the Bible, thus eventually making ancient Babylonian law and Jewish monotheism part of the legal fabric of the United States.

The Roman Empire

Decline of the Republic

Ancient Rome was more stable politically than the Babylonian Empire because its rule was based more on legal institutions than on individual personalities. Although ancient Roman gods played a role in the daily life of the inhabitants, the system of justice that was a social contract hammered out through the interactions of patricians and plebeians gave the regime its ongoing legitimacy. While it was a republic, Rome's legal institutions were able to outlive the life and power of the individuals who occupied various posts. Honoring the laws of Rome was a criterion of staying in office. In the early Republic, virtue and honor were prized and instilled in citizens who took their public duties seriously. Young men in the senatorial class received tough military training as well as training in reading, law, and history.

The expansion of the Republic introduced extremes of wealth and poverty that brought new social and economic conflict. Small farms gave way to plantations and landless peasants migrated to cities looking for work. The general freedom of many citizens degenerated into an oligarchy where a few hundred men had acquired extreme wealth while most workers and provincials suffered and were unable to make any personal progress. The historian Sallust stated that wealth corrupted people. Nobles abandoned their patriotism for the pursuit of personal power and luxury.

Near the end of the Republic, there were huge regional armies under weak central control. Civil wars were frequent from the rule of Gracchi (133 B.C.) until the death of Julius Caesar (44 B.C.). In the late Republic, widespread political corruption and immoral sexual behavior led the upper classes to avoid marriage. The Roman population, already reduced because of civil war, experienced a notable decline in the birth rate.

In 49 B.C. Julius Caesar, who had held many high offices,

marched on Rome to establish order. He ruled as a dictator five years before his assassination by Brutus and Cassius. They tried to restore the Republic, but neither the urban masses nor the military wanted the corrupt aristocracy to regain control. They believed a strong leader was needed and the old system of government could not manage the Empire, now with over 50 million people. A better administration was needed.

Cicero (106-43 B.C.), a famous legislator and orator who had memorized the Twelve Tables at a young age, left us works that go into detail about the degenerating system of justice in the late Republic; how people bought political influence with wealth, and how politicians were misusing their positions to gain wealth. A well-educated "new man," not a patrician, Cicero was able to achieve the high office of consul by age 42. Many laws were being passed for ignoble purposes, leading to his saying, "The more laws, the less justice."

Cicero wrote of the importance of the checks on the power of the Senate by the power of the Tribunes, a concept that influenced the formation of the Senate and the House in the United States Congress. He championed the cause of people who suffered at the hands of corrupt rulers, earning himself both fame and threats on his life. Although he lived to the age of 69, he was beheaded by the order of Marc Antony because he had supported Octavian in the contest for emperor.

Augustus and the Creation of the Empire

After fifteen years of fighting Octavian, an adopted son of Julius Caesar, triumphed as the ruler. In 27 B.C. the Senate proclaimed him Augustus, the supreme ruler.

During the late republic, provincial governorships were seen as stepping stones to higher office in Rome. They were staffed, not by able leaders, but by children of the wealthy and politicians aspiring to become senators. One of Augustus' first goals was to rate the people who held these positions on their managerial capabilities. He installed several of his own supporters whom he had come to trust. He also gave some talented people, who did not have personal wealth, the required amount of money to qualify for positions. He appointed wealthy people, not from the senate, to perform many other administrative duties, from governing smaller provinces, like Pontius Pilate in Judea, to supervising the grain supply.[6] He accepted the principle, inherited from the patricians, that wealthy people had the most at stake, and therefore would make the most responsible administrators.

Augustus' reforms were welcomed in outlying provinces. While he unified Italy culturally, economically, and politically, he allowed defeated kings to continue to rule as subjects, leaving their infrastructures intact. Augustus also initiated laws that encouraged marriage and childbearing, both for purposes of moral reform and to stabilize the birth rate in the upper classes. He provided tax incentives for marriage and those with more than three children received special privileges. He made adultery a criminal offense and sent his own daughter, Julia, into exile for having illicit sexual affairs.

Augustus restored ancient temples and identified with traditional family values, hard work, frugality, and civic responsibility. He gave much of the wealth he had obtained from his conquest of Cleopatra in Egypt to the public treasury and encouraged others to do the same. He was a generous patron of literature and art. He dedicated a new temple to Mars, the Roman war god, and held magnificent celebrations to mark the anniversary of the founding of Rome.

The Empire controlled coinage and taxation, but otherwise the economy was free, operating on principles of supply and demand. The armies were put on regular pay instead of being paid from the spoils of conquest. He established a central military treasury so no general could rebel, and he offered a good retirement after twenty years of military service.

Instead of further conquest of territory, soldiers were put to work controlling piracy on the Mediterranean, and ship trade increased tremendously. The imperial peace gave Romans with vast wealth confidence to invest it in enterprise abroad, bringing many kinds of agricultural goods, timber, marble, and manufactured goods. The peace also brought investment in aqueducts, roads, river transportation, and other improvements in infrastructure that improved health and commerce.

Although Augustus had acquired absolute dictatorial power, he had masked it well, worked as part of a team with other administrators, and won the loyalty of the Roman people. Augustus' accomplishments were great, and, after his death, he was made a god by his successors.

The creation of the Empire gave the emperors and praetors, the executive branch of government, more power to issue decrees or laws, and Roman citizenship was granted to inhabitants throughout the all the territories in the period from 100 B.C. to 212 A.D. These developments made the *jus civile* (the Twelve Tables) obsolete, replacing it with the *jus gentium*. This law was based in the sheer political power of the ruler, and did not have the legitimacy of a social contract. It was only as good as the men who issued it.

Failure of Augustus' Successors

Caesar Augustus outlived most of his chosen heirs. When he died, Tiberius (14-37 A.D.), a son from a previous marriage of Livia, his wife of fifty-one years, was his remaining choice. He had been a successful general and a fine imperial administrator, and was chosen for his skill rather than his direct bloodline. He did not, however, have charisma and he failed to develop rapport with the Roman Senators, alienating some of them. Nonetheless, he left the empire strong and with a healthy treasury. This was not the case with his chosen successor Gaius, nicknamed Caligula (37-41 A.D.), a great grandson of both Augustus and Mark Antony.

Caligula is said to have developed a severe mental illness that turned him into a vicious tyrant. He murdered senators for their property and their wives. He gave provinces to boyhood play-mates and tried to make his horse a consul. He was murdered by one of his own guards. The praetorian soldiers chose Caligula's uncle, Claudius I (41-54 A.D.), who ruled quite well until he was poisoned by his fourth wife, Agrippa, to ensure the accession of her son, Nero (54-68 A.D.), to the throne.

The immature and incapable Nero took the throne at 15. He murdered both his mother and his wife at the urging of his mistress. Fire devastated much of Rome in 64 A.D., while Nero supposedly played his fiddle. He neglected the military legions that had become an indispensable support to the rule of the emperors and eventually alienated them. After Nero died in 68 A.D., four claimants to the throne marched to Rome with their respective military contingents.

Vespasian (69-79 A.D.) eventually triumphed. He was the commander on the Eastern front that had crushed the Jewish rebellion. After he returned to Rome, his son destroyed both the city of Jerusalem and the hilltop fortress of Masada where the Jews made their last stand. Vespasian proved a more capable leader than his recent predecessors, ensuring military loyalty and recruiting support of senators from western provinces. He began a new dynasty, known as the Flavians. His son Titus (79-81 A.D.) was quite popular, but his brother Domitian (81-96 A.D.) was a tyrant distrusted by the Senate and murdered in a palace con-spiracy that included his wife.

The Antonines

After the murder of Domitan, the Senate proclaimed Nerva (96-98 A.D.) as emperor. He adopted Trajan (98-117 A.D.), a highly respected governor of Germany as his successor. This began an imperial line known as the Antonines in which successors were chosen based on qualifications other than blood lineage. Trajan was of Spanish birth, the first emperor born outside of Italy. He expanded the Empire to Romania and Arabia. He treated people fairly, distributed food to poor children, and tried to reason with dissident Christians fuming about the Roman occupation and destruction of Israel. It is not surprising that the eighteenth century historian, Edward Gibbon, would look back on this time as the happiest time for the human race.

Trajan's cousin and successor, Hadrian (117-138 A.D.), continued building roads and walls to secure the frontier. His successor, Antonius Pius (138-161 A.D.), had a peaceful reign, but the peace brought complacency regarding the military. His successor, Marcus Aurelius (161-180 A.D.), was consumed much of the time with fighting German tribes that had crossed into the Empire in the north.

Decline of the Roman Empire

The "good emperors" ended when Marcus Aurelius, rather than choosing a successor based on skill, tried to create a family dynasty by appointing his son Commodus (180-193 A.D.) as emperor. Commodus, who had developed fighting skills against the Germans, returned to Rome to exhibit his strength to the senators. He ruled by threat of force and spent more time with gladiatorial games than rule of the Empire. He was eventually strangled by a wrestling partner, precipitating a crisis similar to 69 A.D. where four emperors backed by military power vied for the throne.

This time Lucius Septimius Severus, a military commander from North Africa, prevailed. He disbanded the praetorian guard, the elite troops who had guarded Rome, and replaced them with his own troops. He took many offices away from Senators and gave them to his own legionnaires. He tried to keep soldiers loyal by raising their pay and giving them non-military responsibilities. This only weakened their military preparedness and inflamed their greed for money and power. His five successors, including both his sons, were all murdered.

After Severus, all power derived from the army. Rome became a military state. Gibbon titled one section of *The Decline and Fall of the Roman Empire* "The Sale of the Empire by the Praetorians."[7] During the period from 235-284 A.D., the troops acclaimed about twenty emperors and another thirty pretenders, many of whom had bribed the military for the privilege. During one period of twenty-six emperors, only one died of natural causes.[8]

Roving armies commandeered supplies and taxes for themselves. The taxation forced many farmers to give up their land and work for others or become robbers. Infrastructure was neglected. The silver content of coins became a worthless one percent and the state, like its citizens, was reduced to the barter of crops and animals rather than use of money. Pay of wage workers became less than the support of slaves, so slavery was greatly reduced. The edicts of the emperors had little to do with justice and were viewed by the population as personal wishes.

The Division of the Empire

At the time when the empire seemed doomed, another able emperor appeared. Diocletian (284-305 B.C.) instituted reforms to stabilize the government, one of which was to name a co-emperor with the title Augustus and two junior Emperors each called Caesar. This rule of four was called a tetrarchy. The administration of the empire was divided among this tetrarchy into an Eastern and Western Empire. Diocletian made economic reforms to stabilize the value of money and balance the government budget. He declared a famous edict on prices that set a maximum price on everything—food, services, and imports. Not all of these policies worked; price setting drove some goods off of the market altogether. But his vigilance to finances had brought some fiscal health to the empire by the end of his reign.

Diocletian retired in 305 A.D. and left two Augusti, assisted by their two Caesars to rule. Things began to fall apart quickly after the death of the western emperor. His son Constantine claimed his father's throne. He consolidated power through military victories, and is known for his victory at the Milvan bridge, where he put crosses on the soldiers' shields and proclaimed the victorious power of the Christian God. Christianity became tolerated and later officially supported under Emperor Constantine I (324-337 A.D.). After another decade, Constantine defeated the eastern emperor and established Constantinople as the new capital of the East. Constantinople was a Christian city, and, by time of Constantine's death, Christianity had become the most popular religion in the Empire.

After Constantine, the Empire remained a police state. To obtain anything, people had to get the favor of the rulers. Bribes were required for the pettiest services. Position and power were everything. Many epithets arose during the time, such as: your Sincerity, your Gravity, your Excellency, your Eminence, your sublime and wonderful Magnitude, your illustrious and magnificent Highness. Magistrates were divided into three classes of importance: the Illustrious, the Respectable, and the Honorable. Gibbon described the whole regime as a theater or pageant filled with pomp and circumstance.[9] The role of patrician was reduced to an honorary one, showing up at a ceremony at the first of the year. Fortunes came, not from how much you worked, but from whose favor one could cultivate. The eighty years after Constantine are described by *Funk and Wagnalls New Encyclopedia* as among the most dismal in the world's history.[10]

The Rise of Christianity

Ancient Rome, like ancient Babylonia, had its foundations in agrarian life. The plethora of gods was believed to determine good harvests or famine, good fortune or bad. As long as the rulers of Rome enforced justice fairly these religious beliefs and practices were of no concern to the stability of the government of Rome.

During the first century B.C., as Roman education and philosophy advanced, the anthropomorphic qualities of the gods and the old rituals associated with them fell into decline. The patricians charged with supervising the rites often no longer believed in them and discharged them only as a public duty. The emperors, still formally charged with ancient priestly duties, reorganized worship towards the imperial house and the emperors themselves became deified.

With Augustus, the Roman project had reached its goal. There are many interpretations regarding the decline of Rome which fit historical observation; failure to solve the problem of succession, the inevitable corruption that comes with power, the failure to inculcate military virtues in senatorial families after the *pax Romana* had been achieved. All of these factors no doubt led to setbacks and difficult times. But even in dire periods, good leaders were able set the empire back on course. After reaching the goal of establishing a magnificent empire, what next?

For most people the "what next" meant personal luxury and pleasure, and inevitably a lesser sense of public service and civic virtue. Others, like the American "hippies" of the 1960s, sought more spiritual and esoteric explanations of life and new purposes for living. The Roman gods were perceived as inadequate because they had been part of the project which was now realized, the seekers were looking for something more.

Those people who sought genuine religious explanations for life and rites to cultivate a spiritual life increasingly found them in the foreign territories. Worship of the Egyptian goddess Isis and the Persian god Mithras were common, and, despite numerous persecutions, the Christianity of Paul steadily found converts. Christianity was built on the monotheism of Israel, but Paul, a student of Greek philosophy, imbued the notion of God with an ontological status. The Christian God of Paul, like Elohim, was the Father of the entire world. Paul emphasized that the primary attribute of Christianity, taken from its founder Jesus Christ, was love. The perfect love of God, known through

Jesus Christ, fulfilled and went beyond the law. The ethic of forgiveness taught by Jesus was considered a higher ethic of justice than "an eye for an eye." Christian believers, who lived according to this "higher law" based on their own conscience, were, like the Jews, able to maintain their integrity regardless of political regime or circumstance.

The early history of Christianity in the Empire is one of separate communities of believers with different customs and teachings. Jews and Christians in Judea shared hostility toward the Roman occupiers and their gods. On the other hand, St. Paul, a Roman citizen, was more interested in converting Romans and living peacefully in the Empire. Most early Christians refused military service and civil positions in Roman government. However, as the destruction of Jerusalem in 135 A.D. faded in their past, Christians began to adapt their lives more to the political life of Rome; and many taught that the creation of the Roman Empire was part of a divine plan to allow for the spread of the gospel. Tertullian, the son of a centurion in Carthage, schooled in writing and Roman Law, converted to Christianity about 197 A.D. and became a priest and one of the early church fathers. He wrote, "this empire has become the garden of the world!"[11]

Gibbon posited five reasons for the expansion and gradual acceptance of Christianity in Rome:

1. Christian zeal
2. The doctrine of future life
3. Belief in miraculous powers
4. The pure, austere morals of the Christians
5. The union and coalescence of a Christian republic, that formed a "state" in the heart of the Roman Empire

The Christian lifestyle impressed Romans. Christians had a doctrine of rebirth, through which people could be cleansed of their sins and start life anew. The community gatherings and rituals helped keep converted criminals and other sinners on a path of righteousness. Christians believed not only in monogamy and sexual purity, but in one spouse for life. They frowned upon or disallowed second marriages. This teaching may help explain why many women, who desired faithful husbands, were among the first converts in the Roman Empire, much the way a similar teaching was a cause for the spread of Protestantism in Latin America in the late twentieth century. Christians lived simply and did not place a high value on physical luxury. Rather, they acted with charity, using what resources they could to help the sick, widows, orphans, and others in need. While Christians often eschewed public service, when they did take positions, they acted with honesty and integrity, and became some of the most trusted members of government.

The legitimacy of the Roman law had been undermined by an accumulating body of arbitrary edicts by military rulers and the rampant corruption in high offices. The moral law of the Christians was appealing, looked more legitimate, and eventually won the hearts of people throughout the Empire—including the "barbarians" in the north.

In the western part of the Empire, the Edict of Milan (313 A.D.) had legalized Christianity and led to increased peace with the growing church. When it became legal for the Church to own property, its assets increased quickly. The Bishop of Rome was renamed Pope with the accession of Sylvester I in 314. This further alienated the bishops of the Eastern Empire, who already had doctrinal differences.

In 325, Emperor Constantine sponsored the Council of Nicea, called to determine the true doctrines of Christianity and eliminate heresies. Constantine's sons became more fanatic; they destroyed ancient temples and showered particular favor on Christians. This was reversed in the following reign of Julian, who was inspired by Greek sophists and sought to restore pagan temples, including the temple in Jerusalem, and to oppress Christianity.

Finally, in 392 A.D., after Christianity's wide adoption

throughout the empire, all other "pagan" cults were forbidden by an edict of Emperor Theodosius I. It was hoped that Christianity would be the unifying and legitimizing force for an empire that had been depleted of every other social anchor. Temples of other gods were converted or destroyed. In Carthage, the Temple of Celestial Venus was converted to a Christian Church. In Alexandria, the pagans would not yield, and the Temple of Serapis and the great library of Alexandria were destroyed.

The Sack of Rome

In 408-410, Alaric, king of the Goths to the north, brought an army to Rome and surrounded and starved the city, causing it to capitulate and hand over much of its wealth. This led to widespread blame and scorn of Christianity, which had abandoned Rome's traditional gods and military values. The shock of this event prompted St. Augustine to write the *City of God,* in which he outlined the duties and responsibilities of the sacred and temporal spheres, of church and state. It led to an arrangement whereby the church held spiritual and moral authority, while the state wielded the sword of temporal authority. The temporal rulers, like other people, rich and poor, were to be bound to one moral law as established by the Church.

From that time, the fate of Christianity as the official religion of Rome was sealed. However, the history of the relationship between church and state was schizophrenic, with different standards officially applied to the two orders of society. The two dominions were co-mingled, not unified. Churches were to guide spiritual communities, but church leaders often held vast amounts of wealth and power, frequently succumbing to their temptations. Priests did not serve in temporal armies, but required their protection. After the ninth century, priests were forbidden to marry, possibly so that heirs would not inherit church property and take it from the Church.

Despite the Christian profession of monotheism, the worship

of various Christian martyrs formed a new panoply of gods. Relics, like finger bones of the Christian saints, were placed on altars to be gazed upon. Gibbon points out that those practices, not a part of the lifestyle or teachings of early Christians, went unchallenged for twelve hundred years, from Constantine to the time of Luther and the Reformation.[12]

The church's spiritual authority served as a moral check on the use of temporal power. It helped to reduce the corruption, selfishness, and arbitrary behavior of Roman leaders. Unfortunately, there was no check on the spiritual power of the popes. They often failed to live according to the standards of the church, and often issued pronouncements that condemned scientists or freethinkers to death. Many people look back on this period as "Dark Ages" because it was a period of increasing doctrinal rigidity and persecution of those who would not give complete faith to the doctrines of the Church.

The Fate of the Roman Empire

The history of Christianity in the West is vast. However, it is important to note that the history of the Roman Empire was that of a system grounded in justice whose fortunes oscillated between wealth and glory on the one hand, and corruption and licentiousness on the other. Its fate was tied to the virtue and skill of its rulers, and when family dynasties were implemented, disaster inevitably ensued. Moral laxity and moral relativism prevailed both at the end of the Roman Republic and the end of the secular Roman Empire. During these periods, rulers used power as they pleased and received little respect from the citizens. By the fourth century A.D., the Empire was a police state, and the legitimacy of the law itself had ceased to exist. Christianity, which emphasized faith in one God and his Son, Jesus Christ, had filled the spiritual void. It taught a higher way of life that people could admire and practice despite the problems of the political order.

Eventually, the old laws, voluminous and often at cross

purposes, were digested and systematically recodified. In the East, the Emperor Theodosius II (401-50 A.D.) published the Codex Theodosianus. Later, under a committee of ten jurists appointed by Justinian, a series of books was published known collectively as the *Corpus Juris Civilis*. In Western Europe between the sixth and eleventh centuries, the principle source of Roman law was the Breviary of Alaric, a code of laws compiled by Alaric II, king of the Visigoths, in 506 A.D. Today Roman law continues as part of many of the legal systems of the nations of continental Europe.

The Western Roman Empire officially ended in 476 A.D. without much fanfare. Theodoric already held the real power and he simply assumed a new ceremonial title. In 800 A.D., Charlemagne reestablished an empire aligned with the papacy in Rome, which had always favored the West, creating a Holy Roman Empire that gave Charlemagne spiritual authority to rule Europe and the Vatican temporal authority in Italy. The Holy Roman Empire officially ended with the Peace of Westphalia in 1648, but remnants remained in Prussia until 1866, when Germany became a modern state. In the East, the Empire lasted until 1453, when Constantinople fell to Mahomet II, who imposed Islam as the official religion.

Christianity continued, although the Protestant Reformation and the mass publication of the Bible made it once again possible for people to practice the moral laws articulated in the Bible, and practiced by Jews and Christians, without mediation by the Church hierarchy.

Questions for Reflection

1. What are the problems of political leadership associated with family dynasties?

2. How might second and third generations of entire societies create problems similar or different to the problems of the descendents of kings?

3. Do you think the United States has solved the problems of succession with its method of electing presidents?

4. Explain the differences of legitimacy of the system of justice in the Roman Republic and the Roman Empire.

5. What are some of the reasons the laws of the Roman Empire lost their legitimation? Why did Hammurabi's Code not suffer delegitimation to the same extent?

6. Do you think the legitimacy of the United States' system of justice is undergoing a transformation like that of the Roman Empire?

7. How did the adoption of Christianity serve to bolster the legitimacy of the Roman Empire?

8. Do you think the Roman government could have followed a different course that would have avoided its eventual decline and fall? If so, what would you recommend could have been done differently?

3

Thoughts After the Roman Empire: Love, Power, and Justice

Limits to Legitimate Justice

THE BABYLONIAN AND THE ROMAN EMPIRES came into existence when the people in power established systems of justice designed to treat every citizen fairly or equally. Laws were designed to be impartial so that the citizens would have no complaint against rulers, who also obeyed, respected, and were held accountable to the laws. In the systems of justice of both empires, the protection of property was given a very high priority. There was not a special exemption for Hammurabi or his aides, nor was there a special exemption for the Roman patricians. A military or police force was always required, in principle, to enforce the laws. However, when the laws and the system of government they derived from were viewed as legitimate and fair by the majority of the people, and the citizens were free to pursue their own lives within the framework the laws established, there was, in practice, not a need to use the police very frequently.

Summarizing, the principles of justice required for the Babylonians and Romans to prosper included:

1. Equal legal treatment of all citizens, rich and poor
2. Protection of personal freedoms
3. Protection of property and upholding of contracts
4. Promotion of intact family units
5. Protection of widows and orphans

A legitimate system of justice is a prerequisite for political stability and peace, but justice alone is inadequate to guarantee the success of a society. A perfect constitution guarantees neither peace nor prosperity. As the histories of Babylon, Rome and other nations attest, the overwhelming power of a conqueror from without or usurpation of power, moral degeneration, and decay from within can lead to the collapse of a society with a legitimate code of justice. The Babylonian Empire is an example of a society in which people accepted the system of justice as legitimate, but outside invaders frequently conquered and imposed their own will on the people. The Roman Republic and the Roman Empire are examplesof a society in which people accepted the laws as just, but periods of misuse of power and moral decay created great distress for common citizens.

However, even in the case of a good system of government and a succession of good leaders, peace and prosperity are not guaranteed. People, technology, social conditions and natural ecosystems all experience change. The conditions that bring great empires and civilizations into existence do not remain constant over time. Among other things, peace and prosperity lead to a larger population that puts pressure on the physical environment, as was the reason for the collapse of the UrIII empire. This can lead to economic and social decline or spur the desire of a nation to go to war to get resources in another country. Also, wealthy societies are envied by poor ones, and they become a target for attack from outside invaders.

In addition to establishing a legitimate system of justice, an enduring society must be able to:

1. Defend itself from aggression
2. Promote righteous and virtuous use of power
3. Prevent corruption and abuse of power
4. Change and adjust to new social and environmental circumstances
5. Cultivate loyal citizens who can prosper in the system that has been established

Leadership Qualifications

Good leadership is essential. The view expressed by both Cicero and Augustine, that justice is essential but that virtuous use of power is necessary, is valid. Justice cannot be implemented without power, and power must be exercised with virtue and skill. The skillful and virtuous use of power has always been seen as a requisite for a good society, but there has never been a great success in maintaining this quality in leaders over time. Therefore the saying of Cicero as paraphrased by Lord Acton: "Power corrupts and absolute power corrupts absolutely."

Traditionally tribes and smaller communities have instituted rites of passage from childhood to adulthood aimed at ensuring that adults would become responsible leaders, willing to work with and live for the sake of the social unit. Drawings on caves in France from Ice Age hunters dated c. 10,000 B.C., portray one ritual as follows:

> The initiation begins with a rite of separation, in which boys are separated from their mothers. Childish things are completely put away. The break is often dramatic and violent. The boys might be seated in a circle around a fire with their mothers placed behind them and covered with blankets or branches. The men approach from the sacred ground, whirling bull-roarers, beating the ground with rods, and throwing burning sticks. The women and children are forbidden to peek under pain of death. The men seize the boys

and carry them off to the sacred ground. There they are made to lie on the ground covered with branches.

The mothers believe their sons will be killed, and indeed they never do get their little boys back.... It is indeed a ritual of death. Their old lives as children are over and they are dead, buried in the dark under branches, waiting to be reborn as men....

The second stage of the rite is a transition, or liminal period. During it the boys are kept isolated on sacred ground...to undergo certain ordeals...to gain requisite skills.

Finally the initiates, marked as men, are incorporated into the tribe. In some places they are painted white to resemble ghosts—a clear indication that this is indeed a resurrection after ritual death. The marks of initiation separate them from noninitiates.... The initiates are reborn as men in these rites.... In many languages the word for human being is the same as that for an initiated member of the tribe.[1]

Anthropologists Arnold Van Gennep and Victor Turner developed a theory of three phases of the rites of passage to responsible adulthood in tribal societies: (1) separation, (2) margin (*limin* or liminality meaning "threshold"), and (3) aggregation, or reincorporation with new status.[2] In the liminal period there is no social status that relates to the status of the child's parents. All initiates go through the same process as equals and brothers and progress is based on passing tests that qualify the child for adulthood.

In modern society the Boy Scouts, though they do not remove boys from parents' homes, attempt to accomplish similar training for adulthood with the moral principles embodied in the scout oath, the scout pledge, scout laws, and acquisition of skills signified by earning merit badges. The 4-H clubs established in the rural United States are another example. In them, the young person pledges his head to clearer thinking, his heart to greater loyalty, his hands to greater service, and his health to better living. Projects prepared for county fairs are aimed to develop skills that will make the young person an economically productive adult.

Four elements are common to such training for leadership:

1. Knowledge of the inherited rules,

2. Development of the skills to provide material resources,

3. Loyalty to the community over one's selfish interests, and

4. Ability to pass on the above three elements to succeeding generations.[3]

These elements are tested in traditional rites of passage and need to be part of any enduring society.

British sociologist Robert E. Goodin noted that ceremonies and rituals involving kingship and other positions of high public office are often confused by modernists as being appeals to religious and supernatural powers, rather than a social ritual whereby the society confers legitimacy on the ruler by accepting his qualifications to rule.[4]

In the case of Hammurabi, the legitimacy supposedly bestowed by the Babylonian god of righteousness, Marduk, could be considered by a Christian as a pagan ceremony or by a modernist as a nonsensical primitive ritual. However, the socially important function of such a ceremony would be to confer legitimacy on the ruler by having the people publicly accept his qualifications.

From the ancient epics of Gilgamesh to English knights slaying a dragons and saving princesses, literature has been written to convey virtues of heroism, skill, and service to the larger society in order to inspire readers with definitions of a good and noble life, proving one's qualification to lead society. Whether these epics convey fact or fiction is not their primary social purpose.

In ancient Roman society, the education and training of the noble class was to prepare young men for economic, military, and government positions. Memorizing the Twelve Tables, being sent to military training camps to endure harsh conditions and learn military skills, learning to manage business and property, studying history and philosophy, practicing virtues, and taking an oath of loyalty to Rome were all part of training for leaders.

The problem for ancient Rome, as conveyed in the writings of Livy and Cicero, or of the Roman Empire as portrayed by Augustine, is that despite the requirements of good leadership, only a few genuine leaders actually served as consuls and emperors. Much of the history of Roman office was based on the luck of being an heir to a dynasty or the victor in a successful military campaign, rather than possessing leadership skills.

The adoption of Christianity as the official religion was an attempt to increase virtuosity in the members of society as well as to morally legitimize the state itself. However, during the millennium after Augustine, Rome never returned to its full glory. Kings and princes professed Christianity but often ruled by tyranny. They continued dynastic practices that led to inept and spoiled rulers. Christian popes and bishops preached love and virtue, but the separation of church and state often left the practice of altruism to monks without any real political impact. Leaders in these "Dark Ages" seldom measured up to the necessary qualifications for a good and peaceful reign.

The Use of Political Power: Machiavelli to Locke

The inept use of power led political theorists like Nicolo Machiavelli and Thomas Hobbes to focus on power rather than justice. They are considered to be the fathers of modern political philosophy, which has put more emphasis on power than justice.

Machiavelli

Nicolo Machiavelli (1469-1527) was a government administrator in the Italian city-state of Florence, a historian, political philosopher, and Renaissance man. His best known and early work, *The Prince,* considered the work of the devil by later Puritan dramatists, is a book of practical advice to rulers. It is influenced by his study of Cesare Borgia, to whom he was envoy, and it develops pragmatic principles of rule for a prince. It treats power, not justice, as the main object of political philosophy. It looks amorally on the use of power, and includes the use of deceit to gain or maintain power. Ruling is an art that requires a prince to know how much force is required to keep order and how much freedom can be given without social degeneration. *The Prince* provides the reader with Machiavelli's broad historical understanding of human nature. It is pithy psychological realism.

However, to understand the political theories that Machiavelli personally advocated, one has to turn to his *Discourses* on Titus Livy's *History of the Roman Republic.* These were written in the context of his personal consultation on the creation of a new constitution for Florence, the state to which he devoted his entire life. In the *Discourses,* Machiavelli explained that the strong hand of a single leader, like Julius Caesar, is often necessary to establish a government. In *The Prince,* Machiavelli argued that those who become a prince by fortune, i.e., inherit or are given the position, are unlikely to achieve legitimacy in the eyes of the ruled. Legitimacy is won through building a solid foundation through one's own effort. The successful leader must devolve power to the citizens to create a stable long-term polity. The following excerpt from the *Discourses* provides us with his basic viewpoint:

> I say that the people are more prudent and stable, and have better judgment than a prince; and it is not without good reason that it is said, "The voice of the people is the voice of God".... We furthermore see the cities where the people are the master make the greatest progress in the least possible time, and much greater than such as have always been governed by princes; as was the case with Rome after the

expulsion of the kings...the governments of the people are better than those of princes.[5]

Machiavelli taught that all human beings seek comfort and wealth, and that this inevitably leads to an attempt to control their own situation at the expense of others. He did not believe religion, which uses love and persuasion rather than force, had the power to guarantee virtuous behavior. He thought it was a fiction for society to rely on it. Rulers who govern over more wealth are more tempted to manipulate it for their own purposes, but all people are basically seeking their own happiness more than that of society as a whole. He notes that people will not obey the laws simply because they are laws. They obey laws only when the laws are backed by the physical force of the ruler, or when they believe that disobeying or obeying the laws would bring the wrath or the favor of the gods.[6] The Romans, he argued, honored their sacred oaths, and obedience to the law was a sacred oath. He concluded that, even if the religious beliefs were false, as long as they were believed by the common citizens, they would serve the order of the state by promoting obedience to the laws.

However, the situation in Florence at his time left him little hope that sufficient virtue could be imparted in any ruler. Machiavelli was a great social historian and analyst, but a product of his times; cynical towards the political value of Christian ideals. He echoed the sentiments of those who blamed Christianity for the sack of Rome. Christianity had failed to make rulers virtuous, and Christians seemed particularly inept as secular rulers where the harshness of a sword was frequently required to keep order.

Although Machiavelli did not see much progress in his own day, his idea of securing a state through power and then establishing a republic that was governed by the consent of the people was implemented by the founders of the United States.

Hobbes

In *Leviathan*, Thomas Hobbes (1588-1679) accepted the selfish tendencies of human beings as the basic state of affairs. He defined the means to obtain what one desires as *power*. The natural state of society is a state of war, of every man against every other man.[7] One of the goals of politics, then, is to hold acquisitive instincts and the use of power in check. This is done by mutual agreement among people, as the Roman patricians had done with the plebeians, or the Barons with King John when they signed the Magna Carta in England in 1215.

Hobbes elaborated on the two kinds of power that could encourage men to uphold their word. One was their sacred oaths to God, and the other the fear of a physical consequence. Hobbes was even more pessimistic than Machiavelli about the ability of an oath to God to keep people in check; he believed threat of coercive physical power and fear of punishment was necessary. Unlike the doctrine of natural law taught by the Church, Hobbes argued that natural right was derived from the state of nature. Therefore natural right equated with what one could take with his power. Civilization was only possible by restraining natural right and substituting legal right as decided by social contract and enforced by the sovereign power. The state of nature is essentially unjust, and real justice cannot exist apart from a sovereign power.

For Hobbes, the articulation of human rights in relation to transcendent or spiritual power was meaningless and ineffective. The only justice that could be enforced was agreed-upon rules that could be written down for a sovereign to uphold. There could be no justice without coercive power.

Hobbes spoke about two types of sovereign power; the first type is the power of a sovereign who seizes power by natural force—subduing one's enemies or inheriting power from one who already has it. The second type of sovereign power is when a ruler is selected by people to enforce a compact they make among themselves. The reason for people to make such a compact is because, without it, they live in constant fear of being defeated by someone with greater power. Therefore the sovereign must have overwhelming power to enforce the compact and keep order.

Hobbes' realism was thoroughly rational and based on a cynical and pessimistic appraisal of human nature. He had no place for religion in his political philosophy; religion was superstition and a cause of strife—not a cure for it. He did not see altruism as a sufficiently powerful force to create justice. Justice was ultimately based on fear of the power of others to kill, steal, or oppress without the protection of the sovereign.

The problem that follows from his philosophy is, "Why would the sovereign enforce the compact when he could use his power to oppress and enrich himself?" Hobbes answered that the sovereign is also motivated by fear. In his case, the fear of a common rebellion that would overthrow his power and kill him if he did not perform his obligations to uphold the law.

Locke

John Locke (1632-1704) accepted Hobbes' arguments about human beings acting selfishly and being motivated by fear; however, he argued that, from an abstract moral point of view, each person has equal rights. These rights exist whether human beings recognize them or not. Locke referred to these "natural rights," neither as the law of the jungle described by Hobbes, nor as a "natural law," such as gravity. We would refer to his conception of natural right as an ideal—endowed by our Creator. Locke equates the "law of nature" with reason:

> The *State of Nature* has a Law of Nature to govern it, which obliges every one: And Reason, which is that Law, teaches all Mankind, who will but consult it, that being all *equal and independent*, no one ought to harm another in his Life, Health, Liberty, or Possessions. For Men being all the Workmanship of one Omnipotent and infinitely wise Maker....[8]

The United States founding fathers used this definition of nature in the Declaration of Independence.

Locke explained that human beings are born with capacities for reason and freedom. They have to be ruled while they are in this developmental state. In the family they are not ruled primarily by force, but through love.[9] A humane grounding is the basis of the family, the most fundamental political institution. Thus we will find in Locke a place for love in the motivation for political action.

Unlike Hobbes, who felt that all religion was illusion, Locke believed that all religion should be tolerated. Religion has a place in providing answers about one's ultimate end and underpins human morality, but it should not be used as a political tool to undermine the rights of some for the sake of others. After British ships sank the Spanish armada in 1588, many artifacts and writings of Ancient Egypt, Greece, and Babylon had begun making their way to England. These had an effect of creating new religious speculation beyond the Catholic and Protestant influences. With the growing wealth of Britain, moral laxity and hedonism were becoming pervasive in the British ruling classes.

Thus, in Locke, we find not only a scholar and political theorist who ascribes political value to both morality and power, but an activist involved in creating a movement based on love for one's fellow man that would provide society with a new kind of leader, a leader he believed worthy of governing a society based upon liberty.

Montesquieu

Charles Louis de Secondat, Baron de Montesquieu (1689-1755), contributed to the study of political philosophy the understanding that political science is more than the study of justice and power; it is more than the study of government. Montesquieu understood that societies are formed by an array of institutions, customs, and laws that form an organic relation, like the parts of a plant or animal. As a result you cannot understand a social problem, or prescribe a legal solution, without understanding the entire nexus of social parts. Societies differ widely and the same solution, or the same law, that works in one society may not apply to another.

In *Spirit of the Laws,* Montesquieu discussed the issue of absolutism versus relativism. If every society was completely different, and there were no underlying principles common to human life, there would be no way one could learn from one society in order to draw lessons for another. On the other hand, the absolutist position, which imposes the view of one social group on all others, really has no way to determine that its view is correct or appropriate for others. Montesquieu therefore sets out to distinguish *first principles,* those applicable to all societies, from *derivative principles,* or laws created within the boundaries laid out by first principles, which he called "positive law."

Montesquieu considered natural law to be that which exists when there is no political state. Hence, the desire for food to quench hunger is a law of nature. Animals are subject to this law, as are human beings. Good positive laws cannot contradict the natural need to eat, i.e., a law that forbade eating and leads to death would be bad.

The end of government, according to Montesquieu, is liberty. However, "peace is the first law of nature."[10] Therefore human beings require security as the highest responsibility of government. However, human beings have "an innate detestation of force" and "love of liberty." All people desire to pursue whatever they wish and speak and write whatever they wish; but this is not possible without each person being an individual despot, carrying out actions that injure others. The goal of his *Spirit of the Laws* is thus to provide advice on how to fashion a government that gives the most liberty without failing to provide security. This became one goal on which George Washington sought advice as the United States Constitution was being drafted.

Montesquieu evaluated different types of governments—

monarchies, republics, and despotisms—and ended up favoring a monarchy, leading some Americans to believe the United States should have a king as well. He looked at the British system, which had managed to restrict the power of the king, as better than what the French had in the beginning of the eighteenth century. He thought the best way to preserve a monarchy from being usurped by a single person is to have a constitution that provides checks and balances on the various components of government, a doctrine that would be introduced into the American Constitution:

> In every government there are three sorts of power: the legislative, the executive, and the judiciary.... When the legislative and executive powers are united in the same person, or in the same body of magistrates, there can be no liberty....
>
> The legislative power should reside in the whole body of people. But since this is impossible in large states, and in small ones subject to many inconveniences, the people should transact by their representative what they cannot transact by themselves.... The legislative body is composed of two parts which check one another by the mutual privilege of veto. They are both restrained by the executive as the executive is, in turn, restrained by them.[11]

The writings of Locke and Montesquieu represent the Enlightenment project in full bloom. It was a project of which many of the American founders were a part. The atmosphere was filled with optimism about the possibilities of creating a new order, both in Europe and America, based on reason. This would bring liberty, peace, and happiness to all people. That optimism was dampened with the lawlessness and tyranny of the French Revolution and later scientific theories that seemed to undermine the natural law theory of Locke and the writers of the United States Declaration of Independence.

More Reflection on Love, Power, and Justice

Before returning to the philosophy of the United States, it is useful to try to understand more fully the relationship between love, power, and justice. The writings of Locke and religious leaders of the time emphasized the importance of love as the social glue of a society. Two twentieth-century writers who thought extensively about this relationship are Paul Tillich and Reinhold Niebuhr, both of whom taught at Union Theological Seminary in New York in the 1930s. These men discussed the essential relationship between love, power, and justice in any human society; where love, power, and justice both complement and limit one another.

Tillich taught that love, power, and justice are aspects of "being itself" and grounded in the ontological nature of society. He understood human society to consist of three spheres: personal relations, social institutions, and the holy. He described the relationship of love, power, and justice to these spheres as follows:

> We must consider the ethical functions of love, power, and justice in the spheres of personal relations, of social institutions, and of the holy. In the first sphere, justice is leading, in the second sphere, power, and in the third sphere, love. But all three principles are effective in each sphere. And the sphere of the holy is a quality in the other spheres, and only in some respects a sphere of its own.[12]

He then went on to explain each of the concepts and their relationship to each other in a systematic fashion.

Personal Relations

Traditional small communities, agricultural villages, and nomadic tribes are rooted in face-to-face relationships in which everyone sees and knows what everyone else is doing. Love, power, and justice in such relations are based on one individual's behavior towards another. The Ten Commandments, for example, are primarily a code of personal behavior, as are the bulk of Confucius' ethical teachings on the right order of relationships and the deference and responsibilities of people in various positions.

In face-to-face communities, where a clear standard of behavior has been adopted by the community leaders and elders, members will make a conscious effort to follow them in order to survive and prosper in the community. Punishment for violations might be more arbitrary in small communities without a legal system of justice than in more complex societies with various social institutions; however, love is usually strong in such situations because people in small communities tend to heavily depend upon one another and no one has the ability to use some form of abstract political power or outside source of wealth to dominate the group. Relations in small communities are more like those of an extended family than a modern state. In such communities, we could see Machiavelli's Prince constrained by the pressure of face-to-face relations to perform the task he was assigned, or fear losing his job, if not his life.

Group Relations

In 1932, Reinhold Niebuhr asked the question, "Why is it that people seem to live peacefully with one another as individuals within a group, but groups of people cannot act with the same sense of justice and decency toward other groups? His book *Moral Man and Immoral Society* was aimed firstly at attitudes of economic groups, or classes, but he also recognized the same problems existed between national and racial groups. He concluded that justice in such cases required the use of political force.[13]

Niebuhr noted that large-scale, complex societies with urban populations and bureaucratic institutions form impersonal relations and require rational principles of justice.[14] The feeling of personal responsibility, strong in face-to-face relations, is watered down with the complicity of everyone else in the group. An individual often feels powerless to oppose the behavior of the entire group and may try to ignore wrong things the group is doing. Often the behavior of the group towards other groups takes place on the periphery of group activity and the individual member is unaware of evil that may be taking place on the fringes.

For example, a worker on a ranch in the United States may not want to think about, or even be aware of, agricultural subsidies that give him a job but take away ten jobs from farmers in an African country. An American citizen may not want to think about how its foreign policy, which varies with the interests of elected national officials, affects the lives of people in other nations. An individual who has invested in mutual funds for his retirement may not be thinking about the retirement of workers of companies acquired or downsized in his manager's portfolio. He wants an income for his personal future and is often oblivious to the behavior of the institutions he has trusted to secure his retirement.

In groups, one's conscience is not sensitized by visual contact with the results of the group's behavior as it in personal relations. In groups, one does not feel a personal sense of responsibility to the unseen person, but must be taught such responsibility as abstract duty.

Another example: The owner of a small company will see all his employees every day and know their families, where they live, and who is sick. They probably eat lunch together at the same table every day. They may be best friends during non-work hours as well. However, the owner of a large corporation may never see most of his employees and certainly will not know about their families. He is likely to have an expensive lunch with other executives or clients while the workers share brown bag lunches in a corner of a warehouse. This scenario is the breeding ground of a labor strike.

Reinhold Niebuhr had the unique advantage of being the pastor of a church in Detroit in which both Henry Ford and plant workers were members of his congregation. He felt he had to help foster a sense of community and conscience within the congregation, to help prevent the class division developing at the Ford production plant. As the pastor, he felt personally responsible for the spiritual salvation of both Henry Ford and the lowest-paid worker in the plant.

Niebuhr was very concerned that the type of community rooted in love was being rapidly lost and displaced by a mass society which only understood principles of power. As the World Council of Churches and United Nations were being organized at the end of World War II, Niebuhr stated that,

> the most immediate cause of our distress could be defined as the inability and unwillingness of modern men and nations to establish and reestablish community, or to achieve and to reconstruct justice under the conditions which a technical civilization has created.[15]

Niebuhr was impressed with the realism of the United States' founding fathers, who created a system of checks and balances on the political power of leaders and institutions of their time. Such checks and balances were crucial if even an approximate justice were to be realized. They were especially necessary in the arena of large institutions and nations. However, like Montesquieu, Niebuhr did not believe that checks and balances on power and a good system of laws alone were adequate for a good society. He spoke about the importance of the voluntary component of love.

Love and Justice

Systems of justice are rational and based on equality. However they do not account for actual circumstances. Individuals, their needs, desires, and circumstances vary. These things are better known in communities. Niebuhr said,

> Love is both the fulfillment and the negation of all achieve-
> ments of justice in history. Or expressed from the opposite
> standpoint, the achievements of justice in history may
> rise in indeterminate degrees to find their fulfillment in a
> more perfect love and brotherhood; but each new level also
> contains elements which stand in contradiction to perfect
> love.[16]

There is a paradoxical relation between love and justice. The equality of rational justice counteracts the human tendency toward injustice which selfishness generates; however, love can provide a more perfect justice than that of blind reason. For example, the justice of an impartial government might conscript two men into military service, yet one has four brothers and two healthy parents, while the other is a son caring for incapacitated parents and young children. Blind justice will treat them equally, but justice enlightened by love will treat them differently.

The ability of individual human beings to comprehend the true needs of others is limited to our interactions with them. The better we understand the situation of others, the more perfect the justice we might accomplish. Niebuhr explained that nobody can design a perfect system of justice. We can always improve and aim at the highest justice, but perfect justice is possible only when perfected by love. In his language, the perfect society is "beyond history."

Without love, justice degenerates into a contest for power. Everyone pulls and twists at the existing system of justice to bend it towards self-interest. Such a society will eventually fall apart. Without love, true justice is not possible.

Societies Always Face Changes

All societies are in constant flux. Our technological civilization, the development of which was hastened by freedoms provided though checks and balances on political power, has created new accumulations of power that must be checked for the sake of justice. The problems of industrial justice that Niebuhr was forced to mediate did not exist in an agrarian-based society. It was not an issue the founding fathers of the United States had to contemplate. New power concentrations require new forms of restraint. A society must be capable of adapting to such changes.

The insights of Tillich and Niebuhr remind us that love, power, and justice are all dynamic elements in any peaceful and prosperous society. No abstract formula can create an ideal society, nor can any static formula serve the ongoing causes of peace and justice. Yesterday's formula for justice can become tomorow's breeding-ground for oppression. Further love, through its connection to the infinite ground of all being, must be infused through any institution of power or system of justice to make it truly good, or to lead to a society that will endure and prosper.

There are those conservative Americans who cherish the Constitution of the United States because the founders set up a system of government that led to hitherto unknown freedom and prosperity. In a way similar to fundamentalist religionists clinging to sacred scriptures, they hold the constitution "sacred," in the sense that "it is all we will ever need," or it is "complete in itself for all time." There are others today who believe that a democracy is "anything the majority of people want" and that the constitution can be changed at will, or ignored, without repercussions. However, both of these views are faulty.

Further, the ideologies bandied about in contemporary America often conceal in their political rhetoric a single element—love, power, or justice, but not their relations to one another. However, love, power, and justice form the legs of a tripod on which a healthy society can stand. If one or two of the legs are kicked out, society breaks down.

True civilizations require a basic system of justice and rules of behavior that are humanized and improved upon over time as new components of society come into existence. Like a building that requires adherence to basic principles of physics to stand strong, civilizations require that love, power, and justice are present and that they stand in proper relation to one another. The United States is not so unique that it is immune from these principles.

Questions for Reflection

1. What qualities of leadership do you think are necessary for a President or a member of Congress?

2. Do you think that the citizens and the media in the United States understand these qualities and apply them in elections?

3. Why were Machiavelli and Hobbes considered the fathers of modern political philosophy?

4. How did the understanding of nature differ for Hobbes, Locke, and Montesquieu?

5. Do you think that love has a place in political life? Can a society based on justice and power alone survive?

6. Explain Montesquieu's distinction between first principles and derivative principles and how might such a distinction affect a judge's interpretation of laws.

7. Explain the view that love can create a higher justice than reason.

8. Do you think that an enduring society needs to have concepts of love, power, and justice grounded in a source that transcends the society itself?

Part II
The American Experiment

4

God, Religion, and the State

We hold these truths to be self-evident, that all men are created equal, that they are endowed by their Creator with certain unalienable Rights, that among these are Life, Liberty, and the pursuit of Happiness.

—United States Declaration of Independence

God Legitimates the State

THE REFERENCE TO GOD TO JUSTIFY A POLITICAL SYSTEM did not begin with the United States. Babylon, Israel, the Holy Roman Empire, and other nations have expressed loyalty to God, or a god. God represents a supernatural or transcendent source of human existence. A people's understanding of that source, and the purpose of human life given by it, sets the framework for what is perceived as legitimate human activity. When a legal system is framed to promote life according to that transcendent purpose, or God's plan for human beings, then it is legitimated in the minds of people who believe in that plan.

The problem for any nation that claims its legitimacy from God is to have the agreement of the people on what comprises God's will. The founding fathers of the United States were well aware of the abuses of political power in the name of God. They knew about persecutions of the Jews, the Albigenses, Jan Hus and others by the Catholic Church, ostensibly at the instruction of God. They were aware of the Salem witch trials, the excommunication of Roger Williams, and other deprivations of rights employed by Protestants in the name of God. Thomas Jefferson, an admirer of Galileo, Newton, and other scientists, was bitterly cognizant of the restraints on science imposed by the Catholic Church in the Middle Ages in the name of God. Despite this knowledge, the founders were willing to legitimate their new republic with a reference to God. With the variety of people living in the colonies, how could they hope to accomplish this?

Nature's God and Particular Religions

Many philosophers have discussed the relation of universal to particular law, but for our purposes it is useful to return to Montesquieu's distinction between first principles and derivative principles, or natural law and positive law. Jefferson viewed his references to God as related to first principles, while the various established religions added their own particular derivative principles. Jefferson can be viewed as referring to natural law when he talked about nature's God. Established religions, on the other hand, contained human opinion about additional qualities of God that could not be verified by reason.

This line of reasoning enabled the founding fathers both to establish a state based on the laws of God and to allow freedom of religion. That people of any religion should follow the laws of the state was not a contradiction in their view, because all religions should accept the first principles—the self-evident truths. Within this general framework, they were free to pursue a life based on additional beliefs derived from their particular traditions and scriptures. The founding fathers met little objection from any quarter on these basic principles. Jonathan Edwards, the most prominent Protestant theologian of the early eighteenth-century Great Awakening was an admirer of science and a reader of Isaac Newton. Jews believed in God and were men of science who, having suffered persecutions under Christians in the past, were more than happy to agree to the premise that all men are created equal. Deists believed in these first principles, even if they were skeptical about many theological dogmas.

Except for references to equal rights and the right to life, liberty, and the pursuit of happiness, there is very little said by the founders about God or God's will. There is no reference to any human founder of a religion—Moses, Jesus, or Mohammed; nor is there reference to any contemporary religious or political leader having some unique channel to God. As soon as a human being, a human document, or a human institution is elevated to divinity, division occurs, because the people who do not relate to that person, document, or institution will feel they are being treated as second-class citizens. Thus, there is a basis for national unity under God and division under established religion. This is why the founding fathers could both imagine "one nation under God" and disallow the establishment of religion.

Life, Liberty, and Happiness

The signers of the Declaration of Independence were using the philosophical concept of Nature's God as articulated by John Locke in his treatise *Of Civil Government.* Locke believed that God was a Creator who endowed everyone with equal rights. He said that reason teaches that "no one ought to harm another in Life, Liberty or Possessions."

In their preamble to the Declaration of Independence, the signers proclaimed the belief that all human beings are created equal, and that they have the right to life, liberty and the pursuit of happiness. This is the foundation of the ultimate purpose of the nation. This foundation for justice can be compared to the preamble to Hammurabi's Code. Hammurabi justified his Code as the law given by Marduk, God of Righteousness. This proclamation made "righteousness" the highest end of the government of Babylon. Righteousness was the yardstick by which all things political were to be measured. The practical result of Declaration of Independence was the Constitution designed to "form a more perfect union" based on the principles for which the United States stands—the equality of all men, and their right to life, liberty, and the pursuit of happiness.

A few years later, the Enlightenment philosopher Immanuel Kant would attempt to ground these ideas in a philosophy of practical reason. He developed a couple of philosophical "golden rules" consistent with the political project of the founding fathers. One rule is to not interfere with the rights of others that you would want to claim for yourself. The second rule is to treat others as ends in themselves and not means to another's ends. Taken together, these rules describe a worldview in which each person is created equal and each person has his own ends to pursue. We should not interfere with others' lives by using them (as rulers too frequently had done) as a means to an end.

The Constitution of the United States can be viewed as a document that set up a government based on similar respect for individuals. The whole system was designed so that people would be free to pursue their own ends. In order to guarantee this pursuit, a system of government was necessary to provide a framework whereby the people would be protected from those who would interfere with that pursuit, whether it is by aggression, theft, or the misuse of power.

For the founding fathers, references to God in public ceremonies were to remain in the realm of first principles and not the promotion of established religion. Thus, a meeting of Congress could be opened with a general request for God's guidance; or one could be sworn into office saying "so help me God." The statement on money that says "In God We Trust," or the Pledge of Allegiance, which includes the phrase "One Nation Under God," are both consistent with the founding principles of the United States and the founding documents of the nation. Not only are these references to God consistent, but they are important reminders to citizens about who they are as a people in order to foster the ongoing legitimacy of the government of the United States. For without such references the people might make laws for selfish purposes, that violate the intrinsic rights of others to pursue happiness.

It is clear from current debates about using the phrase "under God" in the Pledge of Allegiance (a phrase added in 1954) that many proponents and opponents alike misunderstand the basic philosophical distinction between first principles and derivative principles in reference to God. Proponents often want to claim the phrase reminds us we are a "Christian" nation. But the founders did not intend for Christianity to claim any monopoly on God. Opponents, on the other hand, claim the phrase mixes up "religion" with the state. This also belies ignorance of the founders' distinction between the principles about God as a Creator of all that could be derived from reason and science and other theological principles promoted by established religion.

No Law Respecting an Establishment of Religion

The first amendment to the Constitution says, "Congress shall make no law respecting an establishment of religion, or prohibiting the free exercise thereof...." This amendment serves to separate "the establishment of religion" from the state, and from the God of the state as well. The founders' primary concern was that no religious institution would gain political control, curtail any citizen's freedom of belief or speech, or use public funds to promote a religious institution. The clause was not a denial of the existence of a Creator.

The men who drafted the United States Constitution were well aware of the inquisitions and the burning of witches that had deprived people of their freedoms, their equal treatment before the law, and even their lives. These practices violated human rights and prevented people from the pursuit of life, liberty and happiness. The founders knew about the problems created by the established Church of England, funded by tax dollars, which had deprived Puritans and other non-Anglicans, of their freedom in England. They were constantly reminded by Baptists that establishment of religion in the colonies had deprived Roger Williams and others of their religious freedom.

The founders also were faced with the practical consideration that the United States was to be made up of thirteen states in which numerous religions existed. There were Congregationalists in Massachusetts and Connecticut, Baptists in Rhode Island, Quakers in Pennsylvania, Catholics in Maryland, Episcopalians in Virginia, and Dutch Reformed in New York. The founders harbored no illusions about the problems they would face if one of these religions received the recognition of the federal government, but not another. They also had to live with the fact that some states had established religions and others did not. Thus, they forbade Congress from passing any law with respect to established religion.

Jefferson's preamble to the Religious Liberty Act in Virginia and Madison's *Remonstrance* of 1785 were essentially deistic arguments, based on reason and "natural law." They sought to protect the state from established religion. But the reverse was also true, religions wanted to be protected from the state. The pietists feared the establishment of religion would interfere with their own freedom of religion. The following arguments were outlined in Isaac Backus' *An Appeal to the Public for Religious Liberty Against the Oppression of the Present Day* in 1773. His complaint was against the establishment of Puritanism in New England because,

1. they acknowledged that "the civil power" had "a right to set one religious sect up above another,"

2. the right to tax was a claim to the "right to govern in Christ's kingdom which is not of this world,"

3. the established system emboldened people "to judge the liberty of other men's consciences,"

4. "bringing in an earthly power between Christ and his

people has been the grand source of anti-Christian abominations," and

5. "by the law of Christ every man is not only allowed, but also required, to judge for himself concerning the circumstantials as well as the essentials of religion."[1]

The rationalists and the pietists, as different as their beliefs were, could both agree on the First Amendment and the use of the word "God" in public ceremonies. All were in agreement that God created all men equal and that life, liberty and happiness was part of God's plan. This was part of the social contract they all approved at the founding of the United States.

Cultural Pluralism and National Unity under God in Earlier Societies

The United States was not the first nation formed by people of different religious and cultural backgrounds under the concept of a God which included the views of the various groups. Such cultural epigenesis[2] has been an ongoing part of the evolution of Western civilization. The formation of Babylon, Israel, and the Holy Roman Empire all include stories about how the God, whom people of the entire nation are being asked to honor, includes, is descended from, is more powerful than, or is a replacement for the older gods of particular groups. Below are some instances of this process.

Babylonia

The peoples of the ancient Near East had a concept of God and gods, or at least higher gods and lower gods, or gods that begat other gods. There was a general ordering of physical life based on what people believed to be a supernatural order. Four thousand years ago, in "pagan" Babylonia, there was a concept of a creator God, El or Bel, that was transcendent and unknowable, whose will was in some way communicated through other gods, with whom human beings could have some personal relationship. These were the gods of families, temples, and cities. There was no conflict, in principle, between the higher gods and the lower gods, or the prior gods and the gods that descended from them, because they were first gods and derivative gods. Thus the entire Babylonian Empire could accept El as universal, while Babylonians could worship Marduk and live happily alongside people from other towns who worshipped other deities.

On the stele of Hammurabi, there is reference to Bel, "the Lord of Heaven and Earth" who assigned dominion over earthly man to Marduk, "God of Righteousness." In his Preamble, Hammurabi wanted to convince followers of Bel and other gods listed on his stele that following Marduk and the Code being set down is not in opposition to, but the fulfillment of a belief in those gods. This is cultural epigenesis, or the adding on of a new layer of culture over several previous layers to give unity, cohesion, and purpose to previously disunited, and sometimes warring, inhabitants

Yahweh and the God of Abraham, Isaac, Jacob

Today we commonly hear the phrase, "the God of Abraham, Isaac, and Jacob." However, it is not clear that we are talking about the same god, or whether these three generations even worshipped the same God.[3] In Genesis 15:1, Abraham entered into a relationship with the God who was known as the "Shield" of Abraham. Isaac was covenanted with "the Fear of Isaac," and Jacob with "the Mighty One." According to practices of the ancient Near East, they were likely family gods.

The name Yahweh (YHWH in Hebrew) was introduced at the time of Moses. One theory of the origin of the name is that it was the god of the Kennites, a clan of the Midianites. Moses married a daughter of the priest of Midian, Jethro. While tending his flocks, Moses had an experience of YHWH in a burning bush

(Exodus 3:5).[4] The Old Testament explains this as a new name for Israel's God in Exodus 6:2-3:

> And God [*Elohim*] said to Moses, "I am Yahweh. I appeared to Abraham, to Isaac, and to Jacob, as God Almighty [*El Shaddai*], but by my name Yahweh I did not make myself known to them.

Yahweh, the God of Moses, was frequently referred to as "the Lord of Hosts." "Hosts" often referred to armies, so Yahweh might have been the mighty warrior God that led the Israelites to the conquest of Canaan.

The story of Moses leading the Israelites out of Egypt to the Promised Land is an example of the process of epigenesis. Moses asked that all of the people stop worshipping their family and tribal gods and put their faith in Yahweh, the Lord of Israel, who would, if they were faithful to him and followed his commandments, guide them to the Promised Land. Yahweh was mightier than any of the other gods the people were worshipping and he was a jealous God. He gave the Ten Commandments and other laws to Moses, with the guarantee that, if these laws were obeyed, they would lead to peace and prosperity. YHWH was thus the legitimating God of the laws of Israel, at least the state of Judah.

The Ten Commandments were not a set of rules totally foreign to the Israelites. Archeologists and modern historians understand that the Laws of Moses did not appear *ex nihilo,* or out of nothing. They were not written on a blank tablet. Abraham, the common Father of Faith for Jews, Christians, and Muslims today, was probably well acquainted with Hammurabi's Code. This may help explain why there is such a high degree of correspondence between the Code of Hammurabi and the Laws of Moses, which were probably laid down over a thousand years later.[5]

Several scholars have proposed that the slaves of Egypt liberated by Moses were composed of more tribes than just the descendants of Abraham. It was likely that Egyptians made slaves of many groups surrounding Egypt. The Exodus is thus an example of various tribes being brought into a national unity by all adopting the God of their leader, Moses.

Yahweh and Elohim

After their exile from Babylon, the Israelites were faced with the integration of the traditions of the people of Judah, who worshipped Yahweh, and those of Israel, which was made up of Canaanites and the ten Northern Territories of the old confederacy. Thus, it was necessary that Yahweh, the name of the high God of Judah, and El, the name of the highest God of Israel, become one. The literature of the post-exilic period indicates that, for a while, the name YHWH was seldom spoken. It was the most holy word and was reserved for high priests in secret. One explanation for this could be the disunity that could be caused by Israelites who called God by another name. When the temple was rebuilt in Jerusalem however, Lord Yahweh became the object of worship at temple ceremonies. The *Psalms* were sung at the Second Temple. Several of the *Psalms* refer directly to the enthronement of Yahweh in much the way that the enthronement of Marduk was sung at ceremonies in Babylon.[6]

When the Greeks translated the names of God in the Old Testament, Elohim was usually translated as "God," and *Yahweh* was frequently translated as "Lord." The Hebrews used the term *adonai or* "Lord" to refer to Yahweh. According to the narrator of Exodus 3:14, Yahweh was not just any god for Moses, and the state of Judah, but had an ontological status:

> And God [Yahweh] said to Moses, I AM THAT I AM: and
> he said, Thus shalt thou say unto the children of Israel, I
> AM hath sent me to you.

This would not be a surprising statement to read if the entire Pentateuch was written during or after the Babylonian exile in which all of the tribes that made up Israel were developing a common national history. This is an example of the development of a broader conception of God than previously existed for the creation of national unity among several different peoples.

Jewish and Christian Monotheism

By the time of Jesus, the worship of Yahweh had developed into Jewish monotheism, which considered Yahweh more than the personal deity of the tribes led by Moses to settle Canaan. Yahweh had become another name for the God who created and sustains the universe, to whom we can also pray. He was described by Jesus as "our Father in Heaven."[7]

Christianity added another layer of meaning to the Jewish concept of God by importing Jewish monotheism into the Roman Empire. In the Gospel of John, there is emphasis on the cosmic nature of God; "In the beginning was the Word, and the Word was with God, and the Word was God."[8] For John, salvation was not just for a chosen group of people, or a single state, but for the entire world.[9] Paul used Greek conceptions of ontology and universal reality in his description of God. This epigenesis was completed with Augustine's understanding of a real God that has been active in guiding the affairs of all people, regardless of whether or not they recognized Him. He does this in the context of refuting classical Roman conceptions of fate and the panoply of gods described by Cicero:

> The One True God....granted to the Roman people an empire, when He willed it, and as large as he willed it. It was the same God who gave kingdoms to the Assyrians and the Persians.... This is the God who gave corn to the Persians without regard to their worshiping the goddess of corn.[10]

Particular Forms of Christian Religion

Christianity did not, however, develop its monotheism apart from personages who could more directly relate to human beings. Like other religions, various teachers and cultures developed particular doctrines that often divided one group from another. The various branches of Christianity, for example, could not agree on the status of Jesus. Some thought Jesus came to become the King of Israel, others a divine King of Kings, still others said that Jesus was God himself. Early followers in Israel more likely saw him as the future king of Israel,[11] and Matthew attempted to prove this in his genealogy from David to Jesus.[12] This theme has persisted through the ages with legends of Jesus' lineage in France and attempts to place him on his rightful throne in Jerusalem.[13] Luke traced Jesus' lineage to Adam to associate him with the father of the entire human race.[14] In John he is "the Word made flesh." Some Christians have taken the idea that "Jesus is God" to the extreme position of saying that Jesus created the cosmos in which he was born, with no differentiation between Jesus and his Father.

The Catholic Church in the West and the Orthodox Church in the East could never agree on the status of Jesus in the doctrine of the trinity, creating the *filioque* controversy dividing the church in the two halves of the Roman Empire for hundreds of years. People in other religions, especially Islam, have wondered whether Christians have subverted a true monotheism with the deification of Jesus creating, in effect, two Gods.

Further, although Augustine vehemently criticized polytheism, his view of angels, and the role of angels in the Catholic Church, has been viewed as giving angels the same social function as the panoply of lesser supernatural gods in the ancient Near East. This concept was further developed with the idea of patron saints for different churches. Was the role of St. Peter in the Vatican functionally that different from the role of Marduk in the temple of Babylon? Further, was the concept of "guardian angels" or the adoption of personal saints as intercessors for prayer functionally any different from the ancient role ascribed to personal or family gods in the ancient Near East? To the extent that Jesus or any of these other personalities have been equated with God, or eclipse the role of a Creator of all, they have had the potential for divisiveness rather than unity.

In the Middle Ages, when a charismatic leader like St. Francis, St. Dominique, or Jan Hus obtained a significant following with characteristics like a modern sect or cult, the Church would either have it purged as heresy or find room for it under its umbrella by calling it an "order." In the Holy Roman Empire, the Church was thus able to maintain its position at the top of a hierarchy, with the Pope as the highest spiritual leader for the entire Western world. This fell apart with the Reformation.

Religious Pluralism and National Unity Under God in the United States

With the Reformation came the assertion that individuals were each directly accountable to God for their actions, removing the necessity of the priests as intercessors. Their role became religious instruction and ceremonial officiating. The floodgates were opened to all kinds of people receiving many different kinds of revelations. A spectrum of Protestants followed. On the conservative end, in Lutheranism and Anglicanism, the Catholic tradition was only slightly modified and allegiance to Rome severed. On the radical end of the spectrum, zealots took over the city of Münster in Germany, believing it to be the New Jerusalem. In Münster, John of Leyden was proclaimed King of New Zion.[15]

The Puritans

There is no need to go over a detailed history of all the denominations and religious sects that formed between the Reformation and the American Revolution. What is important to know is that the Puritans were one of many groups that ended up in America with an established church, i.e., a church politically integrated with the government of a colony. The Puritans, in particular, thought of America as a Promised Land, a New Israel, or the source of the spreading of God's Kingdom to the world.[16]

The sovereignty of God and the concern with limits on human power can be seen in early preachers like John Cotton:

> Let all the world learn to give mortall men no greater power than they are content they shall use, for use it they will.... It will be necessary...that all power that is on earth be limited, church power or other.... It is counted a matter of danger to the state to limit prerogatives, but it is a further danger not to have them limited. They will be like a Tempest if they be not limited. A Prince himselfe can not tell where he will confine himself, nor can the people tell.... It is therefore fit for every man to be studious of the bounds which the Lord hath set; and for the People, in whom fundamentally all power lyes, to give as much power as God in his word gives to men.[17]

This passage shows that Cotton, like his Protestant peers, was conversant with themes being developed in the political thought of Machiavelli, Hobbes, and Locke; concern about limitations on power and the concept that power lies with the people. But for the religious believer, the Sovereign was not King, compact, or state, but God or Christ. Despite Cotton's reference to the power of the people, the Puritans had set up a theocratic state in which the "will of God" was interpreted quite specifically by men who demanded obedience, as Roger Williams was quite aware. Despite the limitations of their own government, Puritan theology contained notions of freedom and the pursuit of happiness that would dovetail with those of the rationalist writers of the Declaration of Independence a century later.

Other Religions in America

There were many religious groups in America. Episcopalians in Virginia and Catholics in Maryland had a long history of being established churches before coming to America. The Congregationalists were established in New England. Pennsylvania, led by

William Penn, was made up of Quakers, who preached religious toleration. Rhode Island, which had been founded by Roger Williams, who had been exiled from Massachusetts for his religious beliefs, was adamantly opposed to established religion. There were Dutch Reformed in New York who had come from the only country in Europe that enjoyed religious freedom. In addition, there was an assortment of independent groups like the Anabaptists and Shakers who were engaged in social experimentation. Then there were the rationalists; Unitarians, freethinkers, and deists.

John Cotton, Thomas Hooker, Roger Williams, and William Penn, leaders of different religious movements in America, could all agree that the people were an earthly source of political power, but that it was given to them by God and should be exercised according to his will. In the words of Roger Williams:

> In a free state no magistrate hath power over bodies, goods, lands, liberties of a free people, but by their free consents. [Free men are not, however] free lords of their own estates, but are only stewards unto God, therefore they may not give their free consents to any magistrate to dispose of their bodies, goods, lands, liberties, at large as themselves please, but as God, the sovereign Lord of all, alone.[18]

These words convey the sense of freedom and personality in the colonies from the beginning. The early colonists did not have the sense of intrusion into their affairs by the King of England that developed later.

Because the specific religious doctrines of the early Americans differed widely, in the early eighteenth century it was very difficult for anyone to imagine creating any unity on the religiously pluralistic continent. It was a land of multiple experiments. The social and theological basis for that unity came, in addition to a shared geographical experience, from Freemasonry and the Great Awakening.

Freemasonry as General Religion

Freemasonry was based on the traditions of guilds of stonemasons, many of whom had built great cathedrals, castles, abbeys, and fortresses in Europe. They received the protection of King James I in Scotland and in the seventeenth century it became increasingly popular for men of other fields to become masons by paying a fee and becoming an "accepted" Mason. The actual first recorded induction was Dr. Robert Moray in Edinburgh in 1641. Another early inductee was Dr. Isaac Ashmole. Both these men were founding members of the British Royal Society, who brought in other scientists like, Sir Isaac Newton. Masonry became increasingly fashionable and soon the number of "accepted" Masons began to outnumber stonemasons.[19] Gradually masonry came to have little relation with the original practice of stonemasonry and became mainly a philosophical and benevolent society.

Masonry claimed its ancient roots in the building of the temples of Babylon, Solomon's temple, and the pyramids of Egypt. The tools of stonemasonry took on additional symbolic meaning as masons saw their own efforts deriving from God, the greatest builder, and "the Great Architect of the Universe." In addition to erecting buildings, Freemasons spoke about building character and developed a system of three "degrees" to chart one's social progress as a member of the fraternity. Many of the advances in masonry were related to a member learning moral lessons about building character and society.

The Grand Lodge of London was organized in 1717 by a merger of four lodges that published a book of constitutions known as "Anderson's Constitutions" in 1723. In London a number of the lodges incorporated more "freethinking" than the "ancient" rite established. The "moderns" were eventually accused of having sympathies with the revolutionary Jacobins in France and were pressured to conform to the ancient rite after the French Revolution.

Although there were Freemasons in America in 1705, the first official deputation was the appointment of Daniel Coxe, a Catholic, by the Duke of Norfolk in 1730. Although there is not much record of Coxe organizing Freemasonry in America, he was perhaps the first person to advocate that all of the British colonies organize under one political establishment.[20]

Benjamin Franklin helped organize St. John's Lodge in Philadelphia and drafted by-laws in 1732. Benjamin Franklin apparently associated with Masons in London that were known as Modern, and the lodge he founded was also Modern. In 1734 he printed Anderson's *Constitutions of the Free-Masons,* making it available throughout the colonies. Members of his lodge helped to erect Independence Hall in 1734-35. The actual builder was Thomas Baude, secretary of the lodge. It was inaugurated by William Allen, a former Grand Master. Four of those members went on to serve as governors of Pennsylvania. Franklin also founded the American Philosophical Society (eight Masons were members), which had many lawyers, judges, mayors, and sheriffs among its members.[21]

By 1737 the power and secrecy of the Masons had spawned suspicion and persecution. Masons had a run-in with parishioners of the Presbyterian Church because of their tolerance of Deism. Franklin's own mother was upset with his membership in the secret society, believing rumors that the Devil was involved in it. Then the *American Weekly Mercury,* the rival to Franklin's *Gazette,* joined the opponents, initiating a two-month newspaper war. Philadelphia became known as a Mecca for religious sects in the mid-eighteenth century. Gottlieb Mittleberger commented on the pluralism after his 1750 visit to Pennsylvania:

> Greater freedom exists here than in any other English colony, and sects of every belief are tolerated. You meet here Lutherans, Reformed, Catholics, Quakers, Mennonites, Herrenhutter or Moravian Brethern, Seventh Day Baptists, Dunkers, Presbyterians, the New Born, Freemasons, Separatists, Free Thinkers, Negroes and Indians.[22]

The controversies over Freemasonry led the lodge to become more circumspect, but activities continued and a network of social leaders throughout the colonies developed. Franklin lent support to evangelist George Whitefield when, by 1742, established churches would no longer let him use their buildings for his revivals. He and his friends erected a hall in which Whitefield could preach, beginning a forty-year friendship. When Whitefield thanked Franklin for aiding the cause of Christ, Franklin replied, that "it was not for Christ's sake, but your sake." While he was an iconoclast, Franklin believed that open preaching was good for the soul, and he urged his own daughter to "go constantly to church, whoever preaches."[23] Franklin was not an opponent to particular inspired forms of religion, however, he was a bitter opponent of established state churches.

Religion and National Unity

In 1754 Franklin defended a plan for the political integration of the colonies before the Albany Congress,[24] perhaps being the second person (Coxe being the first) to promote the idea. If Franklin's proposal for a federation of colonies had been accepted, the Revolution likely would not have taken place.

Another early center of American Freemasonry was Boston. In 1733, Henry Price founded the first regular lodge in America under the authority of the Grand Lodge of London. By 1750, over 40 lodges had sprung from this lodge. Then in 1755, another branch of Masonry, known as the Scottish Rite, which claimed to be more ancient and authentic, was established, bringing about a protest from the original Masons. Unlike Pennsylvania, the Bostonian Masons often met at Christ Church in Boston and listened to sermons.[25]

Joseph Warren, Grand Master of St. Andrew's Lodge in Boston, was also a member of a radical political group known as the North End Caucus. Warren's friend, Sam Adams, son of the brewer, had become a firebrand revolutionary. Both were also members of the Sons of Liberty. Adams had encouraged the formation of the Committees of Correspondence which proclaimed the battle cry, "No King but King Jesus," up and down the Atlantic coast.[26] These Bostonians, like their Puritan forefathers, had a more particular understanding of religion on their political agenda than the more liberal and diplomatic rationalists like Franklin and Jefferson.

On December 16, 1773, against the advice of Franklin, the group in Boston engaged in sabotage. Both St. Andrew's Lodge and the North End Caucus were "meeting" at the Green Dragon Tavern while outside Samuel Adams, Joseph Warren, and Josiah Quincy were speaking to a large crowd of people. On the cue of Adams, forty or fifty "Mohawks" (actually Warren's Masons, North-Enders, and Sons of Liberty dressed as Indians) rushed out of a back room onto the docks and dumped 342 cases of tea into the harbor.[27] On Sundays, these men had been listening to rousing sermons from preachers saying the people are responsible to no king.[28]

In London, in 1773 or 1774 Thomas Paine, a Virginia-born searcher for truth, met Benjamin Franklin who was on a diplomatic assignment to England. He was captivated by Franklin, a self-made and self-taught American legend. Franklin shared his philosophical ideas and his thoughts on America. He sent Paine back to America in 1774 with letters of introduction to spark his public career. Paine published *Common Sense* in 1776. He is often miscredited with having a wide impact on galvanizing the forces for the American Revolution.[29] However, his tract perhaps convinced the balking Enlightenment rationalists by officially declaring the Revolution already underway in the minds of many Americans. Not to join the Revolution would perhaps have eventually meant political death for them.[30] The time for negotiation had passed; there was returning. Zeal fuelled by religion and by and disillusionment with British rule had reached the point of revolution.[31]

National Religious Revivals

By 1720 the established churches in America seemed to many to focus on preservation of tradition and to be out of touch with life in the colonies. Everywhere there was a sense that material concerns had supplanted spiritual ones. The Puritan ministers often berated their listeners for their failures and sins. Foreign churches seemed devoted to preservation of the language and culture of the mother country. The Enlightenment had made many traditional religious assumptions seem antiquated. Many newcomers to America were not joining churches at all and, even though the number of churches was growing, the percentage of the population attending church was declining. This was a period fertile for religious revival.[32]

The Great Awakenings were a phenomenon that spanned five decades from about 1720 to the time of the American Revolution. They were spiritual revivals that affected established religions differently. Some churches opposed them, other churches were divided by them, and new churches were formed as the enthusiasm spawned new revelations that both borrowed and rejected elements from traditional religion and the Enlightenment. The increased commerce and transportation among the colonies allowed itinerant preachers and waves of revivals to move through the colonies. These Awakenings played a role in creating a new social layer, a cultural epigenesis, over those disparate elements that had settled in America in an ad hoc fashion who now realized they were neighbors.

George Whitefield (1714-1770) was the greatest itinerant evangelist of the eighteenth century, known on both sides of the ocean. Whitefield, the son of an innkeeper, had gone to Oxford to study. There he associated with the Wesleys and the beginnings of the Methodist movement. He took Anglican orders in 1736. Two years later he went to the new colony of Georgia and, using his homiletic talents, organized a home for orphans. He returned to England and found established pulpits closing to him because of his commitment to the Evangelical Awakening, which was becoming controversial. However, he could draw crowds of up to 20,000 people in the open air of London parks. He traveled to America in 1739 (he was to cross the ocean thirteen times) and stopped in Philadelphia on his way to Georgia. His spectacular preaching drew the attention of Presbyterian Awakening leaders William and Gilbert Tennent. He was soon drawing thousands, and creating the controversies that led to his friendship with Benjamin Franklin.

Gilbert Tennent, emboldened by Whitefield's example, traveled to Nottingham, Pennsylvania, in 1740 and delivered a sermon on "The Dangers of an Unconverted Ministry," openly expressing the widely held view that established church leaders were mere academic "Pharisee-teachers" who did not have the spiritual enthusiasm of those who had experienced conversion. This led to a split in the Presbyterian Church between the "New Side" and the "Old Side."

In New England, Jonathan Edwards (1703-1758) was independently creating a stir among Congregationalists. The son of a minister, he had tutored at Yale and intensely probed the writings of such Enlightenment thinkers as Locke and Newton, Edwards took charge of his grandfather's church in Northampton, Massachusetts, in 1729. He became famous in Boston after an address in 1731 that integrated the theme of the sovereignty of God with Calvinist predestination. Hundreds of souls were being converted by his preaching of a theology ripe for the American scene. In 1740 George Whitefield visited Boston and then went to Northampton. There were no buildings that could accommodate the throngs. People came from all over—churched, unchurched. Edwards preached about the Kingdom of God beginning in America:

> When God is about to turn the earth into a Paradise, he does not begin with his work where there is some good growth already, but in a wilderness, where nothing grows,

and nothing is to be seen but dry sand and barren rocks; that the light may shine out of the darkness, and the world replenished from emptiness, and the earth watered by springs from a droughty desert. [33]

Edwards stressed the worship of a sovereign and transcendent God, emphasizing that the human will directs us to worship something and we often find that we devote ourselves to ourselves, other people, or the world. However, we must transfer our loyalties from the partial, the ephemeral, and the relative to the eternal, universal, and absolute God.[34] Edwards has earned the distinction of being called the first American theologian, or the father of American theology.

As Enlightenment thought became increasingly popular in colleges, it was often used by some of the "Old Lights" to rationally defend traditional religion from the "enthusiasm" of the revivalists. Charles Chauncy, minister of Boston's First Church for his long career, espoused rational defenses of Congregationalism that aroused the suspicion of more orthodox believers. The result was another schism among the Congregationalists, leading to the formation of Unitarian Universalism.

The significance of the Awakenings is that they fostered a general redirection of Protestantism across the colonies of America. While they caused fractures in the traditional churches, they reinvigorated the faith and energy of the people and the emergence of what many believed to be the coming Kingdom of God in America. They hastened the separation of church and state in all of the colonies. They also brought black slaves into churches; and new denominations for Blacks and native Americans were formed. The indigenization of American religion had begun to supplant the traditional forms of European Christendom in America.

In the process of spreading faith, the Awakenings helped foster a common identity for the emerging nation, spreading common interests and loyalties among people that had previously lived separately from one another. The Awakenings also fostered the democratic ideal by promoting personal responsibility under the watchful eye of a transcendent God. They spread the idea that America had a special role in the providence of God. The Awakenings took place alongside the spread of the Enlightenment, creating a tension between two styles of religious and psychological life in the colonies before the Revolution.

Common Cause in Overthrowing an Oppressor

Nothing galvanizes the cooperation and friendship of disparate groups like common suffering under oppression. History is replete with examples. In the case of the British colonies in North America, it was the increased and arbitrary taxation on the colonies on the part of King George III. This was seen as both an encroachment on the freedom the colonies had known and the imposition of an unjust tax. The rationalists, like liberals today, were opposed to war and worked to negotiate more independence from the crown. The religious enthusiasts, on the other hand, were impatient and undiplomatic in their language. In England, Edmund Burke, a Whig, became known for his courageous speeches arguiing for a reversal of the policies of the crown and a reconciliation with the Americans who, in his opinion agreed "on nothing but the spirit of liberty."[35]

Burke and Franklin were unsuccessful in bringing about a diplomatic solution to the growing rebellion in America. The Boston Tea Party, which included cooperation among, of all things, religious enthusiasts and Freemasons, was a harbinger of a unique period of cooperation between rationalists and pietists who, in normal times, could not have been more ideologically polarized.

Historian Sidney E. Mead described the apparently strange coalition of rationalists and pietists as the "head" and the "heart" of the revolution.[36] Both groups contained learned men who opposed traditionalism and sought liberty. George Washington, a military officer and landed aristocrat, was also a Whig, who, like Burke and other Whigs, thought British imposition of taxes unfair. By 1775, after blood had been shed in Lexington and Concord, he was willing to accept command of the Continental Army and lead the fight for American independence. Before the revolution, he had been a devout member of the Church of England and neither an anti-religious rationalist nor a left-wing pietist. A gentleman, Washington believed in mutual respect, moderation, and tolerance. He inspired the confidence of both groups.

It has been said that George Washington would not trust any officer under his command who was not a Mason.[37] Masons had to undergo tests of moral integrity intended to make them socially responsible citizens. Masons, as masons, also remained neutral with respect to religious denomination or political party. Freemasonry has been described as "the religion of the American Revolution."[38] The list of members of early American Masonry reads like a *Who's Who* of American founders, and the American presidents, judges and military leaders of the nineteenth century also were frequently masons. Masonry included freethinkers and rationalists as well as Christian pastors and church elders. Common soldiers, on the other hand, were often motivated to fight for independence based on religious convictions stemming from the Awakenings or their desire to be free of British taxes. Despite their differences in belief, the bonds of men of the Continental Army were galvanized by their opposition to a common oppressor.

Questions for Reflection

1. How did the founding fathers separate their references to God from established religion?

2. What factors contributed to the separation of church and state in the United States?

3. How was it that Enlightenment rationalists and pietistic revivalists could reach agreement on the basic idea of the United States?

4. Do you think that science has delegitimated the concept of God that underpins the United States' legal system?

5. Do you think the influx of immigrants from non-European and non-Protestant cultures delegitimates the concept of God that underpins the United States legal system?

6. Freemasons, Boy Scouts, and other social organizations attempt to foster leadership based on obedience to God without discussing religious doctrine. Do you think such a concept should be part of the public education system or that it would violate the principle of church and state?

5

The Formation of the United States

Failure of the Articles of Confederation

THE VICTORY OF THE CONTINENTAL ARMY, with the assistance of the French, at the Battle of Yorktown in 1781 gave the colonies their freedom. However, there was little unity of national purpose. Everyone tried to return to "business as usual."

Each colony wanted to retain its freedom and independence. The following excerpts from the Articles of Confederation are fascinating to consider:

I. The Stile of this Confederacy shall be "The United States of America."

II. Each state retains its sovereignty, freedom, and independence, and every power, jurisdiction, and right, which is not by this Confederation expressly delegated to the United States, in Congress assembled.

III. The said States hereby severally enter into a firm league of friendship with each other, for their common defense, the security of their liberties, and their mutual and general welfare, binding themselves to assist each other, against all force offered to, or attacks made upon them, or any of them, on account of religion, sovereignty, trade, or any other pretense whatever...[1]

The Confederation failed to work. States that had not paid their share of expenses for the war refused to pay anything. Massachusetts ended up paying a disproportionate amount—about as much as New York, Pennsylvania, Virginia, and Maryland combined. Disputes between states erupted with no successful means of resolution; there was no executive or judicial branch of government with the power to compel arbitration. Congress only had power to make war and peace, draft treaties, and maintain a postal service. After several years, George Washington's troops had not been paid. States erected tariffs on one another and coined their own money.[2]

The Constitutional Convention

The Leadership of Washington

George Washington, who had returned to private life at Mount Vernon, was among those dissatisfied with national disunity under the Articles of Confederation. Washington advocated a stronger central government, hosting the Mount Vernon Conference (1785) at his estate, though he apparently did not directly participate in the discussions. In May 1787, at the urging of friends, after first writing to them to say that he would not attend,[3] he went to Philadelphia and was elected to preside over the Constitutional Convention.

What Washington did not know, he made sure to learn from a variety of scholars and leaders whose opinions he respected. Washington's letters from the time contain correspondence with, among others, James Madison, John Jay, and General Knox. In this correspondence, John Jay argued for three branches of government, an upper and lower house, and limits on the term and power of the executive, with the states retaining power according to their domestic governance. General Knox suggested a Federal government that basically replaced the individual state governments. He thought the executive should be elected by the upper house for a term of seven years, but be impeachable by the lower house. James Madison proposed a middle ground between state independence and federal sovereignty and suggested changing methods of representation. He believed that, for a union to work, national supremacy was necessary in all branches of government; by appeal to the federal judiciary and by executive access to a militia, with the right of coercion expressly declared.[4]

The men who gathered in Philadelphia were well educated. Many of them were widely read in the classics and even conversed in a mixture of English, Latin, and Greek. In those days, entrance to Harvard required an extemporaneous reading from Livy, Cicero, or other ancient Roman or Greek writers in the original language. Franklin was not formally educated, but was an inspiration because he was self-taught and had read the classics. He was fluent in several languages, ancient and modern. One did not need an advanced education for most trades, except law and government. Most of the founders were aristocrats, who were both social philosophers and philanthropists. Of the fifty-five men at the convention, fifty were Freemasons.

James Madison's notes provide us with the best record of the proceedings.[5] John Adams and Thomas Jefferson were absent, serving as U.S. ministers to England and France, respectively. Those present felt that the Articles of Confederation were too weak to be rewritten and that they would need to write a new constitution.

Thousands of books have been cited as contributing to the development of the American Constitution. The founders were widely read. They knew the classics, as well as the contemporary writings of Europe. They were knowledgeable of the histories of England and France and corresponded with philosophers of the Enlightenment, both in its French and Scottish forms.

The Convention was stormy. Small states feared domination by large states. Historians tend to agree that it was only George Washington's presence and civility that kept the Convention together. In a July 10 letter to Alexander Hamilton, who had given up and returned to New York, Washington expressed regret for anything he might have done. He commented that

> the Councils…are now, if possible, in a worse train than ever; you will find little ground on which the hope of a good establishment can be formed. In a word, I *almost* despair of seeing a favourable issue to the proceedings of our Convention…. The men who oppose a strong and energetic government are, in my opinion, narrow minded politicians, or are under the influence of local views…. I am sorry you went away. I wish you were back.[6]

The Charismatic Intervention of Franklin

When it looked as though the breakdown of the Convention was imminent, Benjamin Franklin, a seasoned statesman, brought some sense of higher perspective to the delegates with the following statement:

> Our different sentiments on almost every question is methinks a melancholy proof of the imperfection of human understanding. We indeed seem to feel our own want of political wisdom, since we have been running about in search of it…. I have lived Sir, a long time, and the longer I live, the more convincing proofs I see of this truth—that God governs in the affairs of men. And if a sparrow cannot fall to the ground without his notice, is it probable that an empire can rise without his aid? We have been assured, Sir, in the sacred writings that "except the Lord builds the House, they labor in vain that build it." I firmly believe this; and I also believe that without his concurring aid we shall succeed in this political building no better than the Builders of Babel: We shall be divided by our little partial local interests; our projects will be confounded, and we ourselves shall become a reproach and byword down to future ages.

And what is worse, mankind may hereafter from this unfortunate instance, despair of establishing governments by human wisdom and leave it to chance, war, and conquest.

I therefore beg leave to move—that henceforth prayers imploring the assistance of Heaven, and its blessings on our deliberations be held in the Assembly every morning before we proceed to business....[7]

Some of the delegates, like rationalists today, were surprised that such a proposal came from a freethinker who had doubts about much of Christian doctrine. Franklin's beliefs were well stated in a letter he wrote to Ezra Stiles, president of Yale University a few weeks before he died:

Here is my creed: I believe in one God, Creator of the Universe. That He governs it by His providence. That he ought to be worshipped. That the most acceptable service we render Him is doing good to His other children. That the soul of man is immortal, and will be treated with justice in another life respecting its conduct in this.[8]

Franklin had made an appeal to the convention delegates to establish the type of nation God would desire, and not to focus on petty differences. Although his motion for daily prayer was not passed, his speech brought a new sense of humility and sober reflection to those present. It is credited as marking the turning point of the Convention: from that moment the delegates really started to work on the creation of a new constitution.

Under Washington's careful and patient leadership, the Convention eventually gave birth to the Constitution. Conflicts revolved around three central issues. One division came between larger states and smaller states. It was to the advantage of smaller states, like New Jersey, to have equal representation of each state. The larger states with more population, like Virginia, wanted representation to be based on population. A compromise was the two-house legislature, in which the upper house would have equal representation (two senators) and the lower house would apportion seats based on population.

Another conflict existed between northern states and southern states over the issue of slavery. Southern states wanted each slave counted for representation; northern states argued that slaves held as property without the right to vote should not be counted for representation. The "Three-Fifths Compromise" was worked out, whereby every five slaves would be treated as three free men for purposes of representation. Slave states also wanted to continue importation of slaves while free states were opposed to the slave trade. They reached a compromise whereby slaves could be imported for twenty years, but a tax of $10 per head would be levied. These compromises did not resolve deep-seated issues over slavery, which eventually led to the Civil War.

Another debate occurred when manufacturing states suggested that Congress should have the power to levy tariffs on exports and imports. Agricultural states were opposed. The "Commerce Compromise" said that Congress could tax imports but not exports.

Another conflict arose between aristocrats and democrats over the election of the president, with aristocrats favoring election for life and democrats favoring election for a single term. This issue was compromised by have the president elected by the Electoral College for a four-year term subject to reelection. They also disagreed over the election of Congress and compromised with the idea that representatives would be elected by the people, but Senators would be appointed by state legislatures.

The Constitution left to the states control of local affairs, while the federal government was given power to collect taxes, coin money, raise an army and navy, declare war, and regulate commerce. It separated power into three branches designed to check and balance one another, and it set up a process for amending the Constitution.

The Constitution was signed on September 17, 1787, but would not go into effect until it was ratified by state legislatures.

Ratification of the Constitution and the Bill of Rights

When the Constitution was submitted to the people, further discussion developed. "Federalists" favored its adoption, but "Anti-Federalists" believed it gave the federal government too much power. Some Anti-Federalists favored more state power while others, like Jefferson, wanted more power to reside in the people. In New York, the Federalist arguments were made in a number of newspaper articles by Alexander Hamilton, James Madison, and John Jay. They were later collectively published as *The Federalist Papers* and are one of the best sources for additional reading on understanding the Constitution. Some of the vocal Anti-Federalists were Patrick Henry, John Hancock, and Samuel Adams.

Thomas Jefferson, who was in Paris, wrote to James Madison saying that he would not favor ratification until a Bill of Rights was added to the Constitution. After saying what he liked about the Constitution, he set about describing what he saw as its deficiencies, the first of which was "the omission of a bill of rights, providing clearly, and without the aid of sophism, for freedom of religion, freedom of the press, protection against standing armies, restriction of monopolies, the eternal and unremitting force of the habeas corpus laws, and trials by jury in all matters of fact triable by the laws of the land, and not by the laws of nations."[9]

Five states urged that a Bill of Rights be adopted. Jefferson said he did not think Virginia would ratify the constitution until a Bill of Rights was added. Under the leadership of James Madison, ten amendments were passed by the first Congress. The Bill of Rights addressed most of Jefferson's concerns except for restriction on economic powers and standing armies.

The Cabinet, the Courts, and the Treasury

When Washington became the first President, he wanted to appoint an executive officer for each "department" of government. This was not specified by the Constitution. The Congress soon created four departments: the State Department, the Treasury Department, the Attorney General, and the War Department. The heads of this advisory council became collectively known as the Cabinet.

The Constitution stated that there should be a Supreme Court and inferior courts as necessary. In 1789, Congress passed the Judiciary Act, which established District and Circuit Courts and an appeals process from lower to higher courts. It set up the Supreme Court with one Chief Justice and five Associate Justices, and George Washington appointed John Jay as the Chief Justice.

Washington appointed Alexander Hamilton to head the Treasury Department. He wanted the Federal Government to assume the unpaid state war debts, to set up a bank, and to print money. Jefferson opposed this. President Washington listened to the arguments of each and liked Hamilton's plan better. Jefferson's concerns were somewhat relieved by a compromise requiring Hamilton to establishing the financial center in a location different from that of the seat of government. The differences between the Hamiltonians and the Jeffersonians eventually led to the formation of the first two political parties, the Federalist Party and the Anti-Federalists, later known as Democratic-Republican Party.

State Neutrality in Foreign Affairs

President Washington believed that the United States should take a neutral position toward other nations and issued a Proclamation of Neutrality in 1793. Some Americans were more closely allied to France, which had helped the United States in the Revolutionary War. Others favored England because of cultural and economic ties. James Madison questioned whether Washington had the authority to issue such a proclamation without the approval of Congress. In his Farewell Address, Washington again warned the nation to remain neutral and not to enter into permanent alliances with other nations. This policy became the basis for foreign relations for the next hundred years.

The Government as a Referee

At the Constitutional Convention, George Washington had asked for delegates' opinions about how the United States could be established to provide both adequate security and maximum liberty to its citizens. His goal was to create a state that would be the opposite of a tyranny, in which everyone works for the goal of one ruler. In the United States, the role of government was changed from dictator to referee.

In the United States, the pursuit of happiness, like the pursuit of victory in a football game, can only be played when rules of fair play are established and followed. The Constitution established rules that would allow every citizen to "play the game." These rules included three branches of government with various checks and balances on the power of each and a judicial system designed to ensure the rules were followed.

Try to imagine a professional football game played without referees, or a football game in which referees apply different rules to each team. Imagine penalties called only against one team, while the other team is granted a few extra yards each down. Imagine that one team *is* the referee. Without following rules of fair play provided by independent referees, the football game would fall apart. The team treated unfairly would quit and go home, as would most of the fans. And, if the referees demanded more money for their services than the amount of ticket sales, the game could not be played.

The laws of the United States serve as the referee that allows all citizens to pursue their happiness on fair and equal grounds. It must penalize players that use their power unfairly to gain results for themselves at the expense of others. There are limits to this analogy, but these basic principles should apply:

1. The government must ensure fair and competitive play, with all players treated equally.

2. The government must not allow one player to bend the rules in its favor at the expense of others.

3. The government must not become a player itself, pursuing ends independent of the people or at the expense of the people.

4. The government must not charge excessively for its services, becoming a burden on the people's use of their own resources to pursue their own happiness.

The founding fathers wanted to ensure that the people had recourse if the government abandoned its role of providing a fair framework of justice. They were not sure that all of the features they devised would enable the government to remain on its path. In case the legislative, the executive, or the judicial branch were to be derailed from its mission, they created the Bill of Rights (the first ten Amendments to the Constitution) which was described by Thomas Jefferson as "the rights the people have against every government on earth." These non-compromisable rights included: the right of citizens to free expression, to self-defense, to protection of property, and to fair trial.

Edward Banfield, a professor of government at Harvard University, has argued that this makes the difference between "democracy" and "liberal democracy."

> Everyone knows that democracy is rule by the people. It is tempting to suppose that where the people rule there can be no tyranny. But history and reflection tell us that this is not so: a majority may tyrannize cruelly over a minority. What we want is not majority rule simply, but majority rule plus the protection of certain rights that pertain to individuals. This is the difference between democracy and liberal democracy: in the latter there is a private sphere into which the governing authority may not intrude no matter how large the majority behind it.[10]

The Private Sector Makes the Citizen, the Government Provides Security

The United States was established as a liberal democracy, as Banfield defined the term. It was also designed as a republic in that it uses methods of representative rule. The institutions of liberal democracy protect the private sphere, but those institutions can only exist as long as public opinion values the arrangement as legitimate. This means that no attachment to an individual religion, ideology, or tribal or ethnic group can take precedence over the protection of the basic individual rights in the Bill of Rights. In Banfield's words, "what the majority holds sacred may, on occasion, have to be subordinated to what it deems demonic."[11]

The wide support for the laws and institutions that defend concessions of the majority will to individual rights can be called "civility," or good manners. This is the culturally ingrained willingness to tolerate behavior that some may deem offensive but that is protected for the sake of equality in the pursuit of happiness for all. The sharper the conflict in society, the greater the need for voluntary restraint, or a loss of liberty will ensue. Without civility the United States, like Rome after citizens lost faith in the laws, would become a police state to maintain order. Civility includes some bargaining process which accepts concessions, and the possibilities of competing truth claims. When citizens abandon civility, when they refuse to accept the rules, they cease to play the game. They are like ball players unwilling to gracefully accept the decision of a referee.

Every Citizen Is a Player

The underlying concept behind the American experiment is that every person is a player, pursuing his or her own happiness. That means each adult person is responsible for his own behavior, livelihood, self-maintenance, and citizenship. Of course, children do not automatically possess the capacity for such adult responsibilities; they must be taught to accomplish these things by parents, churches, schools, and employers. The inculcation of civic virtue is the responsibility of the private sector. The existence of the state is thus at the mercy of the success of the private sector in accomplishing this job.

When the United States was founded, 98 percent of the population could loosely be classified as Protestant, if rationalists and Deists are considered among Protestants. Protestant culture, like Jewish culture, had been rooted in the morality taught in the Bible, rules of moral behavior that transcend government laws. One main point of Protestantism is that individuals are responsible for self-governance. Protestants believed that, regardless of how one appeared publicly to one's neighbor, God was aware of every action and every thought one had. They believed that eternal life consisted in the purification of thought and action so that life in accordance with God's laws would be automatic.

Since there was no perceived contradiction between the laws of general religion and particular religion and because all states and religions in the union accepted the general ground rules of the government, there was neither much need for a large police force to keep order and citizens did not expect the government to provide for any of their needs except to enforce the law fairly.

The people in the United States in 1789 were prepared for the government they received. Families, churches, communities, and states were, for the most part, producing citizens capable of fulfilling their responsibilities as citizens under the government that had been designed. The religious and cultural ethos accepted and promoted a sense of individual and national responsibility. Originally, although it was something Federalists like Hamilton desired, the government was given no role in developing the economy. Jefferson took a direct hand in making the United States larger and the American Experiment available for more people with the Louisiana Purchase. As a result, there was plenty of available land for a life of farming, which was the form of livihood Jefferson thought most conducive to the formation of good character.

A high degree of education was not required for economic success; one could learn the needed skills in one's family, or train for a trade as an apprentice. Those who worked hard and obeyed the laws prospered. Extended families and church communities were supposed to care for dependents and the less fortunate. The love that generated this care was taught by families, churches and schools. The federal government was not designed as a caregiver, or viewed as responsible for citizen education; it needed only to provide physical security and act as a referee when issues could not be resolved among individuals.

A Game for Farmers, Artisans, and Shopkeepers

The Constitution and the Bill of Rights were designed for a society of farmers, artisans, and tradesmen. In the United States at the turn of the eighteenth century, farms and businesses were mostly family-run enterprises. In this setting all citizens were going about living freely and pursuing their happiness by engaging in (a) farming, that provided their own food and shelter directly through their own labor, or (b) personal and family businesses that earned money that could be exchanged for basic necessities. Like their political power, their economic power was well distributed among individuals and families.

Aristotle, in *The Politics*, had written that "an agricultural population makes the best *demos*."[12] This is because everyone is busy pursuing their own livelihood and is not busy coveting other people's possessions or trying to make a living off of other people's work. Jefferson felt that the American experiment was designed for such people, stating,

> I think our governments will remain virtuous for many centuries; as long as they are chiefly agricultural; and this will be as long as there are vacant lands in any part of America. When they pile upon one another in large cities as in Europe, they will become corrupt as in Europe.[13]

The "invisible hand" behind the economy, articulated by Jefferson's contemporary, Adam Smith, worked pretty well among these family-run enterprises. Smith's *Wealth of Nations* (1776) was the first serious attempt to divorce the economy from government and jurisprudence. Like Newton's "billiard ball" analysis of physics, Smith's economic analysis was accurate under the normal observable circumstances of his time. The country was not prepared for large-scale corporations with "visible hands" that dwarfed the financial power of family enterprises.

The founders of the American experiment designed the Constitution as a minimal document to establish basic ground rules, and they left the details and the solution to other problems to those that followed them. They assumed the federal government would protect the pursuit of happiness, but that the pursuit itself would be left to individual citizens and lower levels of government. They did not expect the federal government would be involved in business, education, welfare, health care, or religion. All of that was to come at the urging of citizens, businesses, and interest groups who wanted to play a different game, a game in which they could use the government to get something for themselves at the expense of other taxpayers or other countries.

Whether the philosophy of the founding of the United States was adequate or appropriate has been continually debated throughout the country's history. These questions surfaced in many different situations and a number of the concerns of future generations required amendments to the Constitution to implement. Consideration of whether these amendments were philosophically sound or whether they were made in haste to accomplish a goal that undercut the basic experiment should be a part of the philosophizing about the United States that goes on in subsequent generations. That is the subject matter of Part III.

Questions for Reflection

1. Why did the Articles of Confederation fail?

2. Do you think that the United States could have been formed without the leadership of George Washington and Benjamin Franklin?

3. In the philosophy of the founders, what were the responsibilities of the federal government?

4. In the philosophy of the founders, what qualities were required of the people if their experiment in self-government was to succeed?

5. Do you think that the limited role of the federal government the founders envisioned was faulty and that the expanded role of the federal government we see today was a necessary development?

6. Do you think the United States government was designed for a different type of citizenry than we have today? If so, would it be more appropriate to try to create citizens appropriate to the government or a government more suited to our population today?

7. Do you think that the present United States economy, based on industry, is so different from the agrarian economy of the colonies that the system of government the founders designed is inappropriate?

Part III
Unplanned Developments

6

Checks and Balances on Political Power

They called it an election, but it looked more like an auction.

—Greg Palast, *The Best Democracy Money Can Buy*[1]

CHECKS AND BALANCES ON POWER were one of the primary concerns of the founders of the United States. The experience of government from ancient times was that "power corrupts and absolute power corrupts absolutely." A central question in fashioning a government, then, is: How can power be limited to the minimum necessary for the accomplishment of a task? The task was not easy, the founders disagreed on a number of issues, and the result was not perfect.

Political power can be compared to electrical power; it will flow through any conductor that exists, and more power flows through larger conductors. This chapter highlights a few examples of checks and balances gone awry. In some cases the power leaks a bit and in other cases it flows freely. The United States Constitution established general checks and balances on power among the three branches of government and between the government and the people. Details were left to the Congress to work out and the courts to interpret.

Checks on the Executive Branch

Historically, the main concern with power in Europe had revolved around the problems with the absolute power of the kings and princes. Some experience with checking this power had been developed over time in England with the Magna Carta and growth of Parliament. The experience of ancient Rome and Greece could also be drawn upon.

The President, as Commander-in-Chief, or as Chief Executive is most likely to misuse his power especially during periods of crisis. James Madison thought that President George Washington overstepped his authority with his Proclamation of Neutrality. Others have accused presidents of overstepping their authority in declarations of war, or international policing actions. Many felt that President Franklin Roosevelt overstepped his authority in New Deal reforms and his election to office for more than two terms.

The founders constitutionally checked the Executive branch, allowing Congress to pass laws over a President's veto and allowing the Supreme Court to decide on the constitutionality of a President's actions. During crises, such as wars or economic depression, citizens feel that their ability to freely pursue life, liberty, and happiness are at risk and they look to decisive leadership to get them safely through the stormy waters and back to peaceful conditions.

The question that thus frequently arises is whether a crisis is real or contrived. In other words, did the President contribute to the creation of crisis conditions that allow him to exercise greater power, or was the calamity due only to outside forces? For example, skeptics have wondered whether Franklin Roosevelt knew the Japanese were going to attack Pearl Harbor and allowed it to happen so he would have public support for a declaration of war.

The September 11 terrorist attacks on the United States reopened this debate. The Patriot Act of 2001 was quickly passed after the attacks, giving the President power to pursue terrorists with few of the traditional constraints related to due process and invasion of privacy. A proposed Security Enhancement Act of 2003, encountered greater opposition because no terrorist attacks on United States soil had been repeated. Secret arrests, imprisonment without due process, and search and seizure of property without court orders all open the door to abuses of the human rights declared in the Bill of Rights.

Another issue is the claim to "executive privilege," first invoked by Dwight D. Eisenhower in 1954. Eisenhower told an army secretary not to testify in a hearing conducted by Senator Joseph McCarthy because it was not in the public interest. Eisenhower invoked the privilege forty times and other Presidents following him have done this as well. The claim to executive privilege has frustrated Congress by preventing it from getting to the truth on issues. However, normally decisions on sensitive issues are determined by a court because the Congress is unable to keep matters secret. The Supreme Court has never made a decision about whether a claim to "executive privilege" is constitutional. Nevertheless, if presidential behavior is despicable enough, Congress can remove the president from office.

Checks on the Judicial Branch

The checks the executive has on the judicial branch are the appointment of judges, and the pardoning of persons sentenced by the court. Congress has the right to confirm the appointment of judges and the right to remove them from office. Congress can also propose amendments to the Constitution (which must be ratified by three-fourths of the states) to reverse positions taken by the courts.

Alexander Hamilton detailed the founders' intentions for the Supreme Court in *The Federalist, No. 78*. He stated that the judiciary is the weakest of the three branches and that it does not have the power to enforce its decisions. The long duration of the appointment of the judges is to ensure a perspective beyond the political pressures of the day. The job of the judges is to interpret the laws during disputes, and when a law conflicts with the Constitution to give the Constitution heavier weight in their judgment.

The power of the Supreme Court was increased under the watch of the Federalist Chief Justice John Marshall, the fourth Chief Justice, appointed by John Adams in 1801. In 1803, the landmark decision in *Marbury v. Madison* gave the Court judicial review over acts of the other two branches of government. While this decision provided a check on the power of the other two branches which can ensure they are acting constitutionally, it also opened up the possibility that the Court would veto actions that were within the bounds intended by the founders.

It is frequently argued that "activist" courts have overstepped their constitutional authority, doing more than interpreting the law and upholding the constitution. Historically, Supreme Court judges have made decisions based on their own personal experiences or ideology. Chief Justice Earl Warren flatly stated "We make law."[2] And at times the Court has made laws in areas that would not have conformed to the founders' idea of the nation.

Because the Court is able to decide which cases it will hear, it has the power to put social issues that the founders left to personal choice and the lower levels of government on the federal agenda, giving the federal government a constantly expanding jurisdiction. Thus, the Supreme Court has issued philosophical and moral opinions on issues the founders purposely left up to the states. This is both the usurpation of state authority and unnecessary embroilment of the Court in social issues purposely left to the states.

For example, in the 1973 abortion case, *Roe v. Wade,* Justice Blackmun, in the majority opinion, argued that the Texas statute on abortion was unconstitutional because it adopted a theory of life that overrode the rights of a pregnant woman. It went on to say that the right overridden was the "right to privacy." This right was never articulated by the founders but developed later. As Robert Bork has said, "The right does not come out of the Constitution but was forced into it."[3] Justice Rehnquist, in his dissent, argued that,

> The upshot is that the people and the legislatures of the 50 States are constitutionally disentitled to weigh the relative importance.... As an excercise in raw judicial power, the Court perhaps has authority to do what it does today; but in my view its judgement is an improvident and extravagant exercise of the power of judicial review...

According to Robert Bork, when Justice Blackmun discussed the case in public after the decision, the only justification he gave was moral, not legal.[4] Potter Stewart, who joined in the opinion, saw abortion as one reasonable solution to population control, and felt that the public was ready for abortion reform, but that the state legislatures were too far behind. However, there is data to show that state legislatures were changing their own laws to reflect public opinion. Justice Earl Warren saw the decision as fitting because lower courts would have a guideline from the Supreme Court that would make their own decisions easier. But did the founders intend for the state courts to get federal guidelines on issues the they had left to the states?[5]

These Justices appeared to be justifying their decision based upon perceptions that did not fit with the founders' intention for the Court. They used their position on the Supreme Court to dictate social policy or make *de facto* law that would interfere with the pursuit of life, liberty and happiness the way approximately half of the people in the United States' population felt. This was a stretch of their authority which, for non-Constitutional reasons, embroiled the Court in social controversy. In addition to being outside the framework outlined by Hamilton, it restricted the freedom of the people to work out controversial social policy, what Montesquieu would call "positive law," at their own pace.

The Bush-Gore Election

The involvement of the courts in the contested vote between George W. Bush and Albert Gore in the 2000 presidential election is an example of where judicial involvement served to undermine the courts' legitimacy in the eyes of many citizens. It began with the Florida Supreme Court's willingness to make a decision on voting procedure, even though the state had procedures that were being followed and many argued such rules cannot be changed in the middle of an election count. That decision would likely have yielded more Democratic votes for Gore. It was pointed out by the media that the majority of justices were appointed by the previous governor, a Democrat.

Then the United States Supreme Court, a majority of whom had been appointed by Republican presidents, jumped in on November 24, 2000, further confounding the process. They said the Florida court had erred in its ruling. Thus the election went to Bush. In a dissenting vote, Justice Stevens stated,

> Although we may never know with complete certainty the identity of the winner of this year's Presidential election, the identity of the loser is perfectly clear. It is the Nation's confidence in the judge as an impartial guardian of the rule of law.

Activism Undermines the Court's Prestige

Court law-making and activism has favored the political party with a majority on the bench. But whether it be a *Roe vs. Wade* or a decision on an election, the long-term consequence is to undermine its own prestige.

Further, judicial "activism" has drawn both the executive and judicial branches into playing that game. The logic seems to go thus: "If the justices are going to be activists, then we want them to be activists for our party." When the nation was founded, the appointment of justices tended to be a more civil process, but the acceptance of the role of justices as policy advocates has caused the confirmation process to become a highly painful ordeal. A more responsible legislature might use its power to check the Supreme Court's authority by using its power to remove activist justices rather than tacitly approving the process, attempting to control Court decisions by packing the Court with activists of its own choosing.

The current process of packing activist courts has served to create a politically polarized Court, when it was designed to take the more passive role of scholarly interpretation. The Court's attempt to decide social issues that are highly inflamatory, and to stretch the boundaries of its intended juristiction, have also undermined its prestige and legitimacy. This process is not new, only the body of "sacred scripture" is different. Like the theologians of the Church or the "ideologists" of Marxism-Leninism in the Soviet Union, "legalogians" could be viewed as ones who engage the sacred scripture of the United States (the Constitution) with a rationalizing process designed to accomplish political goals. Justices can either act as scholars or as "high priests," and, unfortunately, party politics seems to reinforce the latter role and reduce the former.

In the case of the Supreme Court, references to their own previous decisions are often cited with more enthusiasm than is the Constitution. This was the case in *Dickerson v. U.S.* (2000), in which the Supreme Court overturned legislation passed by Congress that attempted to modify the *Miranda* decision.[6]

The founders gave Congress the power to recommend amendments to the Constitution; this power was intended as a check on the power of the Supreme Court. Nonetheless, the Supreme Court ruled that *Miranda*, "being a constitutional decision of this Court, may not be in effect overruled by an Act of Congress." While the Congress cannot pass legislation that overturns the Court without ratification by three-fourths of the states, it is clear that the founders intended the nation to be ultimately ruled by the people through their representatives.

The fact that the founders gave the legislature the responsibility to organize the Supreme Court should be proof enough of their philosophy.

In dissent on the *Dickerson v. the U.S.* Justices Scalia and Thomas called the decision "an illegitimate exercise of raw judicial power." Scalia, in his dissenting opinion, wrote,

> Today's judgment converts *Miranda* from a milestone of judicial overreaching into the very Cheops' Pyramid (or perhaps the Sphinx would be a better analogue) of judicial arrogance. In imposing its Court-made code upon the States, the original opinion at least *asserted* that it was demanded by the Constitution. Today's decision does not pretend that it is—and yet *still* asserts the right to impose it against the will of the people's representatives in Congress. Far from believing that *stare decisis* compels this result, I believe we cannot allow to remain on the books even a celebrated decision—*especially* a celebrated decision—that has come to stand for the proposition that the Supreme Court has power to impose extraconstitutional constraints upon Congress and the States. This is not the system that was established by the Framers, or that would be established by any sane supporter of government by the people.[7]

Checks Between the Upper and Lower Houses

Ancient Rome had an upper and lower legislative house in the form of Centurions, representing the noble class and Tribunes representing the commoners. In theory, agreement by both the Centuriate Assembly and the Tribal Assembly would mean that both the interests of the wealthy and the commoners would be promoted by legislation, and that either group would be a check on the self-interest of the other group.

The founders also designed the United States' legislature to be made up of an upper house, the Senate, and a lower house, the

House of Representatives. The initial theory was that the Senate would be made of seasoned politicians appointed by the state legislatures (Article I, Section 3). As such, they would represent state interests. The House of Representatives, on the other hand, would be elected by the people and represent their interests (Article I, Section 2). The result would be a system of checks by which no legislation would be passed unless it represented the interests of both the states and the people. The system included respect for states' rights, and a mechanism in which the states would have input on issues regarding the centralization and decentralization of federal power.

The Seventeenth Amendment changed this system. A repeal of the seventeenth amendment would be one way to restore some of the checks and balances between the two houses of the legislature.

The Seventeenth Amendment

In 1912 the 62nd Congress proposed that the two senators from each state be elected by the people. This became the Seventeenth Amendment to the Constitution in 1913, with only Utah rejecting the plan. It was done for a procedural reason, because many state legislatures deadlocked on their selections, leaving slots vacant for periods of time. There seems to have been little thought given to the effect the change would make on checks and balances on power.

The result was that senators became representatives of the same interest group that elected the lower house, the people, making the two institutions somewhat redundant. The Senate still differs from the Hose in that senators still serve longer terms and a somewhat broader constituency and they are are generally more seasoned statesmen. But the Seventeenth Amendment removed a check on the power of the people to pass laws that were not in the interest of the state, or perhaps even in their own long-term interest, which they lacked experience to see.[8] It also left senators more vulnerable to the influence of constituent lobbyists.

This is an example of a constitutional amendment that was intended to make a process easier having unintended consequences that undermined a check on power the founders had deliberately put in place.

The best way to provide checks by one house on the other was debated at the Constituional Convention. General Pinkney and Benjamin Franklin, for example, believed that, as in ancient Rome, the Senate should be made up of the wealthy classes and receive no compensation for their service. At the Constitutional Convention their proposal nearly won, five states voted for it and six opposed it. Today, given the sway that wealthy interests have in both houses, this proposal might seem far-fetched; yet it might be a greater check and balance than the current arrangement if the wealthy had less influence on one house of Congress. Then, for a bill to pass, it would need agreement of both the wealthy interests and those of the common man, as did the Twelve Tables in Rome.

Alexander Bickel, in *The Least Dangerous Branch,* argued that the judicial review process established by the Supreme Court in *Marbury v. Madison* had given the role of long-term guardian of values to the Supreme Court because the legislators are focused on immediate practical measures.[9] The founders had wanted the Senate to assume this role while the House of Representatives was to reflect the immediate and practical will of the people. The election of senators by the people made it less likely that the Senate would accomplish this task. However, it is not clear that either the original appointments of senators by state legislatures, or the two-class approach advocated by Franklin would have ensured that the Senate would perform the role of guarding the long-term interests of the nation. The activism of the Court also sheds doubt on whether that body can properly fill the role. One way or another the long-term philosophy and interests of the nation need to be better worked into the machinery of government.

Payroll and Perks

The compensation of legislators was the subject of debate at the Constitutional Convention and the agreed-upon arrangement failed to accomplish its goals. Congress was given the power to enact laws regarding their members' compensation (Article I, Section 6). Congress also has the power to raise taxes to pay for their own compensation, their staff, their offices, and their mail. This amounts to a blank check.

At the Convention, several delegates suggested that the individual states should pay the salaries of their senators; others, including Madison, argued this would not provide enough independence from the states in looking after the common good of the entire nation.[10] Thomas Jefferson believed that, since the members of Congress would pay themselves from funds they would need to raise from taxes they levied on their own constituents, their sense of dignity and honor would lead to modest compensation. The Convention left it up to the new Congress decide how much they would be paid.

The Twenty-Seventh Amendment

At the First Congress, James Madison, seeing the loophole and having second thoughts, proposed an amendment to the Constitution that would force members of Congress to submit to an election before any pay raise could take place saying, "there is a seeming impropriety in leaving any set of men, without control, to put their hands into the public coffers to take money to put in their own pockets."[11] The First Congress adopted this amendment but only six of the then needed 11 states ratified it.[12]

As it turned out, early members of Congress were moved by a sense of honor or fear of voter reaction. There was no annual salary until 1854; members accepted pay only on a per diem basis for days they attended sessions. However, in 1816 a significant per diem raise caused a public protest in which members were burned in effigy. In 1866 members raised their pay 33 percent with little public reaction. The more blatant 50 percent pay raise in 1874, retroactive to 1872, led to 86 members of Congress losing their seats in the next election, but it did not reverse the previous pay raises. Since that time, members have sought to minimize public reaction by devising ways to bury pay raises in other bills, or let deadlines expire that prevent automatic raises from going into effect. In one case, members of Congress publicly voted "no" on a pay raise after a deadline had expired so the raise went quietly into effect anyway.[13] Since 1935, Congressional raises have averaged over 4 percent per year.[14] In January, 2003 the annual salary for Congress was $155,000 while the U.S. median wage stood at $37,000.

The 27th Amendment, proposed by James Madison in 1789, was ratified by enough states to become law on May 7, 1992— two hundred years later—although other legislation had been passed in the intervening years which accomplished most of the intent of the original amendment.

Indirect Compensation

Today direct salary compensation is only a portion of compensation that legislators receive. Over the history of the nation, members of Congress have discovered many creative ways to compensate themselves indirectly. These forms of compensation include: generous health insurance and retirement benefits which guarantee they will live as well in retirement as while they were in office. Franked mail privileges help secure reelection. Office staff often serve as personal assistants and reelection committees. In 2000, the average annual discretionary spending for a member of Congress was about $1 million.[15] In 1998 the 535 members of Congress employed 31,000 people, or an average of 58 persons each.[16] Members of Congress are pampered with taxpayer-paid cars and drivers, health clubs, a bank, and a service center that even prepares their taxes. Many of these benefits would cause the founding fathers to roll over in their graves. These benefits are surprisingly similar to many of the benefits Soviet elite were able to develop over a 50-year period after the Russian revolution of 1917, a class Michael Voslensky called the *nomenklatura,* an invisible aristocracy whose reign is more oppressive than the czars.[17] Instead of the self-sufficient citizen/gentlemen that formed the government at the time of the founding, today's members of Congress, as a class, have become dependent government employees.

Many suggestions have been made to reform congressional salaries and perks, from spending limits to term limits, but such proposals do not address the fundamental conflict of interest that lies at the heart of the problem in the Constitution. While the Constitution only referred to compensation for services to be paid from the treasury, and no benefit packages, legislators have, over the years, continued to serve their own best interests with increasingly less shame.

In retrospect, the original proposal by Mr. Ellsworth at the Constitutional Convention to have the states pay for congressional wages, offices, and staff would have better served that purpose. This would not only eliminate a fundamental conflict of interest and missing check on Congress, but would cause representatives to constantly reflect the interests of their constituents and prevent the formation of an elite Washington class aloof from the people they are hired to represent.

Legislative Accountability and Transparency

The intent of the founders was ultimately to hold the House of Representatives accountable to the people. The Seventeenth Amendment put the Senate on the same footing. However, both houses developed methods to escape accountability of individual members so that votes can be made against the will of the people without fear of reprisal in the next election. This has skirted the intent of the founders to check the power of Congress.

It would be easy for citizens to evaluate the performance of their legislators if each piece of legislation referred to a single item, and if they received a clear record of how each legislator voted on it. This is not the case. In Article I, Section 5, Congress was given a procedural blank check on the policing of its own members:

> Each House may determine the Rules of its Proceedings, punish its Members for disorderly Behaviour, and, with the Concurrence of two thirds, expel a Member.

This power enabled the Congres to develop procedures that obfuscate the record and protect its members from public transparency.

Committees

In 2003, the Congress of the United States passed a Consolidated Appropriations Bill that was 620 pages long and included appropriations for hundreds of items.[18] This one bill contained instructions to the U.S. Treasury on how much should be appropriated for everything in the budget. Thus, a voter would not know whether his representative was for or against a particular item in this bill by looking at whether he/she voted to approve the entire bill.

The process of producing this bill, and many other consolidated (or omnibus) bills, has become very complex over two centuries of government expansion. Most of the work on this bill was done in the House and Senate Appropriations Committees, with input from civil servants in the budget offices of the various departments of government. They often modify the previous year's budget so as not to cause too much disruption of government services or displacement of employees. This requires a lot of negotiation in the committee. The negotiation process often involves compromises that add a certain amount of "pork" to get a majority to approve the bill. When the time comes to vote on such a bill, legislators are pressured by warnings that the schools will close and health benefits will stop if they do not vote to pass it. Many are left unsatisfied that their own agendas were not discussed by the committee, bu,t faced with deadlines, they feel compelled to vote for it.[19]

Thus not only are voters unsatisfied because they are unable to hold their legislators accountable for a vote on various components of the budget, but many legislators are unsatisfied because the process that their predecessors set in motion makes them feel they do not have control. The budget process has become a Leviathan.

Pork

Often to get a bill passed, the legislators who are opposed to it have to be given favors to change their mind. The 1200 page 2003 Energy Bill is an outlandish example. The bill, which was devised by and for the energy industry, could not succeed on its own merit as beneficial to the nation. An omnibus bill, it included everything from nanotechnology research to industry tax cuts. It proposed new spending of $46.7 billion and $18.7 billion in industry tax cuts. The authors of the bill argued that energy blackouts would continue if the bill wasn't passed.[20] Opponents noted that the bill included billions in handouts for projects unrelated to energy to get legislators from those districts to approve the bill. Included were subsidies for a retail center in Syracuse, New York; a Riverwalk in Shreveport, Louisiana which would have a "Hooters" bar; a residential development project in Atlanta, Georgia; a housing project in Colorado; and a multi-million dollar tax break for Home Depot on ceiling fan imports.[21]

"Pork-trading" is not illegal under current legislative procedures; but it is a form of corruption used to pass unworthy legislation. Those who promise the pork are not paying for it from their own pockets. They are spending public money for private purposes and not acting as responsible stewards accountable to their constituents. In this case, the taxpayers would have had to pay billions of dollars for purposes unrelated to solving the problem of energy blackouts.

Orchestrated Legislation

Another procedure used to pass an unworthy bill is to employ "secret" legislation tactics. One famous example was the passage into law of the federal income tax on December 23, 1913, after many legislators had gone home for Christmas. A more recent example is the H-1B visa. These visas were originally designed to bring foreign workers to the U.S. when there were no Americans that could perform the same jobs.

High-tech industries looking to increase profits wanted to fire American workers and replace them with less expensive labor from other countries. For example an American software programmer is paid $60,000 per year, but Indian programmers were willing to come to the US and do the same work for about $17,000 per year. In 2000 Enron had already laid off 4,000 Americans and hired 4,000 H-1B workers. Other companies were seeking the same competitive cost savings at the expense of workers. This legislation was unpopular among states because (i) there were increased welfare benefits associated with the laid-off workers, (ii) increased public services were needed for the new workers that moved into the area, (iii) college students preparing for these jobs would not find any available when they graduated, and (iv) replacement workers paid much less in taxes for local governments because of their lower pay scale. In short, the high-tech company's gain would come at the expense of American workers, American students, and state budgets.

Here is how the H-1B cap was raised:

> On Tuesday, October 3, 2000, at 3:45 pm, a House of Representatives clerk announced the Senate passage of S.

2045 amending the H-1B visa. The Speaker pro tempore announced that she would postpone further proceedings until October 4. Bush and Gore were involved in a presidential debate that evening so most representatives left immediately to provide comments on the debate to media reporters. At 5:30 pm, an e-mail was sent announcing that a debate on the H-1B cap would begin shortly. About 40 of the 435 representatives remained. About 6:30 pm, Rep. Cannon (R-UT) made a motion to suspend the rules and pass Senate bill S. 2045 instead of the House version of the bill which had included protection for US workers. Rep. Conyers (D-MI), a co-sponsor, was allotted most of the remaining time, leaving little debate. Rep. Rorabacher (R-CA) claimed it was a betrayal of the American worker and Rep. Owens (D-NY) complained that they were steamrolling a cap that gave up 600,000 jobs over 3 years. But their protest was to no avail. A voice vote was taken, passing the bill with no record of who voted for it.[22]

This bill originated in the Senate, where it has become easier for corporate lobbyists to "buy" more legislation for their dollar, perhaps as a result of the passage of the Seventeenth Amendment. It is highly doubtful that a Senate made up of appointees from state legislatures could have originated such a bill. Such an action would have guaranteed they would not be reappointed.

This orchestrated legislation was secret collusion between corporate lobbyists and the government legislators charged with making legitimate and just laws. Philosophically, it is similar to the collusion between the Enron officials and the Arthur Anderson accountants charged to ensure Enron's accounting procedures were being properly followed. In both cases many American citizens suffered. In the Enron case, legislators were not openly involved and public outcry led to the passage of the 2002 Sarbanes-Oxley Act designed to penalize and deter such future collusion between accounting firms and corporations. However, a successful outcry over procedures used by Congress in the H1B legislation would be difficult because it would require the voluntary reform of Congress.

A Fraternity of Lawyers and Judges

Because the United States is based on a constitution, its guardians are members of the legal profession. Unfortunately, over time this profession, with the help of the courts, has used its unique position to establish a better situation for itself—at the expense of the rest of society. Not only have the Supreme Court and the Congress rewritten the laws to give themselves more power, but the entire fraternity of lawyers and judges have, over the last century, changed the rules of court procedure to create more work and pay for lawyers. In the process, laws have been obfuscated, rules of evidence made more restricted, and juries have become more easily manipulated. The victim has been justice itself and those who are required to pay the ever-increasing bills.

Take for example the high-profile case of Timothy McVeigh. The Oklahoma City bomber, whose guilt was not more difficult to determine than a low profile case, netted his taxpayer-paid court-appointed lawyers a sum of $15.1 million. This does not even count the funds required to fund the prosecution, the courts, the policing of a media frenzy, or six years of imprisonment and transportation. Former Judge John Molloy has argued that, over a period of fifty years, the purpose of United States' system of justice has gradually shifted its philosophy from getting at the truth, solving crimes, and protecting society to more work and more profit for more lawyers.[23]

Molloy carefully details successive legal desisions that created new laws and procedures, despite the fact that the founders intended the courts to interpret laws. These changes have led to trials becoming more of a contest between gladiator-like lawyers rather than a search for the truth. These decisions include, but are not limited to:

1. *Miranda* rights and rules of evidence that hide many important facts from juries.

2. Abuse of rules of discovery, in which lawyers dig deep into records to find material to incriminate an opponent even though such evidence was not relevant to the case. This makes it easy to go after anyone with "deep pockets" and legally steal a share of their money.

2. Lower ages and qualifications for jury members and more excusing of older professionals from jury duty, leading to less qualified and more impressionable juries.

3. Fewer people on juries, enabling lawyers to hire jury consultants that profile jury members so that arguments can be tailored to the particular views of that jury.

4. Rules that make longer trials, and make appeals easier to employ more lawyers for longer periods of time.

5. Rules of juvenile court that replace the traditional role of a judge trying to make a decision in the best interest of a child with a network of bureaucracy that restricts the involvement of parents and makes the child the pawn in an adversarial legal proceding.

6. Rules of increased jurisdiction that allow lawyers to sue people and companies in other states.

7. Rules of payment and settlement that lead to excessively large settlements and large windfalls for lawyers.

8. Plea bargins that often give a light sentence to the criminal who makes a deal to testify against a partner, making sure someone will be punished, but not necessarily the right person.

The result of these changes in rules has been to make the system of justice in the United States look unlike that in any other country, even the British system which gave birth to United States law. These changes have not improved the chance of getting to the truth or of deterring crime. It has not made the United States system of law more just than other societies. The United States ranks 42nd in the world in murders per population unit, less safe than Mexico (56th), half as safe as Sweden (80th), and one fourth as safe as Switzerland (117th).[24] These figures indicate a level of violence in the United States that would demand some philosophical reflection on the system of law and the philosophy behind the laws that have been written since the founding.

Conclusion

This chapter highlights areas in which inadequate checks and balances were put into effect in the United States Constitution, or in which original boundaries have been overstepped. The surface has only been scratched in describing the multitude of ways that members of government, in all branches, have contrived to obtain personal benefit or the exercise of more power. In addition, the entire legal class has been able to secure benefits for itself because of its ability to shape and interpret law. Inevitably these abuses translate into more taxes and less freedom for the average citizen. It should serve to highlight the need to constantly check power where it can be used to serve those holding the power at the expense of those who want to pursue life, liberty, and happiness with the least burden of government possible.

A few suggestions for reform were made and other solutions should be developed in keeping with the basic philosophy of limiting the power of government to the minimum necessary to promote freedom and happiness.

Questions for Reflection

1. Explain ways in which the executive branch of the United States government has abused its power and ways those abuses could be checked.

2. Explain ways in which the judicial branch of the United States government has abused its power and ways those abuses could be checked.

3. Explain ways in which the legislative branch of the United States government has abused its power and ways those abuses could be checked.

4. Explain how a legal class has been able to gradually bend the entire body of law and procedures of justice to the financial advantage of its members.

5. Do you believe that the Seventeenth Amendment was good legislation or should it be repealed?

6. Different methods have been proposed to eliminate "pork" from legislative bills. These include the line item veto by the president, elimination of committees, and the elimination of omnibus bills. What are your thoughts about political "pork"?

7. There have not been many proposals to solve the conflict of interest that legislators have in determining their own pay, offices, and benefits. Some people have proposed term limits. Do you think that would help, or would you suggest other methods?

7

Regulating Financial Power

THE ENRON AND WORLDCOM SCANDALS OF 2001, followed by the debates about controlling corporate fraud in Congress that led to passage of the Sarbanes-Oxley Act, put government control of financial power on the center of the stage of public political debates at the turn of the twenty-first century. Many Americans wonder if it is too late to do anything or whether corporations have taken control of the United States, if not the world. How much power do corporations really have? What allowed the present situation to develop? Can corporations be regulated?

The Colonies Were Foreign Charters

Prior to the seventeenth century, corporations in the colonies were limited to non-profit institutions like schools and hospitals. However, commercial corporations based in other countries did business in the colonies. When Britain gained control of the seas after the Spanish Armada was sunk in 1588, the East India Company was chartered by Queen Elizabeth I in 1600. The charter was given to merchant adventurers who pooled together private stock to finance trading operations with Asia. England claimed the Atlantic coast of North America. New England colonies were land charters granted by the King of England. These very first European corporations were tools of globalization and coloniza-

TO THE

Tradesmen, Mechanics, &c.

OF THE PROVINCE OF

Pennsylvania.

MY DEAR AND MUCH RESPECTED BRETHREN,

AT a Time when a corrupt and proftituted Miniftry are pointing their deftructive Machines againft the facred Liberties of the *Americans*, the Eyes of all *Europe* are upon us; and much is expected from the known Refolution and Conduct of the *Pennfylvanians*, amongft whom the induftrious and refpectable Body of TRADESMEN and MECHANICS bear a very large Proportion. The Point in Queftion is, Whether we have Property of our own, or not? whether our Property, and the dear-earned Fruits of our Labour, are at our own Difpofal, or fhall be wantonly wrefted from us, by a Set of luxurious, abandoned and piratical Hirelings, to be appropriated by them to increafe the Number of fuch infamous Penfioners, and fupport their unlimited Extravagance? The Refult depends on our determined Virtue and Integrity, at fo important a Crifis.

THE Nature of the deteftable TEA-SCHEME, and the pernicious Confequences of fubmitting to receive IT amongft us, fubject to a Duty payable here, and levied on us without our Confent, have been fo judicioufly fet forth, and demonftrated by abler Pens, as to leave no Room for one of my Capacity to undertake it; and, if the trifling Duty of *Three-Pence* were ONLY to be confidered, it would not be worth our while to oppofe it; nor worth while for the Miniftry fo ftrenuoufly to infift on, and take off, in Lieu thereof, a much greater Sum payable in *London*: But, that by this Breach (though fmall) they will enter the Bulwark of our facred Liberties, and will never defift, till they have made a Conqueft of the Whole.

THESE arbitrary Meafures we have virtuoufly oppofed hitherto: Let us for our own Sakes, for our Pofterity's Sake, for our Country's Sake, ftedfaftly perfevere in oppofing to the End. Corruption, Extravagance, and Luxury, are feldom found in the Habitations of Tradefmen. Induftry, Œconomy, Prudence, and Fortitude, generally inhabit there; and I expect to fee thefe commendable Virtues fhine forth upon the prefent Occafion, with more than brilliant Luftre.

LET not the artful Infinuation of our Enemies, *That the Duty will be paid in England, by the Eaft-India Company, and not in America*, have any Weight amongft us: This is one of their Toils to enfnare us. The Act of 11th of GEO. 3, *expresfly* lays the aforefaid *Duty*, on all Teas imported in *America* from *England*, payable on its landing here: And no private Contract between the *Eaft India* Company and the Lords of the Treafury, to Power under the Crown, nor even the King himfelf, can difpenfe with, fet afide, difannul, or make void fuch a Claufe, or any other in any Act of Parliament, but the fame Power and Authority by which it was enacted. The grand Point in View is, by every Artifice to enflave the *American* Colonies, and to plunder them of their Property, and, what is more, their *Birth-Right*, LIBERTY. It is therefore highly incumbent on us unitedly, with Heart and Soul, to refift the diabolical Delufion, and defpife the *infamous* Projectors.

BUT fuppofing the Act was repealed, and the Tea could be imported free of any Duty, Impoft, or Cuftom; yet, is it not a moft grofs and daring Infolt to pilfer the Trade from the *Americans*, and lodge it in the Hands of the *Eaft India* Company? Let us not be prevailed upon to fuppofe that this will affect the Merchants only:—We need not concern ourfelves with it:—It will firft moft fenfibly affect the Merchants; but it will alfo very materially affect YOU, ME, and every Member of the Community. The *Eaft India* Company at prefent have fhipped their defperate Adventure in chartered Bottoms; it was prudent fo to do, or elfe poffibly their obnoxious Veffels and Cargoes might become a Sacrifice to the Refentment of a much injured and exafperated People. The fame Confideration might probably have induced them to appoint our Merchants as Agents to fupport the firft heat of Action, rightly judging that if we would chaftife our Friends *with Whips*, we fhould chaftife their Factors *with Scorpions*. But if they can once open the Channel of Trade to themfelves, they will hereafter fhip their Teas in their own Bottoms. They have paffed a grofs Affront upon our Merchants in appointing fuch, whom we refpect, Commiffioners. Hereafter, if they fucceed, they will fend their own Factors and Creatures, eftablifh Houfes amongft US. Ship US all other *Eaft-India* Goods; and in order to full freight their Ships, take in other Kind of Goods at under Freight, or (more probably) fhip them on their own Accounts to their own Factors, and under-fell our Merchants, till they monopolize the whole Trade. Thus our Merchants are ruined, Ship Building ceafes. They will then fell Goods at any exorbitant Price. Our Artificers will be unemployed, and every Tradefman will groan under the dire Oppreffion.

THE *Eaft India* Company, if once they get Footing in this (once) happy Country, will leave no Stone unturned to become your Mafters. They are an opulent Body, and Money or Credit is not wanting amongft them. They have a defigning, depraved, and defpotic Miniftry to affift and fupport them. They themfelves are well verfed in TYRANNY, PLUNDER, OPPRESSION, and BLOODSHED. Whole Provinces labouring under the Diftreffes of Oppreffion, Slavery, Famine, and the Sword, are familiar to them. Thus they have enriched themfelves,—thus they are become the moft powerful Trading Company in the Univerfe. Be, therefore, my dear Fellow-Tradefmen, prudent,—be watchful,—be determined to let no Motive induce you to favour the accurfed Scheme. Reject every Propofal, but a *repealing Act* Let not their baneful Commodity enter your City. Treat every Aidor or Abettor with Ignominy, Contempt, &c. and let YOUR whole Deportment prove to the World, "THAT WE WILL BE FREE INDEED."

A MECHANIC.

Philadelphia, December 4, 1773.

A tract against the East India Company printed in
Pennsylvania in 1773.

tion set up to bring wealth to the stockholders. This was a commercial monopoly, which colonists opposed.

The West India Company was established in the Netherlands in 1621 and controlled all settlements in New Netherlands. A patroon system was established whereby large tracts of land on the Hudson River were given to people who could organize these estates for farming. The patroon was bound to provide a farm ready stocked for each of his tenants. The tenants were temporarily serfs, as they were obliged to remain on the land for ten years. Some of these patroons became the wealthy noble families of America; for example, the Van Rensselaers, the Schuylers, and the Livingstons. New Netherlands was run on the model of Old World feudalism. In 1664 the Dutch were defeated by the English and the colony was given to the Duke of York. The Hudson's Bay Company, chartered in 1670, is the oldest existing merchandising joint-stock company in the English-speaking world. The fur trade, exploration, and development of Canada are thoroughly intertwined in its history.

Thom Hartmann, a critic of corporate power, has described the Boston Tea Party as "America's first anti-globalization protest."

> Conventional wisdom has it that the 1773 Tea Act—a tax law passed in London that led to the Boston Tea Party—was simply an increase in the taxes on tea paid by American colonists. In reality, however, the Tea Act gave the world's largest transnational corporation—The East India Company—full and unlimited access to the American tea trade, and exempted the Company from having to pay taxes to Britain on tea exported to the American colonies. It even gave the Company a *tax refund* on millions of pounds of tea they were unable to sell and holding in inventory.[1]

Hartmann further says that not only were Americans worried about paying the taxes, they were concerned because as a large, government-supported monopoly, the East India Company had an unfair advantage over smaller American companies that were unable to compete because of government favoritism. Of course, the King of England was a major shareholder in the East India Company.

The American Revolution brought an end to all of these corporation charters and the colonies adopted new constitutions as states. The operation of the Hudson's Bay Company and the East India Company were outlawed.

Corporations and Monopolies Not Governed by the US Constitution

The Constitution of the United States did not address the issue of financial power, except for the purposes of regulating the printing of money and commerce among the states. There were several reasons for this.

First, many felt that regulation of business should be left to individual states and not viewed as the proper dominion of the federal government.

Secondly, large corporations, to the extent they had previously existed, had their life at the bequest of the King of England, and were viewed as anathema by the Americans. Most Americans were farmers or ran family businesses and wanted nothing to do with corporations.

Thirdly, the issue was divisive between Federalists like Alexander Hamilton and those like Jefferson who opposed concentrations of power. The Federalists were the realists of their day and believed that the United States should be set up as a nation like England. The Anti-Federalists were more wary of centralized government and corporate power and wanted to fashion the United States into a new model of society. Agreement on the federal Constitution was possible by leaving out some of the more contentious issues, such as references to financial power.

Jefferson opposed financial monopolies along with other forms of institutional power and wrote letters to a number of people stating that this ought to be part of a bill of rights.[2]

> I will now add what I do not like. First the omission of a bill
> of rights providing clearly and without the aid of sophisms
> for freedom of religion, freedom of the press, protection
> against standing armies, restriction against monopolies, the
> eternal and unremitting force of habeas corpus laws, and
> trials by jury...[3]

However, in the same letter he wrote to Madison in December 1787 stating this concern, he also said that he thought American governments would "remain virtuous for many centuries," because they were "chiefly agricultural."[4] Thus, while he was strongly opposed to financial monopolies and concentrations of financial power, he did not see this as an immediate threat at the time the Constitution was written.

In his reply to Jefferson, Madison agreed that monopolies "are justly classed among the greatest nuisances in Government." However, he reasoned that since "monopolies are sacrifices of the many to the few," and that since the United States would be founded on the power of the many people rather than the few oligarchs, the greater threat would be that "the few will be unnecessarily sacrificed to the many."[5]

Jefferson was unwilling to ratify the Constitution on behalf of the state of Virginia until a bill of rights (the first ten amendments) had been included. Out of his list above, all but two protections, from standing armies and from monopolies, were included. This was a sufficient compromise for him. So in the end protections against abuse of financial power were left out of both the Constitution and the Bill of Rights.

Madison, along with Jefferson, viewed the United States as a country for self-sufficient citizens. The nation was not designed as one in which people would be working for others, or for big corporations:

> The class of citizens, who provide at once their own food
> and their own raiment, may be viewed as the most truly
> independent and happy. They are more: they are the best

basis of public liberty, and the strongest bulwark of public safety. It follows, that the greater the proportion of this class to the whole society, the more free, the more independent, and the more happy must be the society itself.[6]

Jefferson and Madison had both been reading Adam Smith's *Wealth of Nations,* in which Smith said that monopoly power was counterproductive to wealth generation, that it could not be sustained in a genuinely competitive market, and that it would not exist without the assistance of government.[7] They were certainly not planning to establish a government that would support a monopolistic corporation—not after the Revolution had been fought to throw them off. Further, most of the revolutionary generation detested corporations.

Thus, when the United States was founded each family was one economic unit and one voting unit. The head of each household cast one vote. Most farms and businesses were family enterprises equal to the value of work that family could accomplish or supervise. The person who headed each of these enterprises was the same person that voted. As a result, the interests of the voting constituency and the interests of economic constituency were the same. There were no external financial interests that wielded additional political influence, either in addition to or at cross-purposes with the average voter.

This is not to say that the United States was a land of economic equality. Prominent aristocratic families with large tracts of land maintained considerable influence through their financial power despite the fact that they only had one vote. However, these families were relatively few in number and their effect on government was not nearly as significant as the corporations that were to develop in the next two hundred years.

Opposition to Corporations before the Civil War

At the time of the Revolution, there were a handful of domestic mutual companies, such as the Philadelphia Fire Department organized by Ben Franklin in 1752. These companies were public service organizations in which citizens pooled resources for mutual protection. Mutual insurance companies were some of the first companies founded in America. They were heavily controlled by the states, and charters could easily be revoked. Most had limits to the duration of their incorporation.

There was not a single bank in the United States until 1780. Most of the first bank's stock was owned by the confederate (later called federal) government, and the bank's charter was revoked in 1785. By 1790, four banks had been granted charters by states, but these banks were not purely private institutions. They served as financial institutions for the states that chartered them.

In 1791, a movement to head a federal bank was spearheaded by Alexander Hamilton. It had $10 million in capital stock, of which the federal government owned $2 million and the rest was owned by private investors. It was chartered for 20 years, and the power of the directors frightened many people. The charter was not renewed in 1811.

Five years later, in 1816, a second federal bank was chartered. The arguments were similar to the first, and the needs of a growing economy helped push it through. It was organized similarly to the first, with $35 million in capital stock, one fifth owned by the federal government. President James Madison, who had opposed the first bank in 1791, signed the charter.[8] When questioned by a Philadelphia lawyer, Charles Jared Ingersoll, Madison responded that, although he had appeared to reverse his position, he was yielding to law that had been developed since that time by the legislature. In other words, he was yielding to precedent, viewing the nation more as an organism than as rigidly grounded in opinions of a previous generation.[9] This concept of precedent was to play a major role in the evolution of later laws and Supreme Court decisions involving corporations.

Thomas Jefferson went on record in opposition in 1816 in a letter to George Logan, a fellow anti-Federalist, writing, "I hope we shall crush in its birth the aristocracy of our moneyed corporations which dare already to challenge our government in a trial of strength, and bid defiance to the laws of our country."[10]

Chief Justice John Marshall, a late appointment by President John Adams in 1801, maintained the Federalist position on the Supreme Court long after the Federalist Party disintegrated. He established the power of the Supreme Court to review the constitutionality of actions of the other two branches of government in *Marbury v. Madison* (1803). He also made rulings that established the basis for the United States to become a corporate capitalist society as opposed to Jefferson's vision of an agrarian society.

In 1819, the United States Supreme Court, in *Dartmouth College v. Woodward,* ruled that Dartmouth's charter, granted by King George III, was a contract that could not be revoked by the New Hampshire legislature. A public outcry ensued. States argued they maintained an absolute right to amend or repeal a corporate charter, it was not properly in the domain of the federal government. However, wealthy businessmen saw the decision as an opening to get regulation out of state legislatures controlled by the voters and into a more friendly federal judicial system.

In 1829, President Andrew Jackson made clear his opposition to the federal bank and to the renewal of its charter, saying "such a concentration of power in the hands of a few men irresponsible to the people" was dangerous. This attack on the Bank's power drew public support and, when the charter of the Second Bank of the United States expired in 1836, it was not renewed.

From 1836 to 1863 a number of banks operated under state charters with no central authority. Over several decades, starting in 1844, nineteen states amended their constitutions to make corporate charters subject to alteration or revocation by their legislatures. As late as 1855, the Supreme Court seemed to concur when, in *Dodge v. Woolsey,* it reaffirmed state's powers over "artificial bodies." Critics argued that lack of a central banking authority hurt the stability of the U.S. economy. They also pointed to legislation in Europe more favorable to corporations. However, the United States' economy in the first half of the nineteenth century resembled Smith's textbook model of a fair and competitive economic order—one in which business firms in nearly all industries were many in number and small in size.

A New Industrial Nation

Ever since the founding of the nation, industry was growing and the number of businesses was increasing. The United States expanded geographically, especially with Jefferson's Louisiana Purchase in 1803. The population grew dramatically. Farm production increased, and international trade increased, with U.S. grain feeding both growing U.S. cities and Europe. Manufacturing in the United States, protected by tariffs from British competition, also progressed rapidly. The favored form for large businesses became the corporation.

In the first half of the nineteenth century states held a pretty tight reign on corporations. Licenses could be revoked, stockholders and owners were not shielded from liability for corporate acts, charters were for limited periods of time and had to be renewed, corporations could not own stock in other corporations or real estate that was unrelated to their purpose of business, they could make no political contributions, direct or indirect, and all corporate records were open to the legislature or the attorney general.[11]

The dominant industries in early in the nineteenth century were textile mills in the North and agricultural products from plantations in the South. Ocean shipping was an important industry for both North and South. The invention of the railroad and the telegraph brought industrial growth to the pre-Civil War era analagous to the growth spurts in the twentieth century that accompanied the invention of automobiles and the Internet. The first passenger train in the United States began operation in 1830. Railroads revolutionized transportation, leading to all kinds of new business opportunities. In 1840 2,700 miles of track had been laid, and in 1850 that number had increased to 9,000 miles. By 1860, largely through government subsidies to new rail companies, more than 30,000 miles of track were in use. By 1890, more than 180 million acres of land had been deeded to railroads.[12]

As the railroads grew in size, they grew in power. They hired the best lawyers. Abraham Lincoln was one of them, and he was able to obtain railroad backing as a Republican candidate. Three of his Civil War generals were men he met while representing the Illinois Central Railroad.[13] Railroad money influenced legislators and courts. They negotiated one-sided government and labor contracts as everyone wanted a piece of railroad action. Their virtual monopoly on high-speed transportation in the areas they served led to predatory pricing. By the 1880s, nearly all states had passed laws setting maximum prices railroads could charge.

The Civil War brought increased unity among the Nothern states. Many national activities were conducted under the auspices of the War Department, which had a large budget. Fighting the war required many products of industry and transportation which brought great wealth to many industries. This was a great boon to many industrialists.

The National Banking Act of 1863, along with its revisions of 1864 and 1865, sought to add clarity and security to the banking system by introducing and promoting currency notes issued by nationally chartered banks, rather than state-chartered ones. The Act imposed a 10 percent tax on state banknotes, thus effectively eliminating non-federal currency from circulation. The legislation created the Office of the Comptroller of the Currency, which issued national banking charters and examined the subsequent banks. These banks were now subject to stringent capital requirements and were required to collateralize currency notes with holdings of United States government securities. Other provisions in the legislation helped improve the banking system by providing more oversight and a more robust currency in circulation.[14]

The Fourteenth Amendment

Following the Civil War, in June 1866, the Fourteenth Amendment to the Constitution was passed to guarantee full citizenship to freed slaves. This amendment included the phrase "nor shall any State deprive any *person* of life, liberty, or property, without due process of law."[15] This amendment had broader implications for federal regulation of states' treatment of individuals. It became a landmark by which individuals and corporations, believing they were being treated unfairly by a state, could seek federal intervention. It would also be cited in numerous cases from education to abortion, where individuals took states to the federal courts. In the philosophy of the founders, the states had sovereignty over social laws, and people who could not seek redress in the state in which they lived could move to another state. The Fourteenth Amendment set a precedent for equal protection for all citizens against unjust behavior by state governments.

In 1844 an act in England had been passed that allowed corporations to define their own purpose. Corporations in the United States lobbied hard for perpetual life with rights as persons. As corporations grew larger, employed more people, and provided services that were helping the nation to grow, the government and the courts more easily yielded to their demands.

Lawyers for the railways argued that corporations were full, unqualified legal persons in four cases that reached the Supreme Court in 1877, stating that they should be protected from state taxation and regulation of maximum rates. In 1886 the Supreme Court heard the case *Santa Clara County v. Southern Pacific Railroad,* in which the county had levied capricious taxes against the fences alongside the railroad that passed through it. In his preamble to the opinion, Mr. Justice Waite stated that stated all members of the Court were agreed that the railroad would have the same equal protection rights against confiscation of property as a "person" within the meaning of the Fourteenth Amendment.

"There was no history, logic or reason given to support that view," Supreme Court Justice William O. Douglas wrote sixty years later.[16] To those making the ruling at the time, it seemed obvious that corporations should have these rights, despite the fact that protection of corporations from the states that chartered them had never been part of the nation's philosophy or history. The state's right to oversee corporate rates of return—a right entrusted to legislators by the U.S. Constitution—had been severely limited.

Many of the Supreme Court justices in the 1880s had themselves served as corporate lawyers earlier in their careers. They freely reinterpreted the Constitution, giving some corporations the power of eminent domain. They eliminated jury trials to determine corporation-caused harm and to assess damages. They listened to corporate complaints that pure competition was "ruinous capitalism" and that mergers and divided market shares could prevent overproduction and lead to more acceptable profits. They laid the legal foundation for regulatory agencies to be primarily accountable to the courts—not to the Congress or the people. This created a shield that protected corporations from popular outcries against their behavior and gave them a new field upon which to play; one which has pushed out and swallowed up many individual entrepreneurs and businesses.

To what extent should corporations be viewed persons? In the United States, actual persons cannot buy and sell other people. That is called slavery. What is the result of mergers and aquisitions? Is it aquisition of property or an employee's fate? Is a hostile takeover a form of extortion? Is corporate raiding theft? How are the abilities to pursue happiness by citizens employed by corporations affected when their jobs and retirement funds are bought and sold? Is a publicly traded corporation, which involves the economic fate of many individuals more aptly compared to an institution like a government than a person? Should officers of public corporations have checks on their power more like government officials? How should these large organizations be understood in the context of our laws? A formula was not set down by the founders and the issues are now central to the philosophy of the United States.[17] Like states, corporations are social creations that have the ability to perform a valuable social function. Like states, they also can grow and consolidate power that needs to be checked.

Philosophical Debates and American Lessons

The tremendous wealth and financial power of industrial life created widespread philosophical debates on the ideal relationship of industry to the government, ranging from Marxist socialism on the left to the laissez-faire libertarianism on the right. The former would want to completely nationalize industry and the latter would want to leave it completely unregulated.

Another issue is whether the money of private businesses and partnerships can be used with the same type of influence as corporations, or whether corporations with public shareholders are a different type of entity. Such debates were not a fundamental concern of the Constitutional Convention.

The history of the Babylonian and Roman Empires, as well as the philosophy of Adam Smith, all argue that free citizens and a free market are a better engine of prosperity and economic development than a political command economy. The failure of the centrally planned economy in the former Soviet Union is a further argument against absolute political control of the economy. However, the ideal relationship between corporations, governments, and citizens is far less clear. There were few examples at the time of the founders except for those like the East India Company which were, in their minds, monopolistic instruments of government. Most businesses were private enterprises.

In the United States, some people argued that corporations were the future of the economy and would benefit all, while others argued that the corporations were devices for the rich to consolidate power and oppress the poor.

After the Great Panic of 1857, and the deflation, depression, and labor strikes of the 1870s, the U.S. public was complaining loudly about cartels, corporate trusts, price-fixing, and monopoly. The "robber barons" of the railroad, oil, and steel industries appeared to be getting excessively rich—was this because they had forced the competition out of business? Common law in the U.S. courts was somewhat contradictory. There were two basic views of cartels and trusts: tolerant and condemning.

The Sherman Anti-trust Act

The Sherman Antitrust Act of 1890, named for Senator John Sherman, was the first measure passed by the U.S. Congress to prohibit trusts. Prior to its enactment, several states had passed similar antitrust laws, but they were limited to intrastate businesses. The Sherman Act, based on the constitutional power of Congress to regulate interstate commerce, declared illegal every contract, combination (in the form of trust or otherwise), or conspiracy in restraint of interstate and foreign trade. It banned monopolizing or attempting to monopolize. The act passed both houses nearly unanimously.

However, the "will of the people" was general and it was left to the courts to interpret and enforce the law. The courts did not see things exactly the same way as the voters. Initial setbacks breaking up monopolies came from the Supreme Court's first consideration of the statute, in *United States v. E. C. Knight Co.,* in 1895. Rejecting a challenge to a sugar trust that controlled more than 98 percent of the nation's sugar refining capacity, the Court held that the company was engaged in manufacturing, not interstate commerce. This was good news for trusts. If manufacturing was exempt from the Sherman Act, then they had little to worry about.[18]

The Court began selective use of the Sherman Act in the late 1890s, starting with cases against railroad cartels that related to interstate commerce. However, by 1904, some three hundred large companies still controlled nearly 40 percent of the nation's manufacturing assets. The Sherman Act authorized the federal government to institute proceedings against trusts in order to dissolve them, but Supreme Court rulings prevented federal authorities from using the act for several years.

After the turn of the twentieth century, federal enforcement became a higher priority as the Presidents joined the Congress and the people with complaints about trusts. Republican President Theodore Roosevelt announced that he was a "trustbuster." He and his successor, President William Taft, responded to public criticism over the rapid merger of industries by pursuing more vigorous legal action. Steady prosecution in the first decade of the twentieth century brought the downfall of several trusts.

In 1911, the Supreme Court ordered the break-up of the Standard Oil Company and the American Tobacco Company in landmark rulings that brought down two of the most powerful trusts. But they were ambiguous rulings. In *Standard Oil Co. of New Jersey v. United States*, for example, the Court dissolved the trust into thirty-three companies, but held that the Sherman Act outlawed only those restraints that were anti-competitive. Critics attacked the decision fearing that conservative judges would gut the Sherman Act; others predicted a return to lax enforcement.

The Federal Reserve Board

The federal banks issuing currency to bankroll the United States economy and corporations have continually been the subject of debate, and that debate heated to boiling in 1912, when bankers advocated the creation of a central bank, combining and concentrating the power of the bankers owning the national banks. It would be the establishment of a legal "money trust" at a time when other trusts were being busted. Depending on which theory one reads, the banks were heroes,[19] responsible for the economic development of the United States or villains,[20] responsible for the crash of 1929, the Depression and for the United States' involvement in both world wars. What we do know is that one goal of the Federal Reserve was to establish the U.S. dollar as an international currency.[21] This would support the growing desire of United States corporations to exploit overseas markets.

Neither the banks nor the politicians had previous experience with the scale of lending and type of economic development the United States was experiencing. There were no guidelines or safeguards to prevent excessive and risky lending or collusion in stock market speculation. The banks that issued United States currency and controlled monetary flow were private corporations and not owned by the government. People were suspicious that the owners of these banks were getting rich, or bailed out of trouble, at taxpayer expense.

The move to create a Federal Reserve Board was initiated by bankers and supported by Republicans close to them. The 1912 election, which saw a popular vote for the Democrats, has been interpreted as a popular referendum against the creation of a central bank. Yet, on December 23, 1913, when many legislative opponents of the bill had returned to their homes for Christmas, proponents remained and orchestrated the passage of the Federal Reserve Act. It was quickly signed by President Woodrow Wilson who, critics charged, had been duped by the bankers.

The Sixteenth Amendment

Around the same time, the Sixteenth Amendment to the Constitution, which allows for the collection of income taxes, both from private citizens and corporations, was passed. Ratification was completed on February 3, 1913, with only Connecticut, Rhode Island, and Utah rejecting it. Populist critics and conspiracy theorists see this as another sellout of the people of the United States to a few wealthy bankers who controlled the politicians. The Act of 1862 had given a Commissioner of Internal Revenue authority to collect income taxes during the Civil War. They were eliminated in 1872. Attempts were made to revive income taxes in 1894 and 1895, but the Supreme Court declared them unconstitutional in 1896, leading to the movement for the creation of the Sixteenth Amendment.

The Clayton Anti-Trust Act and the Establishment of the Federal Trade Commission

Criticisms of the Sherman Act brought new federal laws in 1914. The first of these was the Clayton Act, which declared four practices illegal but not criminal: (1) price discrimination—selling a product at different prices to similarly situated buyers; (2) tying and exclusive-dealing contracts—sales made on condition that the buyer stop dealing with the seller's competitors; (3) corporate mergers—acquisitions of competing companies; and (4) interlocking directorates—boards of competing companies with common members.

The Clayton Act qualified each of these prohibited activities. They were only illegal where the effect "may be substantially to lessen competition" or "tend to create a monopoly." This language was intentionally vague; making it a bill the politicians could take to their constituents to prove they were being tough on corporations while leaving the courts to decide whether business would remain as usual. One important limitation was added: the Clayton Act exempted unions from the scope of antitrust law, because corporations had attempted to use the Sherman Anti-trust Act to outlaw labor unions as an anti-competitive combination.

The second piece of federal legislation in 1914 was the Federal Trade Commission Act. That law provided that "unfair methods of competition in or affecting commerce, and unfair or deceptive acts or practices in or affecting commerce are hereby declared illegal." The law also created a regulatory agency, the Federal Trade Commission (FTC), to interpret and enforce it.

World War I and the Roaring Twenties

When World War I broke out, the United States needed industrial products for the war effort. While American ships were being sunk, there were also business reasons for American involvement in the war. One was the potential profit to be made by war production businesses, but another was a feature of global economics. The J. P. Morgan Bank, a substantial holder of shares in the Federal Reserve, had given loans to Great Britain totaling over $2.3 billion. As a result, Wall Street feared a British defeat. As in the Civil War, patriotic appeals to increase output pushed anti-trust concerns aside. Historians have since debated the extent to which corporations are responsible for the United States' entry into World War I.

The profits from the war economy continued into the 1920s. However, in the 1920s several other developments led to the decade being called "the Roaring Twenties": (1) high tariffs on foreign products stimulated domestic industrial production, (2) the mass production of automobiles, which every family wanted, (3) the application of Taylorism and the increase in worker production and efficiency, (4) the building of electrical plants and wiring, which stimulated the invention and sale of electrical appliances, and (5) the development of consumer credit that would underwrite purchases of consumer products.

During the 1920s all kinds of loans, investing schemes, and financial experiments were devised to create wealth without physical labor. Everyone wanted to use their money to make more money. The number of banks had expanded to 30,000 by 1920. There were far too many banks, with many people wanting to get on the bandwagon to start new ones due to the real estate boom of the 1920s. Nebraska had a bank for every 1,000 residents. During the 1920s about 600 banks failed each year. Individual reserve banks, through a loophole, were able to purchase government securities for their accounts as they also sought easy money.[22] Failures increased after the stock market collapse of 1929. Neither the business sector nor the government was prepared for the panics that followed. It became clear that no regulation of banking and business was an unacceptable political policy. There were 5,100 failures and three major panics between 1930 and 1932.

In retrospect, a number of economic scholars have argued that the Federal Reserve Board had had the power to avert much of the trouble, but had failed either to understand its power or to use it.[23] President Calvin Coolidge (1923-1929) thought things were going well and remained popular through government inaction. He is known for his statement, "The business of America is business," which redefined America's purpose to the conduct of business. He won a landslide election in 1924 and let things slide slowly out of control. The lack of controls in the 1920s is cited by many as the reason for the collapse of the stock market in 1929, followed by the collapse of banks and other financial industries. Some opponents of controls have cited the "cyclical nature of business" as a normal occurrence that would have happened with or without regulation, but this was not a sufficient explanation.

It is quite possible that markets for automobiles and appliances were becoming more saturated and, combined with the exhaustion of cheap farmland and the growth of large amounts of consumer debt caused a slowdown in consumer purchasing that led to a period of deflation. This, combined with all of the above problems, led to an inevitable day of reckoning.

The New Deal

When Franklin D. Roosevelt took office, the country was in the midst of economic crisis. He promised change, and that promise caused further crisis as the Emergency Banking Relief Act of 1933 gave him emergency powers over American banking and finance. The Act, approved five days after he took office in March 1933, gave the president power to regulate transactions in credit, currency, gold and silver, and foreign exchange. It also authorized the Secretary of the Treasury to require the delivery of all gold and gold certificates, and provided for the appointment of conservators of national banks in difficulties. Roosevelt acted quickly during his first one hundred days to put the banking system on sound footing, put an end to public panics, and get the economy rolling. It can be argued that the public had become so distraught over the handling of the economy by the courts and the bankers that it gave the President powers the founders of the U.S. Constitution had sought to check.

Banks were all closed and investigated. Solvent banks were allowed to reopen and the Federal Reserve could help them. Senator Carter Glass, a former Treasury Secretary and the author of the bill establishing the U.S. Federal Reserve System, was the primary force behind the Glass-Steagall Act. Henry Bascom Steagall was a House of Representatives member and chairman of the House Banking and Currency Committee. Steagall agreed to support the act with Glass after an amendment was added permitting bank deposit insurance. This act was designed to create permanent federal regulation of banking and credit practices. It allowed more banks to join the Federal Reserve, separated commercial banks from investment banks, and set up the Federal Deposit Insurance Corporation. In 1934 the Securities and Exchange Act set up the Securities and Exchange Commission to register and examine all publicly traded securities and licensed stock exchanges.

The New Deal also involved a number of programs designed to spur employment by creating public works jobs. It created a safety net for the elderly with the Social Security Act of 1935. This provided the basis for the welfare state which grew, establishing increased regulation, taxation, and government social services until the Reagan election of 1980.

Return to the Old Deal

By the 1980s, the regulation of the economy and the welfare state had led to a top-heavy federal government that was becoming increasingly difficult to fund. Taxes were high, and high interest rates and inflation in the late 1970s had made it nearly impossible to buy a home. The voters had been content to live with the welfare state until it caused a fiscal crisis. Ronald Reagan's appeal to "supply-side" economics was a rallying cry to liberate corporations from excessive regulation and taxation so they could once again become engines of the economy. Although President Reagan expressed admiration for Franklin Roosevelt and the New Deal, his policies were to lead to some of the practices of the "old deal" of the 1920s, perhaps even going further by providing tax breaks for mergers and acquisitions. In the mid-1950s, one-third of United States taxes were paid by corporations, by the end of the century that amount had shrunk to one-fourteenth.

Parallel to "Reaganomics" was the development of a whole new breed of business managers (MBAs) being trained in business programs such as in Harvard and other elite institutions. Many were experts in the law and strategy of the new layer of management developing, that of the conglomerate. Soon other institutions throughout the country trained MBAs. These MBAs were trained to look for the bottom line. They held no loyalty to the families, employees, or institutional histories of the corporations they were hired to run. They made no reference to "character" as had J. P. Morgan and many of the wealthy aristocrats of the nineteenth century. They could acquire, divide, sell off, and ransack companies, and fire employees with impunity. They often reaped millions of dollars in compensation as a result.

The economy rebounded in the 1980s and interest rates had returned to normal by 1990. Wall Street had become fashionable and wealth returned to New York City, which had been on the brink of bankruptcy in the mid-1970s. High times in the 1980s and 1990s were also fuelled by the nascent computer and

Internet industries, which created new and booming companies. These were analogous to the auto and appliance industries of the 1920s.

While there were a number of corporate scandals and some punishments for insider trading, as long as the economy was growing, there was little alarm raised by the public. In 1999, in order to pave the way for the Citibank and Travelers Insurance Group merger, Wall Street businesses pushed through the Gramm-Leach-Bliley Act. This act superseded the Glass-Steagall Act and modified the Bank Holding Company Act (1956). It is in the interest of Wall Street to increase profits, not competition. The philosophy was similar to the 1880s. The depth of corporate corruption and the potential unwisdom of some deregulation of large corporations did not get public attention until the details of the Enron and WorldCom scandals began to unfold in 2002.

The Backlash

A backlash among citizens began to grow following the corporate scandals of Enron, Arthur Anderson, and WorldCom, the ever-larger mergers, such as that of J.P. Morgan, Chase, Bank One, or Citigroup Travelers, the globalization and departure of large components of companies like Hewlett Packard, IBM, and Microsoft from the United States, and the passage of H-1B and L-1 visas that lead to the replacement of American workers with less expensive foreign workers. A rash of new books, like David Korten's *When Corporations Rule the World,* Marjorie Kelly's *The Divine Right of Capital,* Arianna Huffington's, *Pigs at the Trough: How Corporate Greed and Political Corruption are Undermining America,* Thom Hartman's *Unequal Protection: The Rise of Corporate Dominance and the Theft of Human Rights,* and *Saving Capitalism from the Capitalists* by Luigi Zingales and Raghuram Rajan, impacted the political rhetoric of candidates for office in 2004.

We have witnessed a history of the interplay of three groups: civil society, the government, and the corporations. When the

United States was founded, there were no corporations and business was part of civil society. The development of industry was the result of inventions and the ability to finance their manufacture. This was done through the creation of artificial "persons" called corporations. The people of the old economy generally opposed the benefits the government gave to corporations, while those involved with the corporate economy favored them.

Like the invention of the state itself, the invention of the corporation has held out the promise of a better life. And like human faith in the state, an artificial "person" itself, human beings have placed great faith in corporations. However, abuses of the state were rampant in the twentieth century and responsible for millions of deaths at the hands of governments. Will unregulated corporations cause some type of chaos? Some fear they will.

However, wishing the death of the corporation, like wishing the death of the state, will not solve the problem. Corporations are now part of the makeup of human life, and they have allowed for much greater prosperity and comfort for the average person of today than most kings and princes of ancient times enjoyed.

The Corporation Game in Modern Society

It is important to gain genuine knowledge about the interplay of civil society, the state, and the corporation rather than throw around ideological rhetoric that masks ignorance with promises of a better future. Historically this rhetoric has come from two polar opposite camps. On the left are the socialists who promote the fiction that corporations are a "thing" that people can take and divide up and everyone will be wealthy. On the right are greedy corporate moguls that would do anything for more money and more corporate power despite its consequences for society. Somewhere in the middle is a reasonable path that allows corporations to freely produce, sell, and earn a profit as long as they do not significantly impede competition or interfere with the ability of others to compete.

The middle path involves a government role as referee. For the market to work its best, the referee needs to supervise a game in which there are many players on the field. The object of the game is this: the players that create the greatest benefit to the society win. The consumers that make up the spectators in the stands pay the players for the products they want. Those corporate players that win are the ones who produce the best results for consumers. The government is the referee on the field that ensures a fair game will be played.

Obviously, in a monopoly there is only one player on the field and there will be no competition. That player will not even have to work hard to be the winner. Unfortunately in this game society gets little because that single player will not bother to produce much, and will not care about the quality, because it is the only thing the spectators can buy. If they want it, they will have to take it, however poor its quality, however high its price.

However, if many corporate players are on the field, and the competition is vigorous, the consumers will be able to encourage them to produce ever better results to make them ever more satisfied. This is a game of strong competition to serve the society, and a game in which excellence, not a monopoly on power, leads to the winner's circle. Results, not power, are the goals of corporations playing such a game.

In a Protestant society, in which one's work is a glorification of God, there is no contradiction between the goals of a good game and the goals of the individual. However, that is an ideal which neither Protestant society, nor any society, could fully achieve. Human beings, by nature, desire more for doing less. Even when they cannot steal from others to make life easy without work, they invent things—from running water, to vacuum cleaners, and better mousetraps—to make life easier. What they cannot take by force, they are forced to do with their brains and skill.

The referee needs to ensure the economic game is not played with force, but played with brains and skill. In other words, corporations should not make wealth off of other people's money, but produce useful products and services with invention and skill. In the Roman Empire, successful rulers were those that skillfully served the wellbeing of the citizens. The same is true for the long-term survival of a corporation.

The United States government does not always act as a good referee, and has not always displayed good referee skills. There are three serious mistakes a referee can make. One is to let some of the players make up rules for him as the game is being played. In this case the government would be swallowing corporate propaganda. Another is to place a bet on one of the players use one's position as referee to rig the game so that that player wins. This is government/corporate collusion and corruption. A third is when the referee becomes a player himself and rules arbitrarily to ensure that he will win. When a person is both a referee and a player, this is the strongest conflict of interest that any game can have. Unfortunately many states do try to engage in both roles.

Basic principles of justice related to corporate regulation can be boiled down to an evaluation of whether they are created to support playing a fair game, or whether they result in one of the three failures of referees listed above.

Failure of justice can originate with the corporation, with the government listening to its propaganda, or with the government that seeks to become a player to enrich itself. It can result from either business in government or government in business, instead of government serving as a true referee.

The following sections are meant to help understand various types of relationships that politicians and corporate representatives can enter into at the expense of the pursuit of life, liberty, and happiness by the citizens. These sections address problems of "government in business" and "business in government," neither of which reflect the government's proper role as an impartial referee.

Government in Business

Government "Businesses"

In this first case, the government attempts to supplant business by creating its own. A government business uses tax dollars, not sound investment principles, to establish a business that attains an unfair advantage through the use of money and legal power. It either becomes an inefficient monopoly or drives competitive companies out of business with its artificial subsidy.

Examples could be the socialist nationalization of an industry, the establishment of a state lottery, a state-established medical research program, or a state insurance agency for provision of special benefits to state employees.

Businesses "Legal" for the Government Only

Another abuse of government power is to declare a particular business illegal for private individuals, but legal for the government. This adds legal power, in addition to tax funding, to a state business, creating a legal monopoly in a sector where competition could exist. An example might be a national airline, owned by a state and given exclusive landing rights at a state-run airport.

Government Subsidies

If a government subsidizes a business, that business will have an unfair advantage over its competitors. While it is not government ownership, subsidy becomes both a form of government control over the subsidized company as well as an unfair competitive advantage for the company in its own industry. Frequently legislators who arrange for subsidies are given kickbacks in one form or another in exchange for unfair laws.

Agricultural subsidies are an example of how a government

can harm poor people in other countries. Using the pretext of "saving the traditional farm," "heartland values," or "national security interests," governments fund large agro-business enterprises that can sell American cows to Africans for less than Africans could raise cows on a free market. One "farmer" in California collects $500,000 per year for not harvesting rice. It turns out the ducks on his swampland are attracted by the rice, and this "farmer" invites "his" politicians to come there duck hunting for free. Such subsidies neither make farming competitive nor encourage entrepreneurs to enter into markets that would naturally be their own. They are simply redistribution schemes that are unjust, thwart economic competition, and undermine a free market.

Official State Approval or Licensing of Businesses

State licensing is often necessary to assure that a product meets minimal safety standards, but state approval processes are often carried out in ways guaranteeing that only big players, existing players, or those giving kickbacks will get approval. Such procedures can be used to establish corporate fiefdoms. For example, when President Bill Clinton took office in 1992, he proposed a plan by which the government would work with a handful of insurance companies to regulate health care. Such a measure would be analogous to the king of a nation deciding who would get which territories.

Government permission to do business is a form of power that can be misused to play favorites and eliminate competition. Every regulatory law is an opportunity for corruption and undermines a free market. The Food and Drug Administration, the Federal Aviation Agency and other regulatory agencies wield power that must be directed toward appropriate ends. These agencies must be good referees and not in the hip pocket of the corporations they are supposed to regulate.

Government Investment in Corporations

The possibility of generating wealth for government treasuries through investment in companies is enticing but ultimately destuctive of society.

First, there is a conflict of interest. A state invested in a corporation has an interest in its profitability, even if that profit is earned in an unfair or non-competitive manner. Such a state is more likely to give that corporation favored status to earn higher profits at the expense of other corporations. If the corporation gets into trouble, the state is less likely to prosecute because it will affect its own budget.

Secondly, investment in a corporation makes the state a player, not a referee. As a result, the state displaces other players or would-be investors in the private sector and deprives them of their right to pursue happiness as investors. The state, by virtue of its size, can displace opportunities for hundreds or thousands of citizens. Thus, rather than enabling the citizens' pursuit of happiness, it impedes it.

Thirdly, since investment is a form of gambling, it is an improper financial foundation for a state. The state should tax citizens according to the success they have in their own ventures, and not take such risk itself. The state has a duty to protect the interests of society, and this requires a stable form of income.

Social Security and Financial Redistribution

Government-provided social security or medical benefits to all citizens both competes with private investment possibilities and limits citizens' ability to plan for their own future. Thus it impedes both the individual's "right to pursue life, liberty and happiness," and the vitality of a free market—the game originally designed by the founders.

By providing social security benefits to all citizens, the government redirects taxed earnings into programs that require many government employees and agencies to manage. These are not invested in any productive enterprise—rather a portion is taken by the bureaucracy. Further, these funds are not under the control of an individual directing them towards the pursuit of his own happiness. They are being directed towards his future state of dependence, as the government has determined it.

Government may have an obligation to see that there is a safety net for the indigent, however social security and medicare should not be a quasi-monopoly plan for the life of retired people.

Tax Structures Can Thwart the Market and Justice

As with subsidies, taxes have consequences in the economic sector. There is a saying that, "If you subsidize something you get more of it, if you tax something you get less of it." A government can also make something tax-exempt to force economic behavior that would not naturally occur.

For example, because they are tax-exempt, employer health plans are widely used. However, they are abused because employers are neither the provider nor the consumer of the product. Such plans tend to get abused by both employees and medical providers at the expense of the corporation, causing non-market prices in the health care industry.

Another form of economic injustice can derive from trusts and other specially regulated institutions that can shield some people from taxation and give them unfair advantages over other people who must pay standard taxes. Such legislation can be as specific as eliminating tax on oil wells in a certain district, or tax on a certain stock, or it can be general enough to include all people who have large amounts of accumulated capital and can afford a lawyer to establish a trust to shield it.

Through a trust, the trustee can determine the expenditure of funds he does not personally own, and he can provide many amenities for himself without declaring personal income. This gives him an unfair advantage over poorer people that cannot establish a trust and instead, receive wages, which are taxed before they can be used to purchase goods and services.

Business in Government

Conflicts of Interest: Corporate Executives in Office

Conflicts of interest are serious impediments to the free market. Potential conflicts of interest exist everywhere. A conflict of interest exists any time a public official is involved in a public policy that affects his personal well-being, or the well-being of a business that he owns. This is a case in which the referee favors certain players on the field.

Just as it is a conflict of interest for a legislature to vote on its own salary, it is a conflict of interest if a politician who owns oil wells is able to legislate for government subsidy of oil. It is a conflict of interest if a board member of a public university votes for construction on a new building on campus that his company will build. It is a conflict of interest if a public utilities commissioner makes a decision on a contract for a utility that he will work for in the future.

A public office is a sacred trust. It must be used to serve all citizens. Use of government to further one's own ends, or the ends of one's corporation, should incur a high penalty. One cannot serve as a referee while advancing one's own cause. Numerous conflicts of interest exist that are legal. They should be made illegal.

Control of Regulatory Agencies

One way that corporations try to control government is by trying to pack the agencies created to regulate them with their own people. Just as packing the Supreme Court with justices who were former corporate lawyers led to legal decisions in favor of corporations, other agencies, such as the Federal Aviation Administration, the Nuclear Regulatory Commission, and the Food and Drug Administration can be packed with "experts" who worked as executives in these various industries. With the promise of a comfortable retirement in return for their service to an industry, "regulators" can become conspirators.

Control of Legislation

Control of legislators through campaign contributions is another strategy of some corporations. This is the same as giving a referee a kickback. Through campaign contributions, corporations or their proxies are able to get politicians to vote for bills they would not otherwise support or initiate. To accomplish their ends, lobbyists try to manipulate political processes as well as politicians.

Controlling the process of legislation is another strategy that requires some cooperation from a few legislators. Secret meetings and the obfuscation of bills are major tactics used to avoid public knowledge of what is being legislated. Over the years, much legislation has been packed into single bills, many now called omnibus bills, shaped more by private "horse-trading" in committees than by open debate on items. Large corporations that can afford to hire people to help ensure the omnibus bills include benefits for them have an advantage over the voters in shaping this legislation. They often propose and help draft legislation.

It is not just large corporate interests that use these strategies to manipulate the political process. Labor unions, teachers, government employees, and non-profit organizations all try to use similar political tactics to influence legislation in order to win an economic advantage at the expense of the society as a whole.

Submitting Fraudulent Claims

Stealing from the government by submitting fradulent claims for work done is another form of business taking advantage of the taxpayer. In some cases, corporations overbill the government for services rendered. In other cases, government employees receive kickbacks to approve payments that would not otherwise be authorized. A recent example of fleecing Minnesota taxpayers was the payment of lawyers who did nothing towards redistricting (redrawing the boundaries of voting districts), but charged and were paid for it anyway.[24]

Governments are a continual target for all kinds of lawsuits simply because they control significant amounts of money, and unscrupulous people continually look for anyone with "deep pockets" they can sue, rather than earning their own income.

Monopoly

Monopolies undermine free markets. For example, if one company owns or controls all timber, all oil, or all power lines, it has consumers at its mercy. It is theoretically able to charge whatever it wants to and not to provide any more service than it wants to. It is to the advantage of any business to attain monopoly status, so that it can become lazy and uncompetitive. It is in the interest of governments, insofar as they act as a referee to promote a fair market, to eliminate monopolies. Trusts are similar to monopolies. This is when all providers of a product agree to cooperate, becoming a virtual monopoly, and fix prices rather than allowing the market to determine them.

The break up of Bell Telephone in the 1970s is an example of legislation that encouraged competition in an industry that had made virtually no progress for forty years, because there was no incentive to spend any money on research or invention. However, renewed competition led to the development of new technologies and industries—including cell phones and the Internet—that would not have been developed by the monopoly, at least not for a long time and then only motivated by public pressure.

Proper anti-trust legislation serves the purpose of the government as referee of a fair and competitive game.

Patents, Research Grants, and Prizes

Patents and copyrights are government guarantors of a limited monopoly. They are granted in order to encourage an outlay of research and development funds for new goods and services. They encourage development of new ideas and technologies by stimulating self-sacrifice and achievement. In short, they encourage competitition. Because a patent has a limited lifespan (17 years), the product that is patented enters the competitive marketplace after that time.

This form of government intervention is socially beneficial. However, the patent process itself, to the extent it is corrupted by larger companies trying to manipulate the process by buying off patent officers or getting around the patents of genuine inventors through unfair legal proceedings is an improper use of patent law.

Research grants are often awarded by governments for ostensibly the same reason as patents—to encourage development of new products. However, government grants tend to foster dependency rather than achievement.[25] First of all, the award givers sit in a position of power to give out awards. They are often given as favors. Further, grant proposals have to be written virtually explaining the result in advance in order to get the grant, thus undermining the concept of free unfettered science. There are reports and strings attached. Bureaucracies are formed. There is also an incentive not to produce the stated goal. If it is accomplished there will be no more grant money required and all those dependent on the give-away would be out of a job.

The bottom line is that research grants usually encourage people to seek money, not to produce a better product. This has little to do with playing a fair economic game that leads to national prosperity.

An interesting example is the result of President George Bush's 2003 "State of the Union" address in which he proposed 26 billion dollars be earmarked for alternative energy and hydrogen fuel vehicles. Immediately, the Republicans proposed legislation that would give the money to the oil companies that put them into office. The Democrats proposed to give the money to the auto industry whose unions helped put them in office. The result had nothing to do with a realistic expectation that alternative fuels would get developed; it was a way to reward special interests in the name of a noble cause.

To foster a real result, competition would need to be created. In this case, as with patents, the goverment could have established some kind of reward that would stimulate a successful result. For example, the government could have offered a prize—say 1 billion dollars or one-twenty-sixth the amount of the proposed research money—to the first company to develop such a fuel. The announcement of such an award would encourage venture capital to flow into research and development to achieve the goal. It would not cost the taxpayer a cent unless a product was delivered.

Conclusion

The United States and the rise of corporations have shared a parallel history. Corporations have proved they can produce railroads, cars, telephones, televisions, computers, airplanes and countless other products at prices that make them widely available. They have become part of the pursuit of happiness of people, even if at times they have created a false sense of happiness by being made ends in themselves.

There is a role for the government to play with respect to corporations. It is to serve as policeman and referee. It should enforce rules of justice that motivate a free and competitive market, giving everyone a chance to achieve economic success by providing a valuable product or service to others. In a free competitive market, people are encouraged to serve themselves through serving others well, and they are rewarded proportionately. Government should be vigilant to ensure that this takes place, and not take actions that make some citizens wealthy at the expense of others.

Government intrusion into the free market comes from two directions, from civil society and from business. The goal is the same: to get something one did not produce and does not deserve through political manipulation. In this regard, the market is sabotaged by socialists and capitalists alike. Redistribution is the goal of the non-producer, the dependent, and the non-achiever.

However, not all government expenditures have negative economic consequences. Funds that support the police and judicial functions that referee the economic playing field are important. Also, funds used to stimulate achievement through education of the underclass, patents, and awards of prizes can add to the size and breadth of the free market that currently exists.

Examination of the ways that government has gotten into business, and business into government, provides an indication of where the nation has drifted off course and provides some suggestions for creating a proper relationship between government and business. Concentrations of power and money are always targets for unscrupulous people. Such people will seek to devise ways to raid government coffers, pension funds, mutual funds, and successful businesses, and to twist the law to accomplish their goals legally. They will always try to create worthy political fictions to mask selfish personal causes. Despite the rhetoric of some corporate lobbyists to the contrary, Adam Smith would probably make most of these same arguments were he alive today.[26]

The United States' founding fathers were especially sensitive to the misuse of political power in their day. But in modern large-scale industrial societies, money is power; it can—and does—buy politicians and armies. Men and women of the twenty-first century need to be as sharply aware of the abuses of money power as our founding fathers were of military and legal power. The legitimacy of any government has always required equal treatment of all citizens. Such legitimacy is not opposed to a free market, but depends on it. It allows all citizens to follow the initial goal of the United States' game—the pursuit of happiness through one's own achievement.

Questions for Reflection

1. Do you think that corporations are necessary to develop the strong economy we have today, or can it be accomplished with private proprietorships and partnerships?

2. Which system of banking do you think is most appropriate for the United States; a government-run national bank, privately run national banks, state banks, or some other system?

3. Do you think corporations should have personhood? If so, in which ways? Do you feel there are inequalities in the way human beings and corporations are treated?

4. Do you think that personal income tax is an appropriate way for the federal government to raise funds? If not, what types of taxes do you think would be better?

5. Is the present approach to monopolies and trusts is satisfactory, or do you think that other measures would be better?

6. Do you think corporations should have greater social obligations?

7. Do you think that the repeal of the Glass-Steagall Act and the merger of Citigroup and Travelers Insurance was a wise move or the result of a lack of vigilance on the part of Congress?

8

Universal Education

EDUCATION WAS NOT INITIALLY PART OF THE FEDERAL AGENDA, although the founders cherished education. They left responsibility for education to families, communities, and states. Education was considered to be a part of the individual pursuit of happiness that would be accomplished by people as they wished. The founders realized that there was a risk that people would not learn good citizenship on their own, but this risk was part of the concept of their experiment with freedom. Education was a potentially divisive issue, as there were debates over whether it should be religious, classical, secular, vocational, public, or private. Framing the Constitution was difficult enough without getting into details like education. Nevertheless, over its first hundred years, the United States developed a system of public schools. It was the state of Massachusetts, with its historical emphasis on religious education, that paved the way for public education for other states.

Education in Colonial Society

In early American society, except for reading, formal education was not needed for employment as a farmer or shopkeeper. The requisite economic skills could be learned from parents, or as apprentices. Pastors and lawyers, of course, had literate professions that required more formal education. But only a tiny percentage of the population were not the producers of goods required for economic life in colonial America.

The Puritans in New England placed an extremely high value on education for religious reasons. They believed everyone needed to learn to read the Bible. Within the homogeneous Puritan settlements public education was originally the norm. Children aged 6-8 in New England attended "Dame schools," often run by single women in homes. In these schools children learned to read, write, and do simple arithmetic. In 1690, *The New England Primer* was printed to assist the teachers. It used religious phrases for each letter of the alphabet, teaching reading and doctrine together. Then the girls would learn homemaking skills from the women, while boys prepared for employment. This could take one of three paths; attendance at a Latin School that prepared them for college (where entrance required fluency in Latin and Greek), working with their fathers learning a profession, or working as an apprentice to a craftsman. Craftsmen often charged a boarding fee to the parents. The Puritans founded Boston Latin School, the oldest existing public school, and Harvard College, the first college in America, in 1635.

In the middle colonies, education was less organized, but because most immigrants were Protestant a high value was placed on reading. Benjamin Franklin, who was self-taught, believed that other Americans could also learn on their own if they had access to books. He founded the first public library in America in 1731 and chartered it as the Philadelphia Library in 1742. He established a plan for an English language grammar school that was different than the traditional Latin schools. A believer in the value of science, he wanted schools equipped with laboratories, workshops, maps and other tools for learning physics, chemistry, and geography. He also allowed girls to attend his school. Franklin's school did not survive, but pointed in the direction others would later take in designing education for Americans.

In the South, children of aristocrats were tutored, bout other children had little opportunity to go to school. Missionaries occasionally taught reading to help propagate their gospel.

Early Thoughts on Public Education

The founding fathers, including the Deists, did not have a serious problem with the type of education early American families and churches provided for children. As discussed in Chapter 4, almost everyone believed in a Creator God and that people were created equal. They all accepted the Constitution of the United States and religious leaders took seriously their responsibility to make sure children in their congregations were good citizens of the United States.

There was a symbiotic relationship between the general religion, or civil religion, that undergirded the state, and the more particular forms of religion that nurtured private faith and childhood development. Even though Benjamin Franklin doubted the divinity of Jesus and Thomas Jefferson was to write a version of the Bible without miracles, both believed that the teachings of Jesus were among the highest teachings known. They believed that, if Americans followed the Ten Commandments and the Sermon on the Mount, they would cause little problem for social order.

Rationalists and pietists alike held that, ultimately, each person's faith was a matter of conscience. Further, the religious revivals of the eighteenth century, spearheaded by Jonathan Edwards and George Whitefield, were seen by rationalists like Franklin as performing a useful service to society, even if some doctrines seemed questionable. The revivals had broken the hold of traditional institutional religion over the people, and created a national spirit that had supported patriotism in the new nation. Franklin chastised Thomas Paine for his more cynical view of religion as stultifying and full of errors.

English, Citizenship, and Science

In Virginia, Thomas Jefferson advocated a general education for all based on English, principles of citizenship, and science. As states developed plans they tended to stress these same goals. However, the general population was not much interested in public schools until the 1830s and 1840s.

Benjamin Rush (1746-1813) was an important figure in the development of educational theory. A graduate of Princeton College who had gone on to study medicine in Edinburgh, he was a professor of chemistry at the College of Philadelphia at the time of the Revolution. He founded the first free medical clinic for the poor in the United States, was a signer of the Declaration of Independence, served as Treasurer of the U.S. Mint from 1797 to 1813, and was strongly opposed to slavery. Like Frankiln, he wanted to see education better serve American needs and support the new democracy. In "Thoughts Upon the Mode of Education Proper in a Republic,"[1] Rush developed a number of points that would be later incorporated into the early United States' philosophy of public education:

- A uniform general education for purposes of citizenship that would render the population more homogeneous.
- A supreme regard for the nation
- Ability to reform the nation as necessary
- Use of the American language, not Latin or Greek
- Focus more on science than foreign languages
- Current foreign languages of French and German preferred to the "dead languages" of Latin and Greek
- High schools should teach grammar, oratory, criticism, higher mathematics, philosophy, religion, chemistry, logic, metaphysics, history, government, and the principles of agriculture and manufacturing
- Students should learn laws of human society to distinguish those that tend to repress and those that lead to liberty

- Train girls in the principles of democracy as well as boys, as women had to teach these principles to their children.
- Development of American rather than European habits

The goal of developing American English as the language of instruction in American public education was aided by Noah Webster, whose *American Dictionary of the English Language* (1828) served the study of language. It was adopted as a national standard by Congress in 1831.

Industry vs. Taxpayers and the Education of the Poor

In 1790 the Pennsylvania Constitution called for free public education for poor children. In 1805, the New York Public School Society was formed by philanthropists to provide education to poor children on the Lancaster model, in which one master teaches hundreds of students in a single room using rote lessons in which older students pass lessons to younger students. These schools emphasized the discipline and obedience that factory owners wanted in their workers.

In Boston, a petition in an 1817 Town Meeting called for establishment of a system of free public primary schools paid by tax dollars. The initiative was put forward by businessmen who would have gained financial relief from the payment for schools for the poor. Wage earners opposed the measure because they did not want to pay taxes. The first public high school in the United States, Boston English, opened in 1820. In 1827 Massachusetts passed a law making public schools open to all students, free of charge.

Practical vs. Classical Education

During the early nineteenth century, as the population continued to shift from farms to industry, industrial leaders were asking for the higher educational system to teach skills more related to vocational skills in agribusiness, commerce, or industry. Like the ideas on education of Franklin, Rush, and Jefferson, this was another attack on classical European education. A debate ensued over the nature of education. In 1828, the Yale Report on higher education was issued in reaction to this trend, advocating the traditional teaching of classics through Latin and Greek that would support creation of a gentleman with a sharp mind and good character.

The Second Great Awakening and a "Christian America"

The Second Great Awakening, which consisted of a new wave of revivals beginning in the early nineteenth century, placed its stamp on the philosophy of education in the United States. As with the First Great Awakening and Protestantism in general, strong emphasis was placed on education so that all Americans could read the Bible. A number of those converted by the revivals wanted to start schools, especially in the more recently settled territories inland, where few existed.

While the First Great Awakening tended to create national unification, the Second Great Awakening turned out be somewhat divisive. The First Great Awakening had emphasized the Kingdom of God in America. While grounded in Calvinism, it was less doctrinal than its strict predecessors, catering to the masses with general moral dictums like Wesley's "earn all you can, save all you can, give all you can." Revivalists like Whitefield were able to work with non-conformists like Franklin, and the formalistic traditional churches were on the defensive. The rationalist wing of eighteenth century Protestantism developed Unitarianism, which among other things, had a humanistic concept of Jesus.

The Second Great Awakening, on the other hand, was, in part, a reaction to the perceived dethronement of Christ. There was a renewed emphasis on the deity and worship of Jesus Christ. Even among the liberal churches, Christ became the centerpiece and the nineteenth century American mainline churches developed a strain of Protestantism called Christocentric liberalism.[2]

The result of these revivals was an emphasis on a "Christian America" that was more specifically Protestant than the founders had envisioned. The goal was to replace the inclusive civil religion of the founders with a Christ-centered Christianity. This was not an attempt, as in the Roman Empire to make a single institutional church responsible for the moral education of the Empire, but it was an attempt to ground the cultural unity of the United States in a Christocentric Protestant vision of society.

Those who did not accept this basic premise of a "Christian America," were subject to exclusion and persecution. Those outside this new contender for control of the philosophy of the United States, included Catholics, Jews, Freemasons, and Unitarians. This was the beginning of a cultural war that has existed in the United States in one form or another ever since. Hence, concomitant with the revivals was a wave of anti-Catholicism, anti-Masonry, and anti-Semitism. Unlike other denominations, the Baptists, who were also theologically Christocentic, continued to champion the freedom of religion for minority religions because separation of church and state was so integrally tied to their own founding and the persecutions they had suffered.

As with the rest of the culture, the Second Great Awakening permeated the public schools; causing widespread persecutions that made it especially difficult for Catholics, but also for anyone else marginalized by the evangelical Protestant culture. Most public schools used Protestant prayers and the King James Bible, and the courts upheld their use, even though Catholics wanted children to learn the prayers and catechism. From 1830 to 1850 one million Catholic immigrants came to the United States. Eventually, the Baltimore Council prohibited Catholics from sending their children to public schools. Catholics sought public funds to create independent schools, but upon failing to get that support, created their own schools.

Horace Mann and the Common Schools

Called "the father of American Education," Horace Mann, a legislator in Massachusetts, had a keen interest in school policy and became Secretary of Education for the state in 1837. He wanted to see public schools available to everyone, rich or poor, that would foster social harmony with children of all backgrounds learning to be Americans together. He believed that, in addition to reducing ethnic and religious strife, such schools would help end the poverty of a perpetual underclass.

> If one class possesses all the wealth and the education, while the residue of society is ignorant and poor, it matters not by what name the relation between them may be called; the latter, in fact and in truth, will be the servile dependents and subjects of the former.[3]

Mann presided over the establishment of the first public "normal school," a school for teachers, in the United States in 1839. He reinvigorated the establishment of high schools and pushed through a law requiring children to attend six months of school each year. Mann and other school reformers like Henry Barnard of Connecticut and Samuel Lewis of Ohio were among the Whigs who eventually pushed through school reform in all northern states. In 1851, Massachusetts passed the first compulsory education law, ensuring that everyone become "civilized" and employable. These centralizing reforms were opposed by populist Democrats, by Catholics, and by some black leaders who wanted control over the education of black children.

By the time of the Civil War, free public school was a reality in the north. It was based on school districts supported by property taxes. In the South, the existence of slavery brought about opposition to widespread public education. The Quakers tried to establish private schools for the slaves until forbidden to do so by nervous slaveholders,

The Civil War consolidated the states into a more centralized nation-state in many ways. In education, one of the first signs was a law passed by Congress in 1864 that made it illegal for Native Americans to be taught in their native languages. The Bureau of Indian Affairs moved many children to off-reservation boarding schools to educate them to be citizens of the Union.

Merger of School Districts and Politicization of Schools

A blow against community control of public schools was dealt at the turn of the twentieth century as many urban school boards in the United States consolidated. Many local district school board positions were eliminated as city-wide positions were seen as a move toward efficiency and standardization. The result was less influence by parents and small business leaders over the public schools in their district, and more influence by more powerful city politicians and the wealthier people that supported them. This led to the possibility of higher-level political battles over theories of education more disconnected from parent input.

One such movement was called the testing movement, founded by G. Stanley Hall, a psychologist and educator at Johns Hopkins University, who was also the founder of the *American Journal of Psychology*. In 1889, Hall became president of the newly founded Clark University in Worcester, Massachusetts, where considerable educational research and studies on adolescent development were conducted. Hall argued that high school should be considered more an extension of elementary school than preparation for college, using ideas about stages of human growth. This research continued and led to the development of tests educators use today, including the General Aptitude Test Battery, the Inkblot Test, and the Thematic Apperception Test, in elementary, middle, and high schools.

Another movement in education that would not have happened without the centralization of school supervision was known as progressivism. A leader in this movement was George

Counts, who earned a doctorate in education at the University of Chicago and afterwards accepted several positions of increasing importance until he began a long career at Teachers College at Columbia University in New York. In his books,[4] Counts promoted the philosophy of John Dewey and the "child-centered" movement, which sought to draw out innate potentials in students, emphasizing social relationships rather than imposing rote memorization and traditional instruction. Like other social idealists of his time, Counts saw progressive education as part of the movement to change society into a more utopian state. Critics cite the outcome of this progressive education strategy as leading to the "dumbing down" of America.[5]

The progressive movement held that schools should identify with other "progressive" elements in society like labor unions, farmer's organizations, and disenfranchised social groups. Thus, progressive education led to a fourth philosophical vision of the mission of schools in America; the first being classical education, the second American civil education, and the third being controlled by a partnership of Protestants and business leaders.

The progressive movement can be seen, in part, as a reaction to the "WASP" (White Anglo-Saxon Protestant) culture promoted by the "Christian America" movement of the nineteenth century. As such, it had a narrowness of its own which tried to create a "secular humanist America" in the twentieth century.

This cultural tension was the center of national debate in the widely publicized case of *The State of Tennessee vs. John Scopes*, alternatively known as "The Monkey Trial." A number of states were considering laws that banned the teaching of evolution and required teaching the biblical account of creation in the public schools. William Jennings Bryan, a three-time Democratic candidate for President, led the crusade for a fundamentalist Christian perspective and the high-profile agnostic Clarence Darrow represented John Scopes, a biology teacher who had taught evolution, in violation of Tennessee law. Scopes' fees were covered by the American Civil Liberties Union (ACLU).

During the Scopes trial, Darrow had Bryan on the stand, interrogating him about his literal interpretation of the Bible— whether Jonah had lived in the belly of a whale, Joshua had made the sun stand still and, eventually, the account of creation in six days. Darrow had the initially smug Bryan on the defensive and the secular reporters lapped it up. The next day the judge struck the testimony from the record.[6] The court did not resolve the issue, but Bryan's intellectual defeat influenced many states not to pursue the legislation. However, Darrow's cynicism towards religion and the Bible was not appreciated by mainstream Americans either.

Only two states, Arkansas and Mississippi, adopted anti-evolution legislation. In *Epperson vs. Arkansas* (1968), the Supreme Court called the Arkansas law unconstitutional because it did not support religious neutrality.

The cultural contests between these two philosophical strains warring for control of education in the United States can be viewed as a degenerated version of a potential conflict that had existed between the pietists and the Enlightenment thinkers at the time of the founding. However, that potential division was overcome by large-minded and large-hearted statesmen like Benjamin Franklin and George Washington, who were able to include both groups in civil discussion as the nation was formed. By the mid-twentieth century, neither group in the cultural war over education was satisfied with education that promoted a general civil religion *à la* Benjamin Rush.

Racial Segregation and Government Involvement

The legacy of slavery in America also became one of the major educational challenges. After the Civil War, freed African Americans mobilized to bring public education to the South, forming alliances with Republican business leaders to rewrite state constitutions and include free public education for all. Reconstruction ended in 1877, when federal troops were withdrawn from the South; Southern whites regained political control and began to segregate the public schools. In its 1896 decision on *Plessy v. Ferguson,* the U.S. Supreme Court ruled that Louisiana had the right to "separate but equal" railroad cars for blacks and whites. This precedent meant that the federal government recognized segregation as legal and many southern states passed laws requiring racial segregation of public schools.

In 1950, the father of Linda Carol Brown, a seven-year-old black girl in Topeka, Kansas, teamed up with the National Association for the Advancement of Colored People (NAACP) to challenge segregated schooling. She had been told she had to attend one of the four black schools in the city, and her father believed this doomed her to an inferior education. Similar suits in Delaware, South Carolina, and Virginia were attached to *Brown v. The Board of Education* by the time it reached the Supreme Court of the United States in 1954. The 1896 decision of the Court was essentially reversed. In the words of Chief Justice Earl Warren,

> To separate [elementary- and secondary-school children] from others of similar age and qualifications solely because of their race generates a feeling of inferiority as to their status in the community that may affect their hearts and minds in a way unlikely ever to be undone. We conclude that in the field of public education, the doctrine of 'separate but equal' has no place. Separate educational facilities are inherently unequal.

The implications of this decision were multifaceted. Not only did it have implications for other "separate but equal" facilities, but it brought the federal government into education more firmly than had been the case before. The Supreme Court decision did not lead to quick implementation. In 1957 Arkansas Governor Faubus sent the National Guard to prevent nine Black children from attending a high school in Little Rock. This defiance caused President Eisenhower to send federal troops to escort the children to school. In areas where the orders were not openly defied, they were often just not implemented. In 1979, Linda Brown Thompson once again went to court because, twenty-five years later, Topeka schools were still segregated.

Desegregation then ran into another issue. In large cities blacks were predominately living in some districts while whites lived in others. Activists sought to equalize education by busing inner-city black students to white suburbs and vice versa, giving blacks and whites access to the same facilities. The plan was expensive and broke apart the community connections that traditionally formed around local schools. Parents were unable to commute the long distances needed to assist in their children's involvement in extra-curricular activities. In 1974 in *Milliken v. Bradley,* another Supreme Court ruling, stated that schools could not be desegregated across school districts. This decision basically left each district to desegregate itself.

The complaint that inner-city schools had fewer resources than wealthy suburbs led many states to propose state-level funding of schools, further removing control of education from parents and local communities.

Public vs. Private Education

In addition to the issue of equal access to public education has been a growing debate over whether all children must attend public schools. The most compelling argument for attendance of all in public schools is their role as an incubator of citizenship. Public schools serve as an equalizer for children by removing them from their social status and inculcating national values and patriotism. Further equalization, some argue, could occur if uniforms were required in school.

On, the other hand, religious and cultural groups that have felt marginalized by the mainstream do not think that public schools have performed satisfactorily. In addition to failing to provide a high standard of learning, even compared to other countries, they have, in fact, been places of bigotry that teach values that undermine the values of parents.

In 1922, when the state of Oregon decided to "American-ize" the schools, a law was passed that parents who did not send their children to public school could be fined up to $100.00 and confined up to 30 days in jail. This was soon challenged both by the Society of Sisters of the Holy Names of Jesus and Mary and a private military school. In *Pierce v. Society of Sisters* in 1925 the Court unanimously decided against the state and in favor of the private schools, arguing that denying freedom for parents to choose the type of education they want for their children is a violation of the Fourteenth Amendment, which guarantees personal liberty. The Court ruled that state governments could enact laws for compulsory attendance, but they could not man-date which school would be attended.

The decision did not change the arguments for and against public education. Critics of the present system feel private schools foster elitism and public schools are often left with the most difficult children to teach. By law they are required to accept disabled children and any student that applies while private schools can be more selective. They are required by mandates to spend money on special education programs that private schools can avoid.

Those who send their children to private schools often com-plain that they have to pay twice for the tuition because they have to make tuition payments to the private school and they have to pay taxes to support the schools they do not use. Many states or local governments give some tax credit to try to address this issue.

In a survey of parents who withdrew their children from public schools and placed them in private schools, the following reasons were given in descending order of importance:

1. Concern about standards of work in school
2. Concern about quality and commitment of teachers

3. Concern about student behavior in school
4. Concern about job prospects after school
5. Concern about moral standards of school
6. Concern about religious atmosphere.

It is worthwhile to note that religion was not the primary issue (scoring sixth). Most parents felt that they, or their religious institutions, could instruct their children in religion as long as the school was not antagonistic towards their religious faith.

Parents also withdrew children from private schools and placed them in public schools. These were the top reasons they gave for doing so:

1. Concern about job prospects of child
2. Concern about quality and commitment of teachers
3. Concern about standards of work in school
4. Concern about student behavior in school
5. Concern about moral standards of school
6. Concern about class size and school facilities[7]

It is clear that both public and private schools have fallen short in meeting the expectations of parents on many occasions and that, for many parents looking for schools, "the grass is greener on the other side of the fence." Both public and private schools have been limited by their resources, and often some aspect of education has been neglected. One solution, it is argued, is to give parents more choices to create more competition.

The Proposal for School Vouchers

One popular, and hotly contested, proposal has been the idea to give each child an educational voucher that would enable parents to select schools for their children and turn in the voucher as payment. This argument is supported by free market theorists that argue that competition would be created among the schools, solving the problem of poor quality education.[8] All schools would become businesses. Parents would use vouchers to send their children to the schools that did the best job at educating. This would also let parents send children to schools that followed an educational philosophy with which they agreed and take away the opportunity for social radicals to influence school curricula through political processes.

As one would expect, this proposal is met with vigorous opposition by current school administrators and teachers' unions that fear losing funds and jobs. Their jobs are currently secured by public funding and, though their wages are generally not high, they receive better benefit and retirement packages than their peers in the private sector. They will use their extensive lobbying power to oppose almost any educational reform except increased taxes to support the present system.

On the other hand, many supporters of the voucher system do not have any idea what it would cost or how it would be administered in a way that did not create another bloated arm of government bureaucracy for the masses like the Social Security administration. Further, there are few instances in which payments by governments do not have strings attached. It would be very easy for a government to withhold vouchers from schools that did not meet its standards, and it would be a slippery slope to withholding from those that the administrator did not like for political or other self-interested reasons. Further, what would prevent schools from charging for extra services to take in more funds than vouchers would provide, causing new forms of discrimination against the poor people whom vouchers are meant to help?

With a universal voucher system, there would be no market mechanism to determine the price of an education. The vouchers would be expected to cover the minimum of whatever is required. This would allow schools to try to name their price, and governments to push it down. A better mechanism, and one more in keeping with the philosophy of the founders, would be to let the market determine the cost of education through private school competition. The government could thus observe the market price and provide vouchers, like food stamps, that could be used by poor children to select an education.

A further aspect of the argument over payment for education is whether parents or the entire society would bear the cost of education. Those who don't have children usually vote against school referendums and want to spend their money on other things. However, school is expensive, parents are often young and struggling financially, and education affects the entire society. One way to give the parents a break and allow the entire society to assist is to allow parents to claim tax credits for each child they send to school. This would offset some of their expense.

Civil Religion and Cultural Literacy in the Schools

One reform of public schools that might be more acceptable to a wider public would be to return to a civil religion more like that taught by the founders and Benjamin Rush and less like the Christocentric "civil religion" that came to pervade American culture in the nineteenth century.

Ignorance of the distinction between the two forms can be seen in the recent battle over former Alabama Chief Justice Roy Moore's display of the Ten Commandments in an Alabama Court House. On the monument was written "The Laws of Nature's God," using the words of the Declaration of Independence that were employed by John Locke, Isaac Newton, and Thomas Jefferson to describe a transcendent Creator. However, the statement was followed by a listing of the Ten Commandments from the Old Testament. These commandments were presented as revelation in the Old Testament and not as the "self-evident truths" promoted by the founders. Despite the fact that most Americans believe in the Ten Commandments, and many of the laws are based on them, it is sloppy scholarship.

This problem was compounded when the revivalists of the

nineteenth century wanted to add New Testament doctrines about the divinity of Jesus Christ to the cannons of "civil religion." Whereas cultural unity can be developed under the umbrella of a transcendent source of creation, the imposition of revealed doctrine or belief is divisive. It can be argued that the attacks against Chief Justice Roy Moore and against including the phrase "under God" in the Pledge of Allegiance, to the extent that they have any legitimate basis for criticism, are grounded in the chauvinism and exclusionism that has attempted to refashion the original broad-minded and inclusive civil religion articulated by the founders in their philosophy of the United States.

These problems have been compounded as scientific theories like Darwinism have appeared to undermine some traditional interpretations of biblical religion. Cultural wars have erupted over the doctrines of evolutionism vs. creationism, with neither the scientists nor the religionists making their case without a faith component. The civil religion of a Benjamin Franklin could have absorbed this debate and encouraged greater scholarship on the part of both groups.

The civil religion of the founders implies three main points:

1. Human beings did not create themselves
2. Human beings desire freedom to pursue happiness
3. Human beings have equal rights

The founders' references to God imply these three doctrines of civil religion. Thus the real question for the opponents of civil religion is whether they would support these three doctrines. Unless they disagree with the concept that human beings have equal rights to pursue happiness, even atheists and evolutionists should have no political objection to the civil religion of the founding fathers. There is also no philosophical reason why a Hindu, Buddhist, Jew, or Muslim would object to these principles being taught in public schools in the United States, what they have objected to is cultural prejudices that are not based in these three points.

In fact, most of the debates over education in the public schools are rooted in a desire to control or influence the education of children in ways that implicitly reject the founders' principles. Advocates of many reforms do not want free competition of ideas or to allow people of all persuasions a fair hearing. However, one of the best forms of preparation for being a citizen of the United States is for children to hear the various ideas and make decisions based on comparison and evaluation of them all. There was a large outcry in the 1970s over the issue of children joining "cults." Those who joined an alternative religion were usually searching for moral or spiritual fulfillment that was a result of either a spiritual vacuum in their lives or explanations about religion that were one-sided and did not match their life experiences.

Moral development of children occurs around the years of puberty. Neither the silence of the public schools on issues of morality (for fear of parent backlash), nor the pushing of a political agenda on students is fair to children in these crucial years of development. They should be taught how people in their society view the world and given intellectual resources for comparison that show respect for all views. A general concept of civil religion that supports the three founding principles outlined above would allow this to occur.

Another approach to this problem was developed by educator E. D. Hirsch in his 1988 book on cultural literacy[9] and his later books on core knowledge. These books in many ways suggest a curriculum that would teach something about all of the people and ideas that make up the United States through an analysis of common language. Hirsh postulated that, at a minimum, in order to function well in the United States, one had to learn basic ideas that were ingrained in the culture. To accomplish this, Hirsch examined written newspaper and magazine articles to determine which terms were assumed by the authors and which words were thought to require further explanation. For example, Christ, Plato, and Confucius were all figures that authors did not feel they had to explain. On the other hand, George Counts would need an explanation. The article might describe him as the father of progressive education in the United States.

Hirsch developed a list of 5,000 terms that compose the knowledge one needs to be "culturally literate." He then developed a curriculum that would, over a period of years from kindergarten through sixth grade, impart the background knowledge of these terms to students. In his book *The Schools We Need and Why We Don't Have Them,*[10] Hirsch argued that the progressive education developed by Rousseau and Dewey and their intellectual descendants failed to recognize the value of this content because of their own ideas of process and innate abilities. They did not place enough value on the role culture plays in human development.

Attacks on Hirsch have come from promoters of progressive education, but teachers in schools that have adopted his theory have found it to be an excellent way to train students to function well in society. Attacks also come from those who argue a strict separation of religion and the state, those who would attack the civil religion of the founders of the United States. This is because a number of the terms refer to the Bible and other religions.

However, if these subjects are taught with neutrality and if knowledge of terms brought to America from other immigrant groups continued to be added, this is one way to teach basic cultural ideas in public schools. The Spirit School, a magnet school in St. Paul based on these principles, has 65 percent Hmong students, with the majority of the remainder being Latino or African American. Parents send their children to this school for the purpose of allowing their marginalized children to become mainstream Americans able to compete with those who learned the culture through their families and cultural organizations, in addition to conventional public schools.

Increased Federal Involvement in Education

In 1965 Congress passed the Elementary and Secondary Education Act (ESEA), opening the door for federal funding of public school programs. In 2003, that amount was about nine percent of every public school dollar. It was only a matter of time before someone in the United States government would decide that strings should be attached to these dollars that would further limit parent and local control over their children's schools. In 2001 the No Child Left Behind (NCLB) Act began to accomplish exactly that.

Proponents argue that the law will boost student achievement, especially among the poor and minority group members for whom ESEA was originally intended, and will bring accountability to states' and districts' use of federal funds. Opponents fear that NCLB's testing mandates and sanctions for school failure will result in student regimentation and parental abandonment of public education. What no one disputes is that NCLB has reshaped federal involvement in American education. It was overwhelmingly passed by both Republicans and Democrats. The new role of the federal government in public education includes:

1. The *federalization* of education under the law;
2. The *standardization* of curriculum, assessment, and accountability;
3. The *systemization* of education from relative local autonomy to an increasingly state-based, federally supported arrangement that oversees school accountability;
4. Increased *privatization* of curriculum and assessment, along with more educational choices for parents.

It is ironic that a Republican president ushered NCLB into law when Republicans have traditionally favored local and parental control of education. The bill means $22.3 billion in new in federal spending on schools. As President Bush explained, the need for strong measures is critical: "The academic achievement gap between rich and poor, Anglo and minority is not only wide, but in some cases is growing wider still."

This legislation that increases federal involvement in education, like the 1954 *Brown v. Board of Education* decision is the result of a perceived failure on the part of the public schools. It is an attempt to provide universal education that will reduce the education gap between rich and poor Americans that Puritans, local governments, private schools, and states have all failed to accomplish.

Critics argue that federalizing education will further dumb down education because it will be further removed from parent and market forces and subjected to an ever-larger bureaucracy that is engaged in testing and analysis for the sake of satisfying a bureaucracy. In several states where standardized tests have been implemented, less time is spent on traditional education and more time on preparation for state standards tests. In short, this process failed before, so let us try harder.

President Bush used the program in Texas to show how the education gap was being closed. What he failed to mention is that, since the 1984 Texas Educational Assessment of Minimal Skills Act was passed, Texas teachers have had to spend a good portion of their time teaching students how to pass the tests. However, Texas students placed 39th compared to other states on basic skills SAT tests.

Another critcism of the program is nepotism and corruption. Neil Bush, President Bush's brother, is founder and CEO of a Texas-based software firm, Ignite! Inc., which collected millions of dollars selling software to prepare students to take comprehensive tests required under "No Child Left Behind." Today United States schools and students typically pay two to three times the competitive market price for books because certain textbooks are mandated. As with other government involvement in business, monopolies and quasi-monopolies arise, driving up prices. NCLB is young and the critics might have made the first attack, but if history is any indication, NCLB, like other federal social programs, is likely to cost more money, produce lower results, and encourage further corruption in the textbook market.

Conclusion

Education in the United States is a contentious and unsolved issue. The founders were divided over the purposes of education and the role of the government in ensuring enough standardization to create good citizens. However, the advent of industrialization, and more recently foreign competition, has required increased levels of education for high performance in the workplace. When the United States was founded, higher education was for leadership and character development and for jobs in the clergy or government. In the minds of average citizens today, a primary reason for education is getting a job in the general economy.

History teaches that the survival of a nation depends on a national faith that both guides and legitimates good leadership and laws. Thus, a democratic nation like the United States requires an educational system that does more than educate for jobs, religious instruction, classical wisdom, or a narrow ideology. The ideas of Benjamin Rush proposed exactly that. His ideas are consistent with the goals of the rites-of-passage for leadership in societies discussed earlier in the book.

Unfortunately Rush's plan was never fully implemented, and the mainstream philosophy around which the United States was organized fractured as various non-inclusive groups sought control of education or reform of society, creating cultural division rather than cultural unity.

In the twentieth century, the federal government became increasingly involved in public school education, but there is little evidence yet that this involvement has actually furthered the educational needs of the nation. Just the opposite, there is evidence that this involvement will mandate more testing for purposes of satisfying the government and less time for the novel and competitive teaching that market forces could bring. Even free-market theorist Milton Friedman proposed a federal voucher system for schools that, on examination, would create the type of bureaucracy free-market theorists normally oppose. It would create competition among schools for federal dollars rather than competition for parents' approval. Normally free-market champions do not propose programs that recommend taxpayer dollars flow through several government hands before being returned to the taxpayer.

A better role of the government, in education as well as other areas of society, is to serve as a referee. This means using its energy to ensure that the players play the game well, not that the government plays it for them. It was suggested that tax credits would be far more efficient than vouchers in accomplishing the proper competition among schools and balancing the financial obligations of parents against other members of society. It was also suggested that the genuine civil religion of the founders be reintroduced if their experiment is to succeed, rather than other pretenders of cultural hegemony that worship something other than a transcendent God that endowed all people with equality and the desire to freely pursue happiness.

Questions for Reflection

1. What are the purposes of education discussed in this chapter? Can you think of others?

2. What has been the United States government's role in public education? Do you think its interventions have been appropriate?

3. Do you think it is possible today to have public schools that teach the civil religion of the founders, or is that irrelevant or a violation of the separation of church and state?

4. What is the educational philosophy of E. D. Hirsh? Do you think it would satisfy the requirement to educate students for good citizenship?

5. What are the arguments for and against a voucher system for public education? What do you think about such a system?

6. How do you think education should be funded? Why?

7. Do you think that a system of competing private schools that met minimum standards of education for citizenship and had a way to include the poor would be better than public schools? Why or why not?

9

Social Welfare

People Falling Through the Cracks

THE AMERICAN EXPERIMENT WORKED PRETTY WELL in its initial years as the people, mostly Protestant, busied themselves pursuing happiness through an ethic of achievement and hard work.[1] This ethic was based on the nature of the United States as a place where Europeans could come and pursue liberty and happiness, and reinforced by the Protestant work ethic which taught that work was the glorification of God.[2]

America received some of the most enterprising and courageous people from other countries. As a frontier nation, it was not hospitable to the weak or helpless. Packing up what earthly possessions one could carry on a ship and saying goodbye to one's home and family, possibly forever, was not an easy thing to do. Many immigrants came without the guarantee of employment. America was a land of opportunity for people tired of oppression in Europe. They could live in freedom and raise children the way they saw fit.

There was opportunity in the United States if one was over the age of 15, healthy, and eager to work. However, if one was dependent, handicapped, or unmotivated, and not the member of a benevolent family or community, there was little public support available. The Puritans who came from England were accustomed to Poor Laws which determined who would get public aid and under what conditions. However, they were not inclined to pursue them. First, the poor in New England were not a threat to public order. Second, there was a general view, supported by the words of Jesus, that "ye have the poor always with you."[3] Third, rigorous Calvinists often questioned whether assistance to the poor would corrupt their moral character; helping the poor person to get work was the preferred solution.

The United States Constitution contained no provision for the poor. Charity was left, by the founders, to private philanthropy and local and state governments. However, it was not many years before Americans became more concerned about poverty. The view that the "poor would always be with you" was becoming less acceptable in a new Republic that viewed all people as equal and sought perfection.

One source of concern came as a fruit of the religious revivals. Samuel Hopkins, a student of Jonathan Edwards, developed Edwards' doctrine of disinterested benevolence into a social theology. He equated sin with selfishness and pragmatically argued that, by serving the whole, oneself was included and cared for, and thus in one's own highest interest. Hopkins was active in the developing anti-slavery and several other social reform movements at the turn of the nineteenth century.[4] A second motive was fear of social unrest and crime coming from a more visible underclass, especially in larger cities like New York and Boston. By the presidency of Andrew Jackson, there was a growing concern that the churches and private sector were not going to fill the role of creating the citizens the nation required. There were ever-increasing numbers of people falling through the cracks and somebody had to take care of them. By the 1820s, poverty became a target for social reform.

The Concept of Almshouses

The first public attempts to deal with the problem were based on the notion that Poor Laws were creating permanent dependency and a perpetual underclass.[5] Rather than giving them handouts the poor needed to be reformed. The Yates Commission in New York and the Quincy Commission in Massachusetts came to nearly the same conclusions; the public would build institutions to reform non-productive citizens. Asylums would reform the mentally impaired, penitentiaries would reform criminals, and almshouses would convert the indigent into workers. Such institutions were developed by communities and cities and aimed at those not being reformed by churches or religious organizations.

Public almshouses turned out to be a failure. Within twenty-five years they were discarded as a viable means of reform. In New York, the mental ward attached to the almshouse still remains in its reorganized form as Bellevue Hospital. There were stories of misuse of money, institutional abuse, untrained and uncaring workers, and unreformable inmates. Public charities have frequently been staffed by people looking for a job, rather than looking for a way to help their neighbors. In the public sector, the failure of the almshouses led to a public search for a better solution and this eventually led to the development of "casework." But that would have to wait until after the Civil War.

The Great Benevolence Movement

By the 1820s the new freedoms provided by the Constitution had led to a sense of optimism. The shackles had been thrown off and there was nothing to hinder progress. Alfred North Whitehead once described it as a peculiar period in which even wise men had hope.[6] No calamities had yet befallen the new nation to dampen that enthusiasm. The period marked the beginning of what has been called the "benevolent empire." The founding fathers had made families, religion, and the private sector responsible for developing the character of citizens, and religious leaders took that mission seriously. Whether it was Congregationalist Nathaniel Taylor at Yale, Albert Barnes at First Church in Philadelphia, Lyman Beecher in Boston, or Charles Finney on the frontier, the basic message was the same; men had to use their freedom for the sake of others.[7]

There was another byproduct of the revivals, the creation of a national Protestant spirit. Revivalists frequently condemned, on the one hand, the Catholics for their allegiance to a foreign power, and on the other, the rationalists, the Unitarians, and the freemasons for their skepticism about the divinity of Jesus. In 1827, a resolution of the convention of Baptist Churches resolved that "all such members as belong to the Baptist church and also to the society of Freemasons, be requested to renounce publicly all communications with that order."[8] A new Christian political party was organized which tried to promote a narrower religious doctrine than the civil religion of the founding. By 1832 there were 141 newspapers promoting anti-Masonry, and the governors of New York and Vermont had been elected on anti-Masonry platforms. The movement reduced the number of Masons in New York from 20,000 to 3,000.[9]

The Catholic Church had far more experience and success in charity work than either the less compassionate view of the Puritans or the less mechanical view of public institutions; but the Catholic Church in the early history of the United States was outnumbered, even when not persecuted. The great benevolence movement began with the American Tract Society, handing out Bibles. Then societies to fight slavery, alcoholism, and poverty, and societies to promote education, prison reform, women's enfranchisement, and peace appeared. These societies were fueled with funds from wealthy philanthropists like Presbyterians Arthur and Lewis Tappan, and the wealthy retired sea captain William Ladd. There was no personal income tax at the time, and some men were able to accumulate vast fortunes. Their philanthropic contributions made them heroes.

The benevolent societies were more effective than public charities because of the love and personal commitment of their members, many of whom toiled long hours for no financial remuneration. Their success also led to reactions from those against whose interests they campaigned. Most notable was the campaign against slavery by northern Christian activists who, motivated by love and a concern for equality, were part of the stimulus for the Civil War.

The Rebirth of the Nation

The Civil War changed everything in the United States. It is the event that turned a collection of states into a genuine nation. Some historians have marked the Grand Review of the Army, in which 200,000 troops marched down Pennsylvania Avenue toward the newly completed Capitol on May 23-24, 1865, as the defining event. The flag was raised to full staff for the first time in four years. National cemeteries were created in which Protestant, Catholic, Jews, Whites and Blacks were all laid to rest side by side. The Memorial Day ceremonies which soon developed were occasions to remember all of these young men who had given their lives for the nation. They entered into the catalogue of American Civil Religion.

The relationship between the states and the federal government changed forever with the war. Although that relationship has never been absolutely delineated by the Constitution or the Supreme Court, the Civil War brought greater centralization and the beginnings of national welfare programs. After the war, the loose connection of states emerged as a more unified modern industrial state.

Social welfare programs, like many government programs, emerged rather innocuously. During the Civil War, the US Sanitary Commission had been organized by the War Department with a semi-volunteer nature; it continued to develop into veterans' programs and public health programs. The end of the war saw the establishment of the Freedmen's Bureau, enacted by the War Department on March 3, 1865. It was the nation's first welfare agency, which was charged with aiding freed slaves and assisting the entry of former slaves into the general economy through financial aid, education, and redistribution of confiscated lands. It also maintained civil records, such as the legal marriages of former slaves.

The Freedmen's Bureau was part of the War Department budget, which quickly evaporated after the war. Although large tracts of land were seized during the war—for example 20 percent of the state of Mississippi—most property was never redistributed to freed slaves. After Lincoln's assassination, Vice President Andrew Johnson became president and quickly gave amnesty and pardons to the Southern plantation owners that had rebelled. Land was returned to almost all of them, except slave-holding Indians that had sided with the Confederacy![10] The pre-war philosophy that welfare was not the responsibility of the federal government reasserted itself in Congress, and in four years the Freedmen's Bureau came to an end.

The Social Gospel

Charitable organizations, primarily connected to churches, once again assumed their role of taking care of people that needed help. Efforts were often uncoordinated and several states established boards of charities aimed at providing some coordination of activities. As the United States became an industrial nation, a whole new set of problems related to industry began to emerge on a larger scale than the churches were prepared to tackle. These issues included urban slums, child labor, industrial accidents, low wages, and disease.

Washington Gladden has been called the father of the social gospel,[11] a movement which grew out of a "Christocentric" liberal theology that tried to wed inherited theology with modern thought. It was careful to distance itself from Unitarianism and Transcendentalism to remain as a reform movement within the mainline churches. A pastor in North Adams, Massachusetts, Gladden became involved in labor issues following a labor walkout in a local shoe factory, which led to the importation of Chinese workers from the West Coast by the owners, leaving the former workers out in the cold. In 1871, he became the editor of *The Independent,* a formerly Congregationalist publication in New York. He began to publish widely on articles from theology to municipal corruption and labor injustice. This led to an illustrious career that made him one of the most prominent ministers and speakers of his day. Gladden attempted to apply the laws of Christian love to industry. While he claimed he was not a socialist, he believed that monopolies ought to be brought under government ownership and that large industries should be cooperatives owned by the workers, rather than by capitalists who exploit labor.

Gladden was not an economist, and his lack of economic and political theory was complemented by the thought of Richard T. Ely, a distinguished economist at Johns Hopkins University, who had been educated in the "historical school" of economics at Heidelberg, where he witnessed the emergence of the modern welfare state in Germany. In 1885, Ely took the lead in forming the American Economic Association, of which Gladden and a number of religious business leaders were members. Although Ely sought to integrate science, religion, and government, he has been called a "statist" by later economists. The first point of the platform of the organization regarded "the state as an agency whose positive assistance is one of the indispensable conditions of human progress."[12]

The Social Gospel continued to spread as the mainstream approach to issues of social justice until the First World War. It was instrumental in bringing wide political support for state and federal laws related to industry and labor; and it was the backbone social organization of the ecumenical Federal Council of Churches in the United States. It was responsible for making the Progressive movement a largely middle-class movement. Neither Adam Smith nor the founding fathers could have imagined the scale of industrial development in the late nineteenth century.

Industrial economic power was not a major issue when checks and balances were written into the Constitution. Without the popular support for federal intervention in industrial labor and anti-trust issues generated by the churches, the labor legislation in this period probably never would have taken place.

Casework

Leadership in the public sector in the 1870s came from the private Charity Organization Societies (COS). Lessons had been learned from the experiences with almshouses that led to a more scientific analysis of social welfare. The COS managed to become a major presence in most cities by the turn of the century, and their method of charity analysis led directly to the method and training of the professional caseworker. The COS developed registries of eligible applicants for assistance and criteria for determining which applicants were most worthy of aid. Still in the private sector, and influenced by traditional moral concerns, the COS warned of unwise forms of philanthropy that could foster dependence and undermine human character. In addition to coordinating private organizations and common recordkeeping, the COS developed links to universities, developing the beginnings of education for the social work profession.

Government Involvement in Social Welfare

Issues of justice stemming from modern industrial life in the last part of the nineteenth century led to the involvement of government in the economic welfare of its citizens in three ways: government regulation, social insurance, and the use of professionals. These progressive issues were put on the agenda by the Republican Party and Presidents Harding, Coolidge, and Hoover.

Regulation was accomplished through lawssuch as the Sherman Anti-Trust Act, labor laws, fire codes, and bank regulation.

Federal oversight agencies such as the Interstate Commerce Commission, the Federal Trade Commission, and the Food and Drug Administration were established.

By 1920, several universities had schools of social work and graduates were being placed in public agencies that were forming. The COS became Family Services, and many services, such as child welfare and mental health were taken on by various governments.

Social insurance was also put on the agenda by the Progressives. Between 1910 and 1921 the majority of states adopted workers' compensation programs. These were insurance programs designed to provide for workers that became disabled. Various old age assistance programs and Aid to Dependent Children (ADC) were also formed in this era. Social insurance did not carry the social stigma of charity, as many of the funds were provided by employers and workers.

Depression and the Welfare State

The "New Deal" promised by the Roosevelt administration was not so much a new idea as the wide scale application of the principles developed in the preceding decades. Labor laws and banking and securities reform were forms of regulation, not nationalization of industry. The Civilian Conservation Corps and other public works projects aimed at creating useful work, not public handouts.

Social security was a form of universal social insurance enacted at the federal level. The Federal Insurance Contributions Act (FICA) initially authorized a modest tax of 2 percent, 1 percent from employees and 1 percent from employers. As an insurance program, the benefits were related to the "premiums" paid into the program. The result was that perennially dependent, non-working, or impoverished people—women, children, and minorities did not receive benefits. Benefits were designed for the mainstream worker.

Most direct handouts were left to the state and local governments, although the federal government began to contribute to state coffers to help relieve the burden on the states.

Expansion and Reform of the Welfare State

The period from Roosevelt to Reagan (1932-1980) was one of continuing incremental expansion of both state welfare benefits and the tax rates required to sustain the benefits. Professional caseworkers provided more rational services than the almshouses of the early 1800s. The impersonal and bureaucratic nature of delivery led to long-term structural inefficiencies and some perpetual welfare dependency. Initially this was overcome by the robust post-WWII economy.

However, by the 1970s there were mounting criticisms that the system was providing a perpetual underclass as third generation recipients had known no other means of existence. Unintended consequences of generous welfare packages surfaced in decisions by teen-age girls to get pregnant out of wedlock in order to qualify for government-paid college educations which childless girls had to pay for. These factors, combined with the loss of traditional factory jobs to other countries, a lower birth rate in traditional families causing a slowdown in workforce entry, and a higher percentage of the population living longer and receiving more social security benefits, guaranteed an eventual collapse of the system, even with a 9.9 percent total FICA rate in 1977 and a shrinking budget for national defense—the original purpose of the nation. Budget projections indicated reform was essential to forestall collapse.

The Reagan administration won a landslide victory in 1980 on the promise that priorities would be changed, the welfare state reduced, and the military restored. Yet after eight years of "Reaganomics," often trying to force harsh and uncompassionate measures, the FICA tax rate stood at 11.4 percent. George Bush won following Reagan, promising a "kinder and gentler" society, followed by Democrat Bill Clinton's continuation of existing policies for another eight years. In 1999 there was a projected long-term unfunded Social Security liability of more than $19 trillion, and the FICA rate in 2004 stood at 15.3 percent.

During the 1990s, individual states like Wisconsin and New Jersey implemented welfare reforms that included welfare-to-work incentives and reduced incentives for having children in order to collect welfare benefits. Savings were realized in reduced benefit payments, and increased tax revenue was generated from those who had returned to the workforce. Shortly thereafter, most states adopted similar reforms. Nevertheless, there are always stories of people falling through the cracks.

When President George W. Bush took office in 2000, he initiated the White House Office of Faith-Based Initiatives. This is not a return to the great benevolence era of the 1820s, as some would like to believe. This is a plan to earmark additional federal funds to faith-based charities that provide social services to the needy, regardless of religion. It is yet another effort to reach people who fall through the cracks of bureaucracy and are being caught by religious institutions as a second safety net. However, funds are being provided from personal federal income taxes that already consume up to 28 percent of workers' pay in addition to Social Security and Medicare payments.

Health Care

A major problem facing many citizens is the cost of health care. At a cost of $1,000 to $2,000 per month for a family of four, health insurance costs at the turn of the twenty-first century became, for many people, a larger share of their income than home mortgage payments. The rising costs also prompted businesses that were paying the major portion of health insurance premiums for their employees to (a) push a larger percentage off onto their employees, (b) lay off employees and outsource their work, or (c) move their facilities to another country where employee costs are less. This caused a further reaction by labor unions, which have now made health costs, rather than wages, the number-one item in contract negotiations.[13]

How did we get to this situation? It is through a confusing course of incremental events that led the entire health care system in the United States away from market forces. However, before surveying that course it is useful to compare health care in the twenty-first century to health care in the eighteenth century. If the goal of the United States is *life*, liberty, and the pursuit of happiness, then we can say that the life expectancy at birth today (77), which more than doubles that at the time of the founding (~37), is an impressive achievement.

At the time of the founding, there were no hospitals and few doctors. Doctors visited people in their homes and carried tool kits for makeshift operations in which sterility was difficult to achieve and infections likely. One of the major deterrents to caesarian deliveries of babies was the high probability that the mother would die from infection. In early America many people on the frontier had little access to doctors or medicine and they died from many diseases and ailments that can be easily treated today.

Like the village blacksmith, the doctor was an individual performing a service. There were no medical corporations that could provide the facilities and range of medical expertise that exists today. Hospitals, to the extent they existed, were primarily Christian shelters of mercy where patients could receive care by other Christians—not so much medical treatment as physical care.[14] It was not until the twentieth century and the development of antibiotics and medical science and technology that life expectancies rose dramatically and hospitals became places of large scale physical healing.

The cost of medical care was not something the founding fathers of the United States considered an issue for the federal government they created. Like a clergyman performing a religious ceremony or a lawyer drafting a deed, a doctor was a skilled person offering a service to those in need of it. This all changed with advances in medicine.

Hospitals also changed—rom non-profit institutions of care by religious organizations to multi-million dollar enterprises run by business managers motivated to maximize profit—even though many have somehow been allowed to keep non-profit status.

The first medical insurance plans in the United States were begun around 1930. Blue Cross, one of the oldest medical insurance companies, started in 1929. Otto von Bismark had tried national health insurance in Germany back in 1884, but it cost people more and delivered less than private insurance. England tried national health insurance in 1911 and failed. It is not surprising, then, that those who pushed for national health insurance in the United States after World War I met with strong resistance, and private insurance was adopted instead.

Employer-Paid Medical Insurance

During World War II, in an effort to control inflation, the United States government enacted a wage and price freeze. This led to the unintended consequence of employers looking for ways, other than direct wage increases, to attract and maintain employees. It became popular to offer medical insurance plans because they were desired by most citizens. While they were initially a loop-hole around wage inflation, after the war they became sought after by all workers because of their value. Labor unions lobbied for them and the government encouraged their spread by pass-ing tax legislation that made these plans more attractive to offer.

There was a problem with this system that nobody at the time seems to have noticed. This was the fact that employers were disinterested third-party payers, neither the buyer nor the seller. Market conditions disappeared as (a) consumers sought more and higher quality medical service than they might have if they had been paying their own bills, (b) doctors and medical providers raised prices for these services without complaint from the consumer, and (c) medical insurance providers raised their own rates to cover this inflation and put in some extra padding for themselves. It was a system pre-ordained to collapse, as prices appeared to have an infinite ceiling.

Eventually, after watching health insurance costs rise exponentially for several years, employers paying for the burgeoning costs of the health care industry found themselves unable to balance their own books. They began cancelling plans, reducing coverage and, in some cases, went out of business. They demanded controls be placed on escalating health insurance premiums.

Managed Health Care

A temporary solution to the crisis was found in the concept of managed health care, but it was, in principle, a patch on a flawed system. Managed health care was a concept by which a large medical group would be organized to provide medical services for lower prices by paying less to participating doctors and hospitals in return for the promise of steady business. Such bargaining brought the cost of medical care closer to a real market price for subscribers within such programs, but other people continued to pay inflated prices. In addition, consumers were faced with fewer options and were required to accept the services determined necessary by plan managers.

Many employers switched to managed health care programs to obtain lower prices. This led to conventional insurance companies either setting up their own competitive plans or, in a number of cases, quitting the health insurance field. However, it also led to frustrated medical providers, who were being forced to work at prices set by managers and cope with volumes of paperwork, frustrated consumers, who felt they were receiving poorer quality and rationed services, and anger on the part of both, as they watched business managers scraping off millions of dollars in profit off the top. There was no one to manage the manager. This is in addition to the 30-60 percent cost of service required to pay the management personnel.

Perhaps one of the most disasterous consequences of a system based solely on managed health care is the high prices that are passed on to non-insured consumers. It is not uncommon for a hospital or doctor to bill individuals an amount four times the price negotiated by a managed care provider. These individuals may include the wealthy, who can pay higher fees, but generally they affect employers who tried to establish their own plan or people too poor to buy health insurance. The result is that the number of uninsured people has been rising, particularly in groups that need medical care the most—children and older adults who are not yet receiving Medicare.

What is Next in Health Care?

Americans are gradually learning that neither third-party payers nor managed health care provide acceptable solutions. Neither system allows true market prices to be available to all people shopping for services. However, socialized medicine has elsewhere led to rationing, poorer service, and lack of medical advances.

In 2003 Congress passed a Medical Savings Account (MSA) act that provides some relief to those not in managed health care programs because these accounts, like incentives given to employers earlier, will be tax-exempt. Former laws almost forced people to use employer-funded plans. However, there are yet many features of the overall health care system that might auger against these plans, notably the high charges billed to consumers without the negotiating power of large health care plans. If a consumer saves 30 percent on taxes on money put in a medical savings account but has to pay four times the price for a service as his insured peer, he will not be motivated to use the MSA.

Another complication is the nature of aging itself. Market-driven insurance plans frequently charge a fee for the cost of service delivered to a particular age group. It is projected that, without other corrections before 2014, a couple one year before retirement would need to pay about $44,000 in premiums—more than many couples would earn.

To make health insurance affordable, future policies, in addition to bringing market forces to bear on the health service industry, should require some weighted averaging across age groups, so that younger and healthier people are helping to pick up the costs of sicker and older people. Each generation, in its turn, would benefit from such policies. This is basically what Medicare does for retired people who, because of their age and the history of the health care system in the United States, are practically forced to accept what the government provides.

Revamping the system along this general philosophy would accomplish a couple of things. First, prices for medical services would come down if market forces were allowed to fully operate. This would have the beneficial consequences of lowering Medicare costs as well, since the government, as well as other consumers, would be able to take advantage of lower prices.

A second byproduct would be the possibility for people to carry life-long insurance policies or develop large enough Medical Savings Accounts that they would not require Medicare. This would be a situation in which people would be free to determine their own medical future and, in keeping with the philosophy of the founders of the United States, be more free to pursue happiness in retirement.

Health care, like social security, public education, or any other service provided by government to the masses, eventually becomes mathematically impossible to fund, as everyone dependent on it—patients, doctors, and administrators—wants the best service and wages they can get. Because the government is a disinterested third party, as are businesses that pay for health care benefits, it does not have a natural ability to create the competitive medical services at competitive prices that a market made up of many buyers and sellers would generate.

Conclusion

Social welfare was not something that the United States founders believed should be provided by the federal government. They believed they had devised a system for people who were largely self-sufficient. They expected the private sector or lower levels of government to provide whatever social welfare was needed. But that would certainly not be a program for the masses. This system worked up until the civil war largely because of the concerted efforts of social and religious leaders in promoting a spirit of benevolence in a largely pre-industrial society. Citizens, motivated by love, added to the level of justice in the nation.

The Civil War and industrial development created a nation the founding fathers would not recognize, and with new concentrations of power they had not imagined. The failure of large industries to provide, of their own initiative, working conditions deemed suitable by the general population, led to a humanitarian backlash that demanded regulation and fair labor laws.

Federal welfare benefits did not develop until the twentieth century. A gradual transfer of economic welfare shifted away from traditional family and community institutions to concepts that related individuals directly to the state. The ever-increasing demand for welfare assistance became viewed as "entitlements." The demand for welfare, in a society that increasingly came to expect universal care without much stigma, outstripped the government's ability to tax and pay for those demands. The Social Security tax rate has continued to rise, and only recently have thoughts about privately held retirement plans been entertained.

President George W. Bush's support for faith-based initiatives is not without precedent. This is how Hammurabi and the Kassite Empires of ancient Babylonia provided for welfare 3,000 to 4,000 years ago. Money was given to temples, irrespective of the gods that were worshipped, in order to support displaced persons, orphans, and other dependents. Of course, there were

differences. People in those temples lived more like one big com-
mune; they did not live the same quality of life that working
families enjoyed. Yet they were cared for and social order was
sustained in a way that was viewed as just and legitimate. The
central government helped provide a safety net.

It is short-sighted to look at social welfare in the United
States as it presently functions and expect that continual incremental adjustments will provide a solution. It is like the late
Soviet Union's attempt to "restructure" its economy time and
time again when its initial premises about human nature were
flawed. A report by Social Security Commissioner Tom Saving
has calculated that, at current rates, the cost of Social Security
and Medicare will consume the entire federal budget by 2070,
leaving nothing for other programs.[15] The masses will have to be
weaned from federal dependency or the United States might find
itself in a situation similar to Russia in 1989.

History has proven that the greatest prosperity has occurred
when people are most free to pursue life, liberty, and happiness
on their own, whether it was in ancient Babylon, Ancient Rome,
or any other society. The goal should not be the provision of any
universal guarantee of welfare that not only expends state coffers,
but also gives people less control over their own lives and fosters
dependency. However, some safety net should be provided.

The plans which are threatening to bankrupt the U.S. treasury are not the plans that provide safety nets for people falling
through the cracks; they are plans like Social Security and Medicare that are aimed at universal care of the masses at the expense
of the next generation. These plans worked from 1935-2000
because the "baby-boom" generation provided more payers than
there were recipients and because rates were continually raised.
However, as the boomers retire and live longer, and the number
of recipients outstrips payers, the present system will not work.
The majority of citizens, as in the time of the founding, will be
forced to plan for their own security in old-age. Most of the population, through some form of mandatory personal retirement

planning, should be able to prepare for retirement with private savings and insurance policies.

The founding fathers could not have imagined a society in which the middle class would be recipients of the majority of federal funding in the form of welfare. They envisioned a society in which people freely lived their own lives based on their own efforts, and any welfare that was needed would be the responsibility of families and communities. However, families and communities did not provide a safety net for all people, and changes in the medical field could not have been anticipated. New government approaches to health and welfare, which account for both individual human behavior and the evolution of medical industries, are required.

Incentives by the government to encourage private planning, and thereby reduce the government's burden should be the goal of Social Security reform and many other social welfare reforms. Key questions asked of any legislation should be: Does it make Americans more independent? Does it make Americans more productive? Does it give Americans more control over their own lives? Some proposals, such as tax deductions for Individual Retirement Accounts, move in that direction. However, it should also be kept in mind that such plans can be abused by unscrupulous management of such accounts. The answer, history has taught, is not to let the government take them over, but to provide regulations and fines that prevent wild speculation, abuse, or careless administration of such funds.

Questions for Reflection

1. The founding fathers saw no reason for the federal government to involve itself with any social welfare program. Do you think changed social conditions have made this necessary?

2. Many institutions of social welfare have their foundation in an institution motivated by love, e.g., the family or a religious organization. Do you think it is possible for a rational bureaucracy to organize such welfare as effectively and justly?

3. Do you think that it is possible to have a free society in which everyone is allowed to pursue happiness and not have an underclass made up of people with lower ambition? Is it even fair to tell young citizens, born into this nation, that in order to succeed, they need the same drive for self-achievement as their ancestors?

4. Do you feel the federal government should provide a "safety net" to catch people falling through the cracks? Why or why not?

5. What do you think the best strategy would be to solve the health care crisis in the United States?

10

The United States and the World

IN THE PHILOSOPHY OF THE FOUNDERS, the United States was formed as an autonomous nation of self-sufficient individuals that could exist on its own, apart from the rest of world, and become a model for the rest of the world. As mentioned in Chapter 7, the Boston Tea Party might be considered the first revolt against globalization. It was a revolt against foreign intervention in both the political and the economic affairs of the United States.

At that time, the world's leading power was England, and it was attempting to establish worldwide dominion through its colonies throughout the world and through its monopolistic corporations, which brought wealth to the king. Today the situation is nearly reversed. In 2002 the United States, the world's sole superpower, initiated a global war against terrorism with England lending its support. Worldwide protests against the World Trade Organization (WTO), perceived as an arm of United States policy, are rebellious against the corporations that vie for control of the world. For many, the United States, once a beacon of hope to other nations, is becoming a source of global domination to be opposed.

How did this reversal occur? Is it an outgrowth of the philosophy of the founders? Is it consistent with their vision of the

United States in the world? Is their philosophy even relevant, given all of the changes that have taken place in the last two hundred years? These are questions with which citizens must wrestle if they are to vote and function responsibly.

Foreign Policy in the First Century

In his Farewell Address, President George Washington spoke at length about foreign policy,[1] asking the United States to "observe good faith and justice towards all nations." "Religion and morality," he said, "enjoin this conduct." Washington advocated neutrality towards other nations, stating that, "The nation which indulges towards another an habitual hatred, or an habitual fondness, is in some degree a slave." Hatred of an enemy or love of an ally both are passions that can lead to irrational behavior not in the interests of justice, peace, or Providence. Giving another nation a favored status can cause corruption which allows citizens to sacrifice the interests of their own nation to those of a foreign power and opens the door for foreign powers to misuse that status with insidious plots. When such an alliance exists, the "real patriots" who resist their intrigues will "become suspected and odious," while the dupes "usurp the applause and confidence of the people."

Washington went on to say that the detached and distant position of the United States from Europe gave it a distinct advantage in enabling it to pursue a neutral course. This neutral course, if followed steadily, would lead to the respect of other nations, unable to sway it from a righteous path. Washington argued that the "great rule" of conduct in commercial relations was to have as little political connection to them as possible. It should be the policy of the United States to "steer clear of permanent alliances, with any portion of the world." To the extent that such alliances exist, they need to be honored to uphold the reputation of the nation. However, he advised that the government extract itself from such encumbrances as soon as possible. He recommended the same in commerce, that no favors or preferences be sought, for whoever seeks a favor must pay with a sacrifice of its independence. This is not the course for a free people.

Washington concluded that a position of neutrality was a duty that would enable the nation to act freely and justly, maintaining peace and friendship with all nations. Washington had entered into many treaties during his presidency. These were basically treaties of friendship that would promote peace and open commerce between the new nation and other countries, not alliances or bestowals of favored status to particular nations. They were formally announcing the existence of the United States and its intent to live peacefully with other nations.

Expansion of the United States in North America

Washington's foreign policy ideals were clear in the abstract, but difficult to maintain. The main factor contributing to wars in the first half of the nineteenth century was the desire of many citizens of the United States to get foreign powers out of North America and to control the entire continent themselves.

While the Atlantic Ocean formed a clear boundary on the east coast, when Washington left office the British were in Canada, the French occupied the Louisiana Territory, the Mexicans controlled Texas, and the Spanish were in Florida. Native Americans inhabited all of these areas.

Skirmishes with the French on the Western frontier disappeared peacefully in 1803 when Napoleon suddenly offered the Louisiana territory to the United States for $15 million. President Thomas Jefferson jumped at the chance and made the Louisiana Purchase.

In 1810, a number of "war hawks," including Henry Clay of Kentucky and John C. Calhoun of South Carolina, were elected to Congress. They aggressively sought to rid North America of foreign occupation. Native Americans in the old French territory and the British in Canada became the defenders against what they saw as United States aggression. Chief Tecumseh and his brother attempted to organize the native tribes to take a stand against the westward expansion. They organized an attack against Harrison's army in the Ohio River Valley in 1811 known as the Battle of Tippecanoe. President James Madison asked for a declaration of war against the Indians and the British in Canada who were accused, perhaps falsely, of arming the Indians.

The Federalists opposed "Mr. Madison's War," but Congress supported the declaration. England responded with the attack and capture of Fort Mackinac and repelled three attempted United States invasions of Canada while, in the Atlantic, "Old Ironsides" captured and burned British ships. The British and Indians defeated Kentucky troops in Michigan at the Battle of Frenchtown in 1813, but United States troops captured and burned York a few months later, giving them control of the Great Lakes, and Tecumseh was killed in Ontario late that year.

In 1814, the Federalists in New England, who disliked this expansionism, began considering secession from the Union, while Major General Andrew Jackson's army battled in the South. The Creek Indians were defeated in the Mississippi territory in 1814. Meanwhile, the British launched a three-pronged attack by sneaking into Washington, D.C., and burning it. They were repelled at Baltimore. Diplomats agreed on the United States-Canadian border. The final battle against the British occurred in New Orleans in January 1815, where the British suffered a humiliating defeat, losing 700 men and injuring 1400, while Jackson lost eight men and thirteen suffered injuries.

From 1810 to 1821, the Spanish Empire in Central and South America was collapsing, as independence movements in most nations were driving the Spanish out. In 1818 Jackson's army invaded Florida, breaking the United States treaty with Spain. The army was opposed mainly by the Seminole Indians living there. The Spanish agreed to leave in 1821. In 1823, President James Monroe subtly warned European powers that any attempt to aid Spain in reclaiming territories in Latin America or any

Russian encroachment in the Northwest would be repelled by the United States. This policy would later become known as the Monroe Doctrine. It was not an alliance with Latin America as much a desire to keep European powers out of the Americas. It was not the type of neutral foreign policy advised by President George Washington, but it was not a policy of foreign adventurism beyond the Americas, either.

In 1823, Stephen F. Austin began settling people from the United States in Texas after land was granted to his father by the Mexican government. Within a few years, relations between these settlers and the government in Mexico City deteriorated, as the Mexican Constitution of 1824 failed to defend the rights and liberties of the settlers. In 1830, Mexico forbade further emigration from the United States. The first Texan casualties were suffered in 1832. Conventions were signed in 1832 and 1833 but fighting again broke out at the Battle of Gonzalez in 1835, marking the beginning of the revolution for Texan independence, which was officially declared in 1836.

Texans battled the Mexicans for the next ten years until United States President Polk, who had won on an expansionist ticket, sought to aid the Texans by annexing Texas as a state. Boundary disputes triggered the Mexican-American war in 1846. A territorial boundary was finally settled with Mexico with a payment of $10 million to the Mexicans in 1850. Meanwhile, gold was discovered in California and Americans rushed there to strike it rich. Polk sent General Zachary Taylor to the Rio Grande, bringing pressure on Mexico. Mexico agreed to cede New Mexico and California to the United States in 1848 for $15 million.

Disputes also continued with Canada over borders west of the Great Lakes. These were settled with treaties in 1842 and 1846. Alaska was purchased from Russia for $7.2 million and became property of the United States in 1867, finalizing the territory of the United States in North America.

Tariffs and Protectionism

When the United States was founded, tariffs were the primary source of federal revenue; there were no income or capital gains taxes. The political struggles between the Jeffersonians and the Hamiltonians over the appropriate size of the federal government often related to tariffs. Rates initially ranged from five to fifteen percent. To the advocates of centralized governmental power, the tariff was the economic lifeblood of government.

John C. Calhoun voted with others to increase tariffs in 1816 and 1820 to pay for the expenses of the War of 1812. Rates then ranged from twenty-five percent on textiles to thirty percent on manufactured goods. The tariffs, it was discovered, also protected industries in the North from competition by foreign companies and, by the mid-1820s, the New England states were fully behind them. Henry Clay, an influential political leader, was the spokesman for a new "American system" which adopted protectionism as the proper role of government. This position, which was the opposite of what industrial leaders hold today, promoted protectionism because their industries were national, not global enterprises. The reversal of economic policy which was to take place in the Republican Party was based on corporate self-interest and not adherence to a consistent economic philosophy.

The South, which relied heavily on exports of cotton, viewed increased tariffs as harmful to sales. After more tariffs were added to more classes of goods in 1824, and the average rate of tariffs reached forty-nine percent in 1828, Calhoun witnessed increased hardship on the South. The cotton industry, a major player in South Carolina's economy, had begun to falter. An ardent supporter of the Southern aristocracy and the institution of slavery, Calhoun changed his position and, while Vice President, called the 1828 tariff the "tariff of abomination." From then on, tariffs thus became a divisive issue between the North and the South.

John Calhoun wrote a famous document, "The South Carolina Exposition and Protest," in which he stated that the tariff of

1828 favored the North over the South and was no longer solely for the purpose of federal revenue—the original purpose of tariffs. His answer to the problem was to give each state the power of nullification of the tariff, or the power to veto a federal law, and in that manner check the power of the federal government. Daniel Webster took an opposing view, arguing that the federal government of the United States was sovereign and that its jurisdiction should overrule that of states. President Andrew Jackson said that nullification was paramount to treason and threatened to hang Calhoun and his followers. Calhoun thought he was trying to avoid disunion by giving the South enough freedom to avoid the economic strangulation it was feeling. That was the real motivation to secede. Not only slavery, but the issue of trade and tariffs, was thus an important reason for the Civil War. There were both domestic and international conditions that pushed the United States into a civil war.

Democrats were less connected to industry and tended to favor lower prices and thus supported reduction of tariffs. Their interests coincided with the South on the issue of tariffs. In 1846 the Democrats were in control of Congress and reduced tariffs to levels which have sometimes been called "free trade," but this was really moderate protectionism.

The Civil War was very expensive, and to pay for it every form of raising revenue was tapped. Tariffs were at least tripled during the war and left at high levels until the end of the century, partly because the federal government enjoyed the funds they made available. In the years of prosperity from 1880 to 1890 large quantities of imports led to high revenues and a swelling of the federal treasury.[2] In 1892, when Democrats came into power, tariffs were lowered nearly fifteen percent. In 1896, Republicans returned to power and raised tariffs to their historical highpoint of more than fifty percent.

The United States as a World Power

In 1890, the Civil War was behind the United States, its territorial boundaries had been established, and its treasury had a surplus. The next logical focus was beyond its borders, and few people captured that spirit better than popular naval historian and writer Alfred T. Mahan. The coming sea change in the philosophical outlook of the United States is well articulated in his *Atlantic Monthly* article, "The United States Looking Outward":

> Indications are not wanting of an approaching change in the thoughts and policy of Americans as to their relations with the world outside their own borders. For the past quarter of a century, the predominant idea, which has successfully asserted itself at the polls and shaped the course of the government, has been to preserve the home market for the home industries. The employer and the workman have alike been taught to look at the various economical measures proposed from this point of view, to regard with hostility any step favoring the intrusion of the foreign producer upon their own domain, and rather to demand increasingly rigorous measures of exclusion than to acquiesce in any loosening of the chain that binds the consumer to them. The inevitable consequence has followed, as in all cases when the mind or the eye is exclusively fixed in one direction, that the danger of loss or the prospect of advantage in another quarter has been overlooked; and although the abounding resources of the country have maintained the exports at a high figure, this flattering result has been due more to the super-abundant bounty of Nature than to the demand of other nations for our protected manufactures.
>
> For nearly the lifetime of a generation, therefore, American industries have been thus protected, until the practice has assumed the force of a tradition, and is clothed in the mail of conservatism. In their mutual relations, these industries resemble the activities of a modern ironclad

that has heavy armor, but an inferior engine and no guns; mighty for defense, weak for offense. Within, the home market is secured; but outside, beyond the broad seas, there are the markets of the world, that can be entered and controlled only by a vigorous contest, to which the habit of trusting to protection by statute does not conduce.

At bottom, however, the temperament of the American people is essentially alien to such a sluggish attitude. Independently of all bias for or against protection, it is safe to predict that, when the opportunities for gain abroad are understood, the course of American enterprise will cleave a channel by which to reach them. Viewed broadly, it is a most welcome as well as significant fact that a prominent and influential advocate of protection, a leader of the party committed to its support, a keen reader of the signs of the times and of the drift of opinion, has identified himself with a line of policy which looks to nothing less than such modifications of the tariff as may expand the commerce of the United States to all quarters of the globe....

The interesting and significant feature of this changing attitude is the turning of the eyes outward, instead of inward only, to seek the welfare of the country. To affirm the importance of distant markets, and the relation to them of our own immense powers of production, implies logically the recognition of the link that joins the products and the markets—that is, the carrying trade; the three together constituting that chain of maritime power to which Great Britain owes her wealth and greatness. Further, is it too much to say that, as two of these links, the shipping and the markets, are exterior to our own borders, the acknowledgment of them carries with it a view of the relations of the United States to the world radically distinct from the simple idea of self-sufficingness? We shall not follow far this line of thought before there will dawn the realization of America's unique position, facing the older worlds of the East and

West, her shores lapped by the oceans which touch the one
or the other, but which are common to her alone....[3]

Mahan's writings both anticipated and helped shape the
twentieth-century course of the United States as a global superpower, literally reversing much of its nineteenth-century focus.
Tariffs decreased gradually after 1896 as protectionism was
scuttled in the interest of global markets. In 1913 they would
be largely replaced by an income tax. Mahan had stated that the
best way to project a nation's power in the world at that time
was through the development of a navy that was based at various ports around the world. After the British navy destroyed the
defenses of Alexandria, Egypt in 1882, the United States Congress was convinced, with the help of Mahan, to appropriate
$1.3 million for the construction of four armored steam and sail
powered gunboats: a dispatch boat, the *U.S.S. Dolphin,* and three
cruisers, the *Atlantic,* the *Boston,* and the *Chicago.*[4]

The Spanish-American War

The first concrete projection of United States power came with
the Spanish-American War, which was begun without clear
provocation. In 1893, after the depression wreaked havoc on the
Cuban sugar economy, Jose Marti led a second bid for Cuban
independence that was brutally put down by Spanish General
Valeriano Weyler, who was referred to as "Butcher Weyler" in
several major United States newspapers.

President William McKinley, desiring order in the hemisphere and under pressure from business leaders who had
invested in Cuba sent the battleship *U.S.S. Maine* to Havana
harbor to observe activities. He sought to broker peace between
Spain and the Cubans. But before he received word from Spain
an explosion sunk the *U.S.S. Maine.* It has never been determined whether this was an internal explosion or an act of Spanish belligerence. However, in the United States press it seemed
clear Spain was the culprit, and an initial Board of Inquiry

blamed it on a Spanish mine. Spain had already recalled Weyler and given the Cubans partial political autonomy, but events were in motion.

In April 1898 McKinley got a Declaration of War from Congress, which voted to recognize Cuban independence. A war fund of $50 million was approved and another $22.6 million was authorized for naval vessels. The United States blockaded Cuba and, when a Spanish ship was captured, Spain declared war. Theodore Roosevelt, Assistant Secretary of the Navy, had given war instructions to Commodore Dewey in Asia to take the Philippines if war with Spain broke out. By the end of the year, the war was over and the United States had given Cuba independence and received Puerto Rico, the Philippines, and Guam as colonies. President McKinley also quietly annexed Hawaii in 1898, giving the United States enough ports to become a Pacific power.

In November 1899, Lance Paul Larsen took the issue of the legitimate annexation of Hawaii to the newly open International Court of Arbitration at The Hague. He argued that the United States had violated the 1849 Treaty of Friendship, Commerce and Navigation. That treaty had been issued in the mode established by George Washington. In 1893 the United States had violated this treaty when its navy, in search of ports, unlawfully occupied Hawaii.[5]

Legal Ideology and International Arbitration

In an insightful paper on the relationship of international lawyers to foreign policy at the turn of the century, Jonathan Zasloff argued that the United States foreign policy before World War II was shaped by "classical legal ideology."[6] This worldview, unlike political realism, held that lawyers and lawyer-diplomats could solve international conflicts without the use of force. This is because, unlike the zero-sum theory, in which one nation's win is another nation's loss, lawyers could arrange settlements in which both parties could win.

Zasloff argued that this theory was based on the success that corporate lawyers had in negotiating of industrial disputes in the nineteenth century. In a climate of developing oligopolies, pure competition à la Adam Smith was relabeled "destructive competition" or "ruinous competition." It leads to ruin, industrialists argued, because factories are designed to mass produce products, and each competing corporation will inevitably overproduce and then go out of business. This could be avoided if lawyers could help the industries each accept an agreed-upon market share or a merger that would buy out one supplier and give the market to another before either had overproduced.[7] The result of this collusion would be a win-win situation for the producers, but not the consumers.

If similar arbitration strategies were applied to international disputes through neutral lawyers, it was reasoned, they could be settled peacefully with both parties accepting the result. The result was the belief in a system of world peace that did not require the power of state coercion, a key element of political philosophy since the time of Hobbes.

The Hague Conference, organized by Russian Czar Nicholas III in 1899, showcased this philosophy as it sought to reduce armaments and bring about international peace through arbitration. The movement inspired great hope in philanthropists like Andrew Carnegie and Alfred Nobel. The 1899 conference fell short of its goals, but established a Permanent International Court of Arbitration that would settle disputes for parties that voluntarily agreed to accept its decision as binding. There was no military arm to enforce it. Andrew Carnegie donated $1.5 million to build a Peace Palace that could house an international court and library at The Hague.[8]

In 1902 President Theodore Roosevelt took the initiative in opening the International Court of Arbitration at The Hague, which had not yet been called upon by any power in its first three years of existence. The United States and Mexico agreed to lay an old difference of theirs, concerning the Pious Foundations of

California, before the Hague Tribunal. When this example was followed by other powers, the arbitration machinery created in 1899 was finally called into operation. (The Hawaii issue was buried.)

Roosevelt also played a prominent part in extending the use of arbitration to international problems in the Western Hemisphere, concluding several arbitration treaties with European powers too, although the Senate refused to ratify them. A similar problem was to occur throughout the twentieth century as the president, acting as the representative of the United States, brokered agreements that Congress would not ratify.

In 1904 the Interparliamentary Union meeting in St. Louis, Missouri, asked Roosevelt to call another international conference to continue the work begun at The Hague in 1899. Roosevelt responded immediately, and in the autumn of 1904 Secretary of State John Hay invited the powers to meet at The Hague. Russia, even though it had organized the first conference, refused to participate while engaged in hostilities with Japan.

In June 1905, President Roosevelt offered to serve as a mediator between Russia and Japan, asking the belligerents to nominate plenipotentiaries to negotiate the conditions of peace. In August they met at Portsmouth, New Hamsphire, and, after some weeks of difficult negotiations, concluded a peace treaty in September 1905. Roosevelt was awarded the Nobel Peace Prize for this feat.

The Churches and the World

The churches in the United States were also interested in the larger world, although not for the same reasons as government and business leaders. One of the products of the nineteenth century religious enthusiasm had been missions in foreign lands. American missionaries had worked with missionaries from other nations and other denominations. They were developing a global outlook and sharing their views with their home churches. In 1893 the churches in the United States organized the Foreign Missions Conference, aimed at developing relationships with governments in foreign lands. Theological differences were put aside for the sake of practical cooperation.

In 1905, after the Spanish-American War, Supreme Court Justice David J. Brewer, whose father was a Congregationalist missionary, asked the church body whether it could help keep the United States government out of future wars. They participated in the 1907 Lake Mohonk Conference on International Arbitration. Many Christians believed international lawyers had hit upon the key to peace. The chairperson of the first Federal Council of Churches (FCC) committee on international relations was Henry Wade Rogers, Dean of the Law School of Yale University. This speech reflects his optimism:

> We may take it for granted that the nations, ours included, will continue their efforts to substitute arbitration for war, and to create an international court....
>
> Two years ago, Mr. Foster, a distinguished Ex-Secretary of State, declared that there was not a human probability of the United States being involved in a war, and he said it was high time the peace loving people of America should call a halt to our naval expenditures....
>
> The United States should go to the next Hague conference and say: "We are doing it. Follow in our footsteps...." I hope that is the sentiment of this Nation. Then the words might be truthfully applied to our country: "Blessed is the peace-making republic, for it shall be called the Republic of God."[9]

Under Roosevelt the United States Navy had built up from fifth in the world in 1901 to second behind Britain in 1907. Despite this naval power, Roosevelt was a believer in international arbitration; and, at the Second Peace Conference at The Hague in 1907, the United States was willing to submit to an international court of justice. Not enough other nations were prepared to go this far. However, given its history, the Senate may not have ratified any treaty that compromised United States sovereignty.

In 1911, when President Taft signed "practically unlimited" treaties of arbitration with England and France, church leaders organized an ongoing Commission on Peace and Arbitration. Dr. Frederick Lynch, a graduate of Yale Divinity School, became the secretary of the commission and he produced a book titled *The Peace Problem,* of which Andrew Carnegie bought large quantities to distribute to ministers. Carnegie also established the Carnegie Endowment for International Peace, and donated $2 million in 1914 to endow Church Peace Union.

Church hopes were dampened in 1912 as the four-year-old commission witnessed its first defeat on disarmament proposals in Congress. They decided to set up a government watch-dog group. The FCC report stated that the United States could either employ "the way of statesmanship or the way of the battleship."[10] Missionaries also pushed the churches to request that justice for oppressed peoples be put on the agenda for the third Hague Conference, indicating their growing impatience with the status quo.

The final blow to hopes for peace through arbitration came in 1914. As the World Alliance for International Friendship, promoted by the Church Peace Union, gathered in Constance, Germany, World War I broke out on the continent and forced the meeting to adjourn to England. In his history of the ecumenical movement, Samuel Cavert said, "the churches…in the main accepted at its face value the high-powered propaganda that this was the 'war to end war.'"[11]

In 1916, the churches abandoned the hope for peace through arbitration and they renamed "The Commission on Peace and Arbitration" to "Commission on International Justice and Goodwill." Their experience led them to conclude that power and money controlled the Congress. The failure of governments to produce a just settlement in the Versailles Treaty led to further disillusionment. Christian love had been unable to prevail. Many Christians, feeling betrayed by governments and powerless to change them, opted for pacifism. Reinhold Niebuhr wrote in a Christian magazine, *The World Tomorrow*, that "every imperialist was able to fool the church in the name of patriotism."[12]

Voters in the United States turned back toward isolationism, feeling that the cost of getting involved in world affairs was too high. This was the prevailing mood of the nation until Pearl Harbor was bombed.

The League of Nations

Both churches and statesmen felt that the saving grace of the Versailles Treaty was the League of Nations. In 1919, many people, like Henry Atkinson of the Church Peace Union, felt the issue was black and white: "Those who are against the League of Nations are for War."[13] The FCC sent a letter to President Wilson in Paris calling the League the "political expression of the Kingdom of God on Earth."[14] Often uncritically, huge numbers of people were eager to sign any petition against militarism or support any organization that was hoped to curb it.

President Woodrow Wilson was the primary force behind organizing the League of Nations in Versailles, but in 1919 the Senate voted not to join the League. During the 1920s and early 1930s the League successfully oversaw the settlement of a number of minor disputes, but the League, like the Permanent Court, lacked any mechanism of enforcement. It was powerless when Poland and France both defied decisions that they disliked. By 1935, when Italy invaded Abyssinia (Ethiopia) with impunity, most people had given up on the League of Nations. Once again unchecked political powers had run roughshod over the moral appeals of the international community.

Global Banking and Business

The retreat of the United States from the world was only partial and temporary. J. P. Morgan's bank had raised $500 million to lend the English and the French in World War I (despite protests from German-Americans), and after the war the bank emerged with greatly enlarged power.[15] The J. P. Morgan bank began to see itself as the financier of the world. Italy owed the United States government $2 billion in war debts, but Tom W. Lamont, Chairman of J. P. Morgan, lobbied hard on Mussolini's behalf in order to lend $100 million. Italians accused the bank of propping up fascism.[16] By 1927, Lamont had received the Japanese Order of the Rising Sun for loans made to Japan after the earthquake of 1924.[17] American bankers warned against the Germans borrowing too much to make war reparation payments, yet they continued to make them loans.[18] United States corporations traded freely with Japan until 1941, helping to fuel its military adventures, even though diplomatic relations were strained.

The United States had emerged from World War I as the greatest financial and creditor nation and the largest producer of consumer goods and foodstuffs in the world. It had the largest stocks of gold. The production output of the United States was larger than the next six Great Powers taken together.[19] The United States did not understand the effects its unregulated economy would have on the rest of the world. Its financial collapse in 1929, which affected the entire world economy, was met with experimentation. The protectionist Smoot-Hawley tariffs of 1930 led to less international demand for American goods, and boomeranged on the economy the legislation had intended to help. By 1933, the nation's GNP was only one-half of the 1929 output. Europeans accused the United States of being preoccupied with domestic recovery and having little concern about how its policies impacted other nations.[20]

Separation of Politics and Economics

John Maynard Keynes, in 1920, wrote his famous book, *The Economic Consequences of Peace,* in which he lambasted the Great Powers' Versailles Treaty. They were operating under an illusion that the political and economic spheres could be divorced from one another:

> The fundamental economic problem of a Europe starving and disintegrating before their eyes was the one question in which it was impossible to arouse the interest of the Four.[21]

Globalization was upon the world, but those in charge did not know what it meant. The philosophy of Adam Smith was designed for family-sized economic units of production that could adjust rapidly to supply and demand. But the economy was massively different in 1900. In the United States, corporations did not want to be regulated, and policymakers continued to heed the advice of George Washington to divorce politics and economics.

Between the wars, money and materials flowed wherever a profit could be made, like water seeking its own level, despite political policies or consequences. Despite rising Japanese militarism, the United States opposed sanctions and allowed oil, steel, and other materials to flow into Japan. Despite opposition to Germany in World War I, the United States' admiration for German idealism and scientific achievement returned in the 1920s. Like an ostrich burying its head in the sand, Americans sought to avoid the thought that the belligerence of the Nazis or the Fascists would lead to negative consequences for America.

Foreign policy makers in the United States government in the interwar period were lawyer-diplomats from the school of classical legal thought, which held to the theory that disputes could be settled without the use of force. These included Charles Evans Hughes, Frank B. Kellogg, and Henry L. Stimson.[22] In *The Pathway to Peace* (1925) Hughes argued,

The notion of law as imposed and maintained by force may have its advantage in dealing with a small minority of infringers, but in the long run this notion derogates from its authority and counts for much of the natural revolt against legalistic conceptions.... Taking the long view, it may not be regarded as a defect or a misfortune that we escape the notion of the imposition of force in the field of international law.[23]

This view contained two naïve assumptions. One was that the system of international law would be viewed as legitimate by all parties. The second was that impartial judges could make right decisions and expose a truth that nobody would deny. Today every parking lot manager knows that reserved spots will be stolen if there is no tow-truck on call to enforce the policy. Every accounts receivable department knows that many accounts will remain unpaid unless there is a bill collection agency that will cause damage to the party who does not pay its account. Despite its impressive navy, the United States was a young lamb in the midst of seasoned wolves when it emerged from a hundred years of relative isolationism. Another example is Henry Stimson's infamous 1929 decision to end the United States code-breaking service on grounds that "gentlemen do not read each others' mail."[24]

For the first four decades of the twentieth century, the United States pursued a policy which its founders could not have comprehended—solutions to world peace that employed no checks and balances on power. Of course, many Americans would not have agreed on these policies either, but, for most citizens, foreign policy was a remote topic to which lawyers and politicians were welcome. The national culture, for the most part, was still isolationist, and most citizens were focused on pursuing a life at home.

Realism and Power Politics

One early advocate of realism and power politics was a prominent New York theologian, Reinhold Niebuhr, who broke from the pacifists in the early 1930s and then from the Marxists a couple of years later. He developed a "Christian realism" which emphasized that Christian utopians had left the important element of power out of their political philosophy. He returned to an emphasis on Hobbes' and Jefferson's concern about power. Niebuhr's thought had an impact on Hans Morgenthau, who later articulated the doctrine of "political realism" in international affairs.[25]

Morgenthau stated that the main signpost of political realism is "interest defined in terms of power." This had been the driving force behind Hitler, Mussolini, and Stalin, and other nations had been forced to own up to this fact in World War II. Arbitration and diplomacy alone were inadequate. The United States and its war allies thus set about creating a new international framework, the United Nations, which would replace the practically defunct League of Nations with a charter that gave it a Security Council with the military muscle to enforce world order. The Security Council was not democratic, but each of the five main powers (the United States, England, France, Russia, and China) would have veto power so that force would not be used unless there was overwhelming agreement on a crisis.

The United Nations

The United Nations had a General Assembly, where delegates of the nations of the world could meet and express their opinions. It was a body that could pass legislation that was more an expression of world conscience than world law because adherence was basically voluntary.

The principle of national sovereignty was absolute at the United Nations. The United Nations was organized much more loosely than the initial confederation of American states after the Revolutionary War. It was not designed as a governing body. It had no internal checks and balances on power because no real power was delegated to it, except for the Security Council. It more like a club. The principle of sovereignty guaranteed autonomy for each nation to organize and rule itself as it wished. This guaranteed that major powers like the United States would retain their sovereignty, but it also guaranteed small nations the right to national self-determination.

The United Nations was anti-colonial in nature and pressured powers that still retained colonies to give them independence. Guilt had been fostered by missionaries and other travelers to foreign countries who believed the philosophy that all people have the right to pursue happiness, and the big powers were wrong to hold colonies. This contributed to the concept of such absolute national autonomy that even massive abuses of power and rights violations within newly independent states were tolerated by the United Nations.

However, under the umbrella of security that was provided, many cooperative and voluntary activities could develop and serve international human needs. The United Nations Economic and Social Council, the World Health Organization, the UN Development Program, and the UN High Commission on Refugees are examples of the cooperative and humanitarian programs that developed. Other non-governmental organizations and quasi-governmental organizations could also function in cooperation with the United Nations. Examples include the International Court of Justice, the International Labor Organization, the International Postal Union, and the International Civil Aviation Board. All of these programs served practical international functions. The international relations theory that developed from this arrangement was called "functionalism."

From the inception of the United Nations, there was a movement to attach to the Charter a Universal Declaration of Human Rights somewhat analogous to the United States Bill of

Rights. The Federal Council of Churches in the United States was very active in promoting this. One of the primary lobbyists was Dr. Otto Frederick Nolde, former Dean of Lutheran Theological Seminary in Philadelphia. He was head of a Joint Committee on Religious Liberty and a champion of the cause of religious liberty in Latin America, where Catholics had shut out most attempts by Protestants in the United States to do missionary work. He helped organize a National Study Conference in Cleveland which recommended adding to the Dumbarton Oaks Proposals the phrase: "A special commission on Human Rights and Fundamental Freedoms should be established." He then organized a large group of nongovernmental organizations (NGOs) who also stood to gain from this amendment, and pushed it through at the San Francisco Charter meeting.[26] In August 1946, the Commission on Churches in International Affairs (CCIA) was established as a joint agency of the World Council of Churches and the International Missionary Council. Nolde was its director.

Eleanor Roosevelt was chosen to chair the committee that would draft the United Nations' Universal Declaration of Human Rights; she worked with Nolde and other delegates to develop the final document. Interestingly, the Latin American nations were the most fervent supporters of the Declaration, likely because they wanted to be seen as supportive of their "big sister" who had done much to produce the document. The Universal Declaration was initially supported by the State Department as John Foster Dulles, then an assistant to the Secretary of State, had earlier chaired the Federal Council of Churches' Commission on a Just and Durable Peace and developed their "Six Pillars of Peace."

However, the United States Congress, as in previous cases, refused to recognize any United Nations' decision seen as compromising national sovereignty and power. One reaction has been referred to as "Brickerism." Senator John W. Bricker of Ohio, in 1952, proposed to amend the United States Constitution so that no treaties or international agreements made by the executive branch of the government would have binding power within the United States unless domestic legislation was passed that would also be valid in the absence of a treaty. The executive branch of the United States government was accused of going too far in compromising national sovereignty.

When the National Council of Churches (NCC) sought United States support for and leadership of the United Nations, a group of Christian businessmen, fearful that international business regulation might curtail their profits, formed the National Lay Committee under the leadership of J. Howard Pew, a Sun Oil executive. When the NCC began to lobby against the Bricker amendment, the national lay committee, which controlled a substantial portion of the financing for the ecumenical body, threatened to turn off the funds, effectively blocking the proposal. Pew also founded a more conservative magazine, *Christianity Today*, in an attempt to draw Christian readers away from the more liberal *Christianity and Crisis* that had been founded by Reinhold Niebuhr.

The relationship of the United States to the United Nations in its first fifty years has been a love-hate relationship. The United States (and most other nations) use it when it can promote national self-interest and oppose it when it appears to threaten or curtail national interest. The United States became an immediate signatory to the Genocide Convention, which was not ratified until forty years later. It ratified the 1966 International Covenant on Civil and Political Rights, but did not ratify the convention on Economic and Social Rights which was consistent with Franklin Roosevelt's views, but not those of the majority of Americans.[27]

The Security Council no longer represents the power arrangements of the world, and since the 1980s it has been called to act on ethnic strife and genocide within nations, thus acting against the principle of national sovereignty enshrined in its own charter. The method of representing regimes rather than demographics in the General Assembly, is criticized for leaving out more than half of the world's people from United Nations' discussions. The result has been the need to reform the international body.

Outsiders, members states, and the Secretary General's "Millennium Declaration" all recognize the need for reform. However, agreement on an underlying philosophy that can make these changes possible has not been forthcoming, and calls for change have quickly stagnated, making the structure of the international body increasingly dysfunctional for the tasks being demanded of it.

Multinational and Global Corporations

The rise of multinational corporations in the twentieth century and their dominance in the twenty-first century is one of the most challenging issues faced by both the United States and the world. Unleashed by free trade laws and the reduction of tariffs, corporations that once operated within national bounds and sought tariff protection from most states, have grown to giants in wealth and breadth that spans the globe. They are able to escape the jurisdiction of nations that attempt to regulate them, and dictate terms to nations that seek employment and consumer products for their citizens. These corporations have no particular loyalty to the nations that gave them birth. They are products of the unregulated pursuit of wealth, which both promises and threatens the quality of life of human beings.

In *A Theory of Global Capitalism*,[28] William I. Robinson argues that corporations have evolved from multi-national (trading with foreign markets) to global, virtually ignoring the nation state as they view the world as one nation. There is no analogous government to regulate these behemoths. Robison conjectures that the United States will not lose its superpower status to another nation but to the new global class leading this social evolution.

The world is not a level playing field. Some economists, especially those at foundations supported by large corporations, believe that the "invisible hand" of economic justice will operate in an unregulated world of corporate giants. Other economists, especially those with neo-Marxist sympathies, view the situation as one of growing injustice, creating ever more slavelike conditions for workers and creating increased polarization between the global proletariat and the global bourgeoisie. Their goal is the destruction of global corporations and a return to smaller economic industries that nations can control.

Representatives of these two opposing views receive the greatest amount of press coverage, but neither represents a view whereby an international governmental body acts as a referee that can help create a level playing field and ensure competitive game-playing by as many players as possible. For it is conditions of maximum competition that will create the greatest productivity with the lowest excess profit for a few elites. Economists in the first camp would want corporations to try to play a game without referees, in which case the strongest ones will gain monopoly or oligopoly rule. Economists in the second camp, reacting out of fear of the evil potential of multi-national corporations, are more like the Luddites of early nineteenth-century England, who sought to break power weaving looms and other industrial equipment that displaced manual workers.

One nation alone, even a superpower, cannot referee the "game" of global economic competition. However, that regulation has not yet developed in a satisfactory way. On the one hand, the International Monetary Fund and the World Trade Organization originated with bankers and multi-national corporations and are not ultimately able to police themselves if our 4,000 year analysis of power is correct. On the other hand, politicians claiming to represent poor people or nations use slogans that play on envy and resentment, and often ask for economic redistribution like children wanting more of their parents' money without understanding the effort that goes into obtaining it.

There is a game to be played, and it should be an honest and fair game, but it has not yet been organized. There are few rules, not many players are on the field, and no referees—just spectators and players with various opinions. A fair game would likely involve restrictions on the collusion of nations and corporations that many governments, including the Congress of the United States, are currently unwilling to accept. History shows that such acceptance comes only when conditions get bad enough that the entire social systems enter into a decline—like the Depression begun of the 1930s or the two world wars. Those who feel their ability to pursue happiness is being thwarted or blocked by the corporations and elite that rule the present order will push for a change.

Although the United States gave birth to a number of the multinational corporations and set them free when they reversed their strategy from protectionism to laissez faire at the turn of the twentieth century, many Americans are increasingly concerned about the loss of jobs, and traditional tax revenue as other countries seek to lure corporations away. Today United States corporations are continually relocating to nations that provide workers for lower wages, demand less social and environmental responsibility, and provide greater tax incentives. It is an unregulated game in which nations are now the consumers and the corporations seem to be a prize (even though they may be a wolf in sheep's clothing). In the 1960s and 1970s, blue-collar manufacturing jobs left the United States and at the beginning of the twenty-first century several million white-collar jobs are following a similar path.

On the one hand, the argument is made that ultimately the world market will be equalized and everything will be more fair, but on the other hand there is concern about the damage left in the wake of the transition and whether a competitive or monopolistic economy will be the result. The complete separation of government from the regulation of economic life would undoubtedly lead to conditions like those after the Versailles

Treaty that ended World War I, which left Germany in a hopeless situation, with its people unable to freely pursue happiness. It turned out that the League of Nations did not solve this problem, nor is the United Nations equipped to do so.

More international organization is required, and a proper political philosophy that has learned from the experience of the United States might help that come about with proper checks and balances on power and the appropriate relationship between love, power, and justice on the international level. But that elaboration is beyond the scope of this book, which is on the philosophy of the United States.

Toward a Philosophy of United States Foreign Policy

In his *Perpetual Peace,* Immanuel Kant saw the cunning of history that would draw nations into cooperation despite the fact that some amount of sovereignty would need to be yielded. He argued that a global federation of nations would have to be voluntarily entered into by each nation, acting on its own perceived interest. Like Hobbes' "state of nature," the world of nations is in a situation of anarchy in which individual nations will come to organize, for their own protection, through a social compact under the rule of an international sovereign, in which they agree to yield a measure of sovereignty in exchange for a measure of security. For Kant, this would not lead to some form of global tyranny because membership would be voluntary and nations could withdraw if they were not satisfied.

The case is being ever more forcefully made that terrorism and violence in the world are, in part, the result of oppression and frustration of peoples who feel they do not have the opportunity to freely pursue happiness. Many of these people suffer under dictators who oppress by force, or like the Palestinians, they live as second-class citizens without hope of freely pursuing the dreams that are available in many other places in the world.

United States foreign policy has never had a clear philosophical objective to which the nation as a whole subscribed. In its first hundred years, the country was isolationist and a clear foreign policy was not required, but in the present global age, the United States can earn respect from the rest of the world only if clear, just, and fair policies, not national self-interest (read expansion), can be pursued regardless of which political party is in control of the government at the time.

Many people admired the ancient Roman Empire and wanted to join it to escape from the oppression they experienced in surrounding countries. The system of justice in the early Roman Empire was legitimate in their eyes. So too, the United States earned the respect and admiration of nations around the world before it developed a history of the arbitrary use of power, and its legal system began to lose its connection to universal principles of justice derived from "cosmic law." Political philosophers should not underestimate the importance of power in world affairs, but neither should they underestimate the importance of legitimate principles of justice, and the role of love in overcoming the shortcomings of both justice and power.

In his recent book, *War on America Seen from the Indian Ocean*, James Mancham, the first president of the Seychelles and a friend of the United States, gives a telling account of the arbitrariness of United States foreign policy. In his case, an embassy was established and money poured in when the United States wanted to install a satellite dish in the Seychelles to track United States space exploration. When the need no longer existed, the United States packed up and went home. Meanwhile, India and China retain consistent relations with the Seychelles and appear as much more trustworthy long-term partners.[29]

Mancham's experience reflects countless thousands of experiences of people living all around the world who admire the freedom and wealth of the United States and desire many of the consumer products Americans enjoy. They understand that national self-interest is a legitimate foreign policy goal of any state, but they do not see the values upon which the United

States was built reflected in its foreign policy. Many people think that a free election, a free press, and a free market will lead to peace and prosperity, or at least that is what they hear American diplomats telling them, despite their better knowledge.

In 1989, when the communist regime in Russia collapsed, Americans had an excellent opportunity to assist in the creation of a society where life, liberty, and the pursuit of happiness were the primary values, encouraging proper regulation of business and checks and balances on power. However the simple thought that a turn to capitalism would save the Russians—both promoted by the United States and believed by many Russians—led to the return of old rulers with new titles and the rise of one of the healthiest mafias in the world. This could have been prevented if the advent of capitalism had been accompanied by a philosophy and political structures that would prevent abuse of political and economic power.

The case of Haiti is an example where the United States attempted to export democratic structures without establishing the prerequisites for a culture for democracy. Using a simplistic understanding of democracy as "free elections and a free press," in 1994 the United States led a United Nations military expedition into Haiti to restore the presidency of Jean Bertrand Aristide, who had won a popular election. What most people failed to note was that the economic producers in Haiti did not feel the election was legitimate because the Aristide regime had made promises to the poor who elected him on the basis of economic redistribution policies that would undermine the national economy. Hence, Aristide was legally in power, but not legitimately in power. There was no legitimate basis for the elections that had occurred, no universally agreed upon social contract such as the patricians and the plebeians had accepted as the legitimate basis of the Roman Republic.

To improve its image in the world, the United States State Department should develop a consistent policy towards other nations that not only superficially promotes the structures of democracy, but ensures that legitimate systems of justice are recognized as such by the majority of citizens and allow all citizens the opportunity to freely pursue happiness. This must be an unwavering goal, whether the Republicans, Democrats, or some future party is in power.

Rather than seeing other nations as allies that can add to United States' power to stand against a global menace or as markets to be exploited, they must be seen first as nations that are made up of people who want to be free to pursue happiness just like the people of the United States, the ancient Romans, or anyone else who has lived on the earth has desired to do.

Questions for Reflection

1. Explain why George Washington believed both enemies and allies would compromise the nation in the larger world. Do you feel this dictum should be applied to international trade and the idea of "most favored nation" status?

2. Do you think that the United States Constitution has adequate safeguards related to foreign policy, or that continual expansion of the United States in the world is not adequately checked?

3. Why did Republicans support protectionism in the nineteenth century, but oppose it in the twentiethth century? Do you think that protectionism is a valid policy?

4. Explain why the executive and legislative branches have taken opposite positions on joining an International Court, the League of Nations, and ratification of the UN Universal Declaration of Human Rights. Do you believe one position is more correct? Why?

5. Why do you think the churches, which had much influence over voters, failed to influence the ratification of international laws related to the League of Nations and the United Nations?

6. Do you think that the policy of separation of economics and politics contributed to the two World Wars, or that the United States would have eventually entered those wars anyway?

7. Is "power politics" inevitable in international relations or can the world develop a more just and peaceful order? Is a political philosophy to guide such a world order possible?

Conclusion: Philosophy and Legitimacy of the United States

A NUMBER OF CONCLUSIONS CAN BE DRAWN from this study of the philosophy of the United States. The most major point is that, while the founders of the United States held different personal philosophies, they agreed on a common philosophy for the United States. That philosophy focused on creating a limited government to harmonize relations between states and to represent the United States to the world.

The United States was not wholly an experiment, even though it contained numerous experimental features, the most significant being its representative system of government with checks and balances on power designed to devolve ultimate power to the citizens. Other governments the founders studied, including the Roman and the British systems of government, had some checks and balances on power, but those systems did not sufficiently place checks on power or ultimately devolve power to the citizens.

Explicit in the Declaration of Independence and implicit in the Constitution is a philosophy of justice that is derived from "the Laws of Nature and Nature's God." The "self-evident" truths upon which the United States was based were the equality of all people and their right to freely pursue happiness.

Legitimacy of the Government

The peace and order of any society require that the government be viewed as legitimate. Legitimacy implies that the citizens view the government as good, fair, and trustworthy. Legitimacy is moral, not legal. It cannot be imposed by power. What is legitimate and what is legal are not necessarily the same, although in an ideal society the law would be viewed as legitimate. Ultimately, legitimacy should be the top priority of any government

The Babylonian Empire's laws were viewed as legitimate because they were believed to come from gods that governed human beings. In the history of Israel, this evolved into a monotheism that developed a conception of legitimate justice based on God's Law that transcended human governments. The monotheistic faiths—Judaism, Christianity, and Islam—have provided people with an independent framework for judging the legitimacy of laws based upon the higher laws that come from God. These faiths have motivated believers to behave according to higher laws of service and altruism in spite of their natural selfish desires.

The Roman Empire, which was begun as a legitimate social contract, lost that legitimacy over time because (a) the Empire contained many new people not party to the original contract, (b) the contract was not related to a higher essential goodness or justice, and (c) rulers promulgated arbitrary and selfish laws for their own purposes. The Roman Republic, originally legitimate, needed few police to keep order, however the aged and illegitimate Roman Empire required a police state to keep order. The adoption of Christianity, which was viewed as the embodiment of divine law by the general population, lent some additional legitimacy to the regime, although the laws were not considered as legitimate until they were later recodified.

When the United States was founded, its laws were considered good and just both because it was a social contract agreed to by all, and because that social contract was viewed as a reflection of self-evident truth and derived from the Creator. The federal government was minimal and its philosophy rather simple. It only governed relations between states, and represented the United States to the world. It was not hard for all citizens to view the United States as a legitimate government. It did very little to impede the freedom or the pursuit of happiness of individual citizens.

Competition Among States

The states were another matter. The laws of most states derived from the British system of law, but a number contained controversial laws supporting slavery or established churches. They also contained laws concerned with the behavior of individual citizens. To the extent that state laws regulated business, enacted welfare programs, mandated public education, or in some other way imposed mandates on people, they were more subject to disputes in which their legitimacy would be questioned.

Leaving the governance of individuals to state and local governments got the federal government off the hook. Letting the states deal with social issues allowed the federal government to remain untainted and aloof from such domestic legitimacy challenges. If the federal government had not usurped state power, it would not have gotten into many of the quagmires unseen and unplanned by the founders. In theory, in a system of competing state governments without federal interference, people could move from one state to another if they did not believe the laws in one state were legitimate. Such competition would tend to be more flexible and force states to efficiently provide necessary services. To the extent that states still have autonomy, this still happens. For example, Wisconsin's welfare reform program in the 1990s was soon adopted by other states. Where unified standards are imposed at the federal level, this type of adjustment cannot take place.

Leaving social governance to the states, as the founders

wished, may not be desirable in every case. Clearly federal intervention was necessary to end rights violations against Southern slaves and their descendants. However, a state with a philosophy that upholds equality and the free pursuit of happiness will suffer the least attacks on its legitimacy if it follows the principle of subsidiary, which devolves responsibility to the smallest social unit capable of exercising it properly.

The increased centralization of power in the United States has been a two-way street. Those in power inevitably desire to expand their power. However, states and citizens in the United States have yielded much of that power in a selfish attempt to get federal funds to support them. Even though the federal government does not get free money to hand out, there has been an illusion that it is bigger and therefore has more to give away. In the end, whoever gets federal funds takes them from someone else—another state, another class, or a future generation. This amounts to a redistribution scheme that usually circumvents true justice and delegitimizes the government itself.

Legitimacy of the Supreme Court

The Supreme Court has to take a good measure of the responsibility for increased centralization of the federal government. Its willingness to hear cases that relate to the state regulation of individual behavior has been stimulated, in part, by clear injustice on the part of some states, particularly on civil rights issues. However, this opened the door for the Court to hear other decisions that had little to do with clear injustices on the part of a state. On many topics related to social issues on which people are divided and there is no clear connection to the Constitution, for example abortion or capital punishment, it would be much better for states to determine their own laws. By making rulings guaranteed to be viewed as illegitimate by half of the citizens, the Court undermines its own prestige. For, as this book has argued, the fact that a law exists does not make it legitimate. An arbitrary decree is worse than no decree, for it is a decree, not based on a higher philosophy, but on the opinions of political appointees.

While the Supreme Court justices are appointed by the President, their constitutional mandate was not political. However, by allowing itself to enter the level of political discussion, rather than retaining a scholarly distance, the Court undermines its legitimacy as a body.

Another problem for the Court has been to view the Constitution, not as the embodiment of a philosophy, but as sacred scripture upon which exegesis can be performed to justify a desired opinion. In numerous cases a desired outcome was sought, often for political reasons, and then the "scripture" was searched to justify that outcome. Since the founders themselves were divided on the role of corporations in society, they left the Congress to enact laws regarding such topics, deriving legitimate authority from the people they served. The Court's decision—whether made out of good intentions or as an act of abuse of power—was out of its philosophical bounds and procedurally illegitimate—even if it was considered "legal."

Not all "activist" decisions of the Court have been bad, not all have been good. The point is that such activism is the role of the legislative branch of the government, not the Supreme Court. By making such decisions, and thereby as Chief Justice Warren freely admitted, making laws, the Supreme Court does an end-run around the Constitutional process. The original role assigned to the Supreme Court by the founders was to interpret, not make, the law. The Court could restore its legitimacy by returning to fulfillment of that role assigned to it by the philosophy of the founders as embodied in the Constitution.

Legitimacy of the Congress

The United States Congress undermines its legitimacy every time it passes legislation that creates unequal opportunities for one person or group at the expense of another. One primary concern of this book has been the creation of a federal legislative class which takes for itself advantages it does not first provide for those it is designed to serve. Every time Congress uses its unchecked power to raise salaries and benefits for its members to a level higher than that enjoyed by the average citizens, it is perceived as an act of injustice by citizens and undermines the legitimacy of the body—and the system itself.

The founding fathers evaded the issue by saying that "gentlemen" would do no such a thing. However, the elected representatives have. It was an unchecked area of power and subject to abuse. In the view of the citizens, who in theory own the country, government officials and representatives are stewards of tax money, not the owners. Federal benefits might be legal, but they are not legitimate unless they are viewed as just. They are not viewed as just if they are based on provisions passed in hidden legislation.

Pork, political favors, omnibus bills, account shifting, and other tactics employed to pass hidden legislation are not consistent with the founding philosophy that representatives are responsible to the voters. These tactics evade representative accountability because a clear record of how an individual representative stood on a particular issue is not available. The founders devised a system in which representatives were to be accountable to their constituents, but history has erased a good portion of their intent. Transparency, accountability, and clear separation of issues would greatly improve the legitimacy of the legislature.

Legitimacy in the Eyes of the World

There was little problem with America's image in the world in the nineteenth century, when the United States was a new nation trying to secure its own borders and throw out colonial powers. Nothing appeared illegitimate about that. However, its rise to superpower status without a clear foreign policy that would give people in other nations the same treatment it gives its own citizens is problematic.

Outward expansion, beginning with the Spanish-American war, the birth of multi-national corporations, the refusal to sign treaties, and reversals in foreign policy based on the self-interest of the ruling party all send the message that the United States and its corporationsis out to get what they can for itself. On the other hand, there are many citizens in the United States that give large amounts of service and charity to the world. The United States provides the greatest amount of private relief in the world, and many individuals volunteer to help people in other countries—for example doctors and dentists, who travel to foreign countries and heal those in need.

This paradoxical image is fostered, in part, due to the structure of the American government. Legislators, in an effort to ensure reelection, will try to bring as much money to their districts as possible. This means using their power to make arrangements to get money from anywhere they can. They not only bargain with one another for federal funds, but it is in their joint interest to seek money from the rest of the world. The extent to which this actually happens depends upon the shrewdness of other nations, however in principle there is no constitutional check on the exploitation of other peoples by the United States.

The history of the executive branch leading the United States into arrangements with the community of nations, like the League of Nations, the United Nations, or the World Court, only to have the Senate veto the arrangements, has created major image problems for the United States in the world. Is the United States properly structured to be a player on the international stage? Can any sovereignty, even temporarily, be given in an international agreement?

If the United States genuinely makes the goals of equality and the pursuit of happiness applicable to nations other than itself, it must place restrictions on its relations with other nations similar to those it places on relations with its own citizens. This requires checking a power that was not checked by the Constitution and therefore is not easily achieved.

9/11 was a Wake-Up Call

The September 11, 2001, attacks on the United States were a wake-up call. This was the first time the continental United States was attacked by a foreign power. This power, al-Qaeda, based its attack on the illegitimacy of United States actions in the world. Because the United States' foreign policy since World War II has been based on national self-interest and its use of power has often seemed arbitrary, it has been increasingly unable to defend itself against a growing concern in the world over the legitimacy of its actions.

History has shown that delegitimation of government behavior leads to a greater need for police and military power to keep order, while legitimation leads to less need for such power. However, police states work against the ideals of equality, freedom, and the pursuit of happiness. The fulfillment of the ideals of the United States at home thus requires their promotion for all people throughout the world. This can be enhanced through supporting or joining international activities consistent with its philosophy and not joining any activities that would deny any people the right to life, liberty, and the pursuit of happiness.

A consistent foreign policy that represents this philosophy is sorely needed. The United States must put this ahead of the perceived short-term interest of a particular political party, President, or military officer. Twentieth-century presidents and officials in the State Department have periodically recommended such activities only to be vetoed by the legislature. However, this issue has never been explained satisfactorily to the public.

The founding fathers established a relationship between the states of the United States which required some compromise of the interests of individual states. Only the firm hand of George Washington and the call of Benjamin Franklin to noble ideals won support for that compromise of state sovereignty to a higher sovereignty. The United States should imagine itself as one of those eighteenth-century American states when it enters into discussions of world organization. I would add the right of secession (a right not allowed the South before the Civil War) so as to bring the world community together voluntarily and not by force of arms.

The Role of Government as Economic Referee

It should be emphasized that a government's main role should be that of a referee. Its job is to ensure that citizens freely and fairly play the game of pursuing happiness without abusing the rights of others in the process. Despite how some people view it, a government is not a producer of goods and services, it is not a substitute for parents or communities, it is not a corporation competing with other corporations to rule the world. It is a referee that serves at the behest of the organizers of the game—the people. It is acountable to the owner of the game—the Creator.

The government should be a legitimate referee; one that is fair and just; one that operates by rules that the players can clearly understand; and one that employs proper checks and balances on power in its rulebook—the Constitution and its amendments. A government cannot be both a referee and a player without causing severe impediments to the game.

This book discussed several issues that the federal government of the United States came to face. In the case of corporations, economies of scale led to tremendous productivity and financial power. They are tremendous engines of wealth that everyone is fighting to control and profit from. Stockholders want them to increase their wealth, executives think all the profit is theirs, workers believe they deserve a greater share of the profits, consumers want prices to be kept down, governments want to tax or own them, big corporarations want to buy smaller ones.

Because corporations are human creations, to the extent they are "persons," they should be like robots. However, they have often become masters rather than servants. They have been given independent life and they have caused both good and harm, both justice and injustice. Governments must ensure that their behavior is legitimate, that they compete with one another fairly, and that they do not prevent individual citizens from being players on the field. They are not people and should not be treated as people, they are organizational structures often the size of states, engines of production. They were not endowed with equal rights by Nature and Nature's God, and the Fourteenth Amendment should not be twisted to say that they were.

In a situation of pure competition, there are not huge profits for anyone: stockholders, executives, or workers. This is because competition forces corporations to lower profits to attract consumers, or another corporation will be formed that will accept lower profits. Huge profits can accrue only when competition is not fair: there are power imbalances, control of resources, special patent rights, and so forth. In other words, excessive profits mean that the market is not working properly, and that implies the government is not fulfilling its proper role as a referee.

A parallel can be drawn between the human faith in nation-states two hundred years ago and the faith in corporations today. Both were viewed as saviors or gods that could make life better for human beings. Both were treated with absolute awe by some people. Hegel spoke of the state as the final end of the march of "the Absolute" in history. Certainly the impartial and bureaucratic apparatus of the state can lead to more efficient and just organization of society. However, because of its success, people wanted it to be a parent and care for them, to be a tool for subjugation of other peoples, or to use its power for other illegitimate activities. The end result of placing faith in the State as a false ultimate was national and world wars between states.

Similarly, the corporation, another human-created social organism, has captured the imagination and faith of human beings because of its tremendous wealth-producing potential. Again, human beings have, as a result, placed excess faith in these entities and allowed them to become gods in their own right. Courts and governments have given them the license they need to operate, but they have done more. They have given them enormous freedoms and powers based on the promises that they will produce more for less.

The chairman of Enron or Worldcom, like King George III of England, is a human being that, when not subject to checks and balances on power, will use that position to enrich himself. This is human nature, as the founders of the United States understood very well.

It was not until the powers of governments were sufficiently checked that corporations could rise. They arose in an economic power vacuum. Like the armies that consolidated the lands of individual people and ethnic groups into vast empires, the corporate raiders of today seek to conquer family and small businesses and create vast economic empires. And like the physical empires that were able to create more fair and secure environments during their more noble periods, so large economic corporations, with economies of scale, might be able to be vast engines of human prosperity. However, they must be refereed, not worshipped as gods.

Today corporations have jumped the political borders of nation states and have become social organisms larger than many states. Even the United States may find itself a hostage to this new international elite if it fails to join in the creation of international regulation and enforcement mechanisms that can serve as referees on the global playing field.

Love, Power, and Justice

The final point to be made is not to forget that love, power, and justice all have parts to play in a good society. Justice is the goal of a nation. Justice is a prerequisite to peace and order. Justice is not just the laws recorded and enforced, but behind the laws lies an ideal of justice that no human can grasp perfectly. However, if the laws treat all human beings as equal, promote freedom for each person to pursue happiness within bounds that do not harm others' ability to pursue happiness, and provide ways for disadvantaged members of the society to become as full participants as possible, these laws will be viewed as legitimate and little policing will be required.

But human beings are not perfect, they desire to get more and work less. This leads to invention and industry, but, if unchecked, it also leads to taking and subduing others to enrich oneself. Hence, power must be checked.

But just laws and checks on power are inadequate for a society to sustain itself. Ultimately, for a society to grow, just like for money to accumulate, more must be put in than taken out. This is where love comes in. Altruism, patriotism, love of family, community, and other human beings makes the decisive difference. Love turns rational justice into true justice by personalizing and targeting human needs. Love fulfills justice. Love makes competitive behavior civil.

Neither states or corporations can make people love. Rational state justice and productive economic corporations will not, by themselves, lead to true justice of peace. The cultural instituions of civil society: families, schools, religions, and other social organizations, like the Freemasons, the Boy Scouts, or 4-H clubs, are the third component that the nation requires.

The United States was founded on the premise that these institutions would play their role alongside government, creating the individuals capable of running and maintaining society, creating the leaders who would use their government positions to serve their fellow human beings, not to enrich themsleves.

The history of the United States is one in which the original justice has been pulled at and tugged at by the selfish pursuit of wealth and power. This must be balanced by unselfish and patriotic acts of love and service. The more legitimate the laws and the government, the more pride citizens will take in it, and the more they will freely give to support it, defend it, and make it prosperous.

Appendices

THE DECLARATION OF INDEPENDENCE

Action of Second Continental Congress, July 4, 1776,
The unanimous Declaration of the thirteen United States of America

WHEN in the Course of human Events, it becomes necessary for one People to dissolve the Political Bands which have connected them with another, and to assume among the Powers of the Earth, the separate and equal Station to which the Laws of Nature and of Nature's God entitle them, a decent Respect to the Opinions of Mankind requires that they should declare the causes which impel them to the Separation.

WE hold these Truths to be self-evident, that all Men are created equal, that they are endowed by their Creator with certain unalienable Rights, that among these are Life, Liberty and the Pursuit of Happiness —That to secure these Rights, Governments are instituted among Men, deriving their just Powers from the Consent of the Governed, that whenever any Form of Government becomes destructive of these Ends, it is the Right of the People to alter or to abolish it, and to institute new Government, laying its Foundation on such Principles, and organizing its Powers in such Form, as to them shall seem most likely to effect their Safety and Happiness. Prudence, indeed, will dictate that Governments long established should not be changed for light and transient Causes; and accordingly all Experience hath shewn, that Mankind are more disposed to suffer, while Evils are sufferable, than to right themselves by abolishing the Forms to which they are accustomed. But when a long Train of Abuses and Usurpations, pursuing invariably the same Object, evinces a Design to reduce them under absolute Despotism, it is their Right, it is their Duty, to throw off such Government, and to provide new Guards for their future Security.

Such has been the patient Sufferance of these Colonies; and such is now the Necessity which constrains them to alter their former Systems of Government. The History of the present King of Great-Britain is a History of repeated Injuries and Usurpations, all having in direct Object the Establishment of an absolute Tyranny over these States. To prove this, let Facts be submitted to a candid World.

HE has refused his Assent to Laws, the most wholesome and necessary for the public Good.

HE has forbidden his Governors to pass Laws of immediate and pressing Importance, unless suspended in their Operation till his Assent should be obtained; and when so suspended, he has utterly neglected to attend to them.

HE has refused to pass other Laws for the Accommodation of large Districts of People, unless those People would relinquish the Right of Representation in the Legislature, a Right inestimable to them, and formidable to Tyrants only.

HE has called together Legislative Bodies at Places unusual, uncomfortable, and distant from the Depository of their public Records, for the sole Purpose of fatiguing them into Compliance with his Measures.

HE has dissolved Representative Houses repeatedly, for opposing with manly Firmness his Invasions on the Rights of the People.

HE has refused for a long Time, after such Dissolutions, to cause others to be elected; whereby the Legislative Powers, incapable of the Annihilation, have returned to the People at large for their exercise; the State remaining in the mean time exposed to all the Dangers of Invasion from without, and the Convulsions within.

HE has endeavoured to prevent the Population of these States; for that Purpose obstructing the Laws for Naturalization of Foreigners; refusing to pass others to encourage their Migrations hither, and raising the Conditions of new Appropriations of Lands.

HE has obstructed the Administration of Justice, by refusing his Assent to Laws for establishing Judiciary Powers.

HE has made Judges dependent on his Will alone, for the Tenure of their Offices, and the Amount and Payment of their Salaries.

HE has erected a Multitude of new Offices, and sent hither Swarms of Officers to harrass our People, and eat out their Substance.

HE has kept among us, in Times of Peace, Standing Armies, without the consent of our Legislatures.

HE has affected to render the Military independent of and superior to the Civil Power.

HE has combined with others to subject us to a Jurisdiction foreign to our Constitution, and unacknowledged by our Laws; giving his Assent to their Acts of pretended Legislation:

FOR quartering large Bodies of Armed Troops among us;

FOR protecting them, by a mock Trial, from Punishment for any Murders which they should commit on the Inhabitants of these States:

FOR cutting off our Trade with all Parts of the World:

FOR imposing Taxes on us without our Consent:

FOR depriving us, in many Cases, of the Benefits of Trial by Jury:

FOR transporting us beyond Seas to be tried for pretended Offences:

FOR abolishing the free System of English Laws in a neighbouring Province, establishing therein an arbitrary Government, and enlarging its Boundaries, so as to render it at once an Example and fit Instrument for introducing the same absolute Rules into these Colonies:

FOR taking away our Charters, abolishing our most valuable Laws, and altering fundamentally the Forms of our Governments:

FOR suspending our own Legislatures, and declaring themselves invested with Power to legislate for us in all Cases whatsoever.

HE has abdicated Government here, by declaring us out of his Protection and waging War against us.

HE has plundered our Seas, ravaged our Coasts, burnt our Towns, and destroyed the Lives of our People.

HE is, at this Time, transporting large Armies of foreign Mercenaries to compleat the Works of Death, Desolation, and Tyranny, already begun with circumstances of Cruelty and Perfidy, scarcely paralleled in the most barbarous Ages, and totally unworthy the Head of a civilized Nation.

HE has constrained our fellow Citizens taken Captive on the high Seas to bear Arms against their Country, to become the Executioners of their Friends and Brethren, or to fall themselves by their Hands.

HE has excited domestic Insurrections amongst us, and has endeavoured to bring on the Inhabitants of our Frontiers, the merciless Indian Savages, whose known Rule of Warfare, is an undistinguished

Destruction, of all Ages, Sexes and Conditions.

IN every stage of these Oppressions we have Petitioned for Redress in the most humble Terms: Our repeated Petitions have been answered only by repeated Injury. A Prince, whose Character is thus marked by every act which may define a Tyrant, is unfit to be the Ruler of a free People.

NOR have we been wanting in Attentions to our British Brethren. We have warned them from Time to Time of Attempts by their Legislature to extend an unwarrantable Jurisdiction over us. We have reminded them of the Circumstances of our Emigration and Settlement here. We have appealed to their native Justice and Magnanimity, and we have conjured them by the Ties of our common Kindred to disavow these Usurpations, which, would inevitably interrupt our Connections and Correspondence. They too have been deaf to the Voice of Justice and of Consanguinity. We must, therefore, acquiesce in the Necessity, which denounces our Separation, and hold them, as we hold the rest of Mankind, Enemies in War, in Peace, Friends.

WE, therefore, the Representatives of the UNITED STATES OF AMERICA, in GENERAL CONGRESS, Assembled, appealing to the Supreme Judge of the World for the Rectitude of our Intentions, do, in the Name, and by Authority of the good People of these Colonies, solemnly Publish and Declare, That these United Colonies are, and of Right ought to be, FREE AND INDEPENDENT STATES; that they are absolved from all Allegiance to the British Crown, and that all political Connection between them and the State of Great-Britain, is and ought to be totally dissolved; and that as FREE AND INDEPENDENT STATES, they have full Power to levy War, conclude Peace, contract Alliances, establish Commerce, and to do all other Acts and Things which INDEPENDENT STATES may of right do. And for the support of this Declaration, with a firm Reliance on the Protection of divine Providence, we mutually pledge to each other our Lives, our Fortunes, and our sacred Honor.

THE UNITED STATES CONSTITUTION

We the People of the United States, in Order to form a more perfect Union, establish Justice, insure domestic Tranquility, provide for the common defence, promote the general Welfare, and secure the Blessings of Liberty to ourselves and our Posterity, do ordain and establish this Constitution for the United States of America.

Article. I.

Section. 1.

All legislative Powers herein granted shall be vested in a Congress of the United States, which shall consist of a Senate and House of Representatives.

Section. 2.

Clause 1: The House of Representatives shall be composed of Members chosen every second Year by the People of the several States, and the Electors in each State shall have the Qualifications requisite for Electors of the most numerous Branch of the State Legislature.

Clause 2: No Person shall be a Representative who shall not have attained to the Age of twenty five Years, and been seven Years a Citizen of the United States, and who shall not, when elected, be an Inhabitant of that State in which he shall be chosen.

Clause 3: Representatives and direct Taxes shall be apportioned among the several States which may be included within this Union, according to their respective Numbers, which shall be determined by adding to the whole Number of free Persons, including those bound to Service for a Term of Years, and excluding Indians not taxed, three fifths of all other Persons. The actual Enumeration shall be made within three Years after the first Meeting of the Congress of the United States, and within every subsequent Term of ten Years, in such Manner as they shall by Law direct. The Number of Representatives shall not exceed one for every thirty Thousand, but each State shall have at Least one Representative; and until such enumeration shall be made, the State of New Hampshire shall be entitled to chuse three, Massachusetts eight, Rhode-Island and Providence Plantations one, Connecticut five, New-York six, New Jersey four, Pennsylvania eight, Delaware one, Maryland six, Virginia ten, North Carolina five, South Carolina five, and Georgia three.

Clause 4: When vacancies happen in the Representation from any State, the Executive Authority thereof shall issue Writs of Election to fill such Vacancies.

Clause 5: The House of Representatives shall chuse their Speaker and other Officers; and shall have the sole Power of Impeachment.

Section. 3.

Clause 1: The Senate of the United States shall be composed of two Senators from each State, chosen by the Legislature thereof, for six Years; and each Senator shall have one Vote.

Clause 2: Immediately after they shall be assembled in Consequence of the first Election, they shall be divided as equally as may be into three Classes. The Seats of the Senators of the first Class shall be vacated at the Expiration of the second Year, of the second Class at the Expiration of the fourth Year, and of the third Class at the Expiration of the sixth Year, so that one third may be chosen every second Year; and if Vacancies happen by Resignation, or otherwise, during the Recess of the Legislature of any State, the Executive thereof may make temporary Appointments until the next Meeting of the Legislature, which shall then fill such Vacancies.

Clause 3: No Person shall be a Senator who shall not have attained to the Age of thirty Years, and been nine Years a Citizen of the United States, and who shall not, when elected, be an Inhabitant of that State for which he shall be chosen.

Clause 4: The Vice President of the United States shall be President of the Senate, but shall have no Vote, unless they be equally divided.

Clause 5: The Senate shall chuse their other Officers, and also a President pro tempore, in the Absence of the Vice President, or when he shall exercise the Office of President of the United States.

Clause 6: The Senate shall have the sole Power to try all Impeachments. When sitting for that Purpose, they shall be on Oath or Affirmation. When the President of the United States is tried, the Chief Justice shall preside: And no Person shall be convicted without the Concurrence of two thirds of the Members present.

Clause 7: Judgment in Cases of Impeachment shall not extend further than to removal from Office, and disqualification to hold and enjoy any Office of honor, Trust or Profit under the United States: but the Party convicted shall nevertheless be liable and subject to Indictment, Trial, Judgment and Punishment, according to Law.

Section. 4.

Clause 1: The Times, Places and Manner of holding Elections for Senators and Representatives, shall be prescribed in each State by the Legislature thereof; but the Congress may at any time by Law make or alter such Regulations, except as to the Places of chusing Senators.

Clause 2: The Congress shall assemble at least once in every Year, and such Meeting shall be on the first Monday in December, unless they shall by Law appoint a different Day.

Section. 5.

Clause 1: Each House shall be the Judge of the Elections, Returns and Qualifications of its own Members, and a Majority of each shall constitute a Quorum to do Business; but a smaller Number may adjourn from day to day, and may be authorized to compel the Attendance of absent Members, in such Manner, and under such Penalties as each House may provide.

Clause 2: Each House may determine the Rules of its Proceedings, punish its Members for disorderly Behaviour, and, with the Concurrence of two thirds, expel a Member.

Clause 3: Each House shall keep a Journal of its Proceedings, and from time to time publish the same, excepting such Parts as may in their Judgment require Secrecy; and the Yeas and Nays of the Members of either House on any question shall, at the Desire of one fifth of those Present, be entered on the Journal.

Clause 4: Neither House, during the Session of Congress, shall, without the Consent of the other, adjourn for more than three days, nor to any other Place than that in which the two Houses shall be sitting.

Section. 6.

Clause 1: The Senators and Representatives shall receive a Compensation for their Services, to be ascertained by Law, and paid out of the Treasury of the United States. They shall in all Cases, except Treason, Felony and Breach of the Peace, be privileged from Arrest during their Attendance at the Session of their respective Houses, and in going to and returning from the same; and for any Speech or Debate in either House, they shall not be questioned in any other Place.

Clause 2: No Senator or Representative shall, during the Time for which he was elected, be appointed to any civil Office under the Authority of the United States, which shall have been created, or the Emoluments whereof shall have been encreased during such time; and no Person holding any Office under the United States, shall be a Member of either House during his Continuance in Office.

Section. 7.

Clause 1: All Bills for raising Revenue shall originate in the House of Representatives; but the Senate may propose or concur with Amendments as on other Bills.

Clause 2: Every Bill which shall have passed the House of Representatives and the Senate, shall, before it become a Law, be presented to the President of the United States; If he approve he shall sign it, but if not he shall return it, with his Objections to that House in which it shall have originated, who shall enter the Objections at large on their Journal, and proceed to reconsider it. If after such Reconsideration two thirds of that House shall agree to pass the Bill, it shall be sent, together with the Objections, to the other House, by which it shall likewise be reconsidered, and if approved by two thirds of that House, it shall become a Law. But in all such Cases the Votes of both Houses shall be determined by yeas and Nays, and the Names of the Persons voting for and against the Bill shall be entered on the Journal of each House respectively. If any Bill shall not be returned by the President within ten Days (Sundays excepted) after it shall have been presented to him, the Same shall be a Law, in like Manner as if he had signed it, unless the Congress by their Adjournment prevent its Return, in which Case it shall not be a Law.

Clause 3: Every Order, Resolution, or Vote to which the Concurrence of the Senate and House of Representatives may be necessary (except on a question of Adjournment) shall be presented to the President of the United States; and before the Same shall take Effect, shall be approved by him, or being disapproved by him, shall be repassed by two thirds of the Senate and House of Representatives, according to the Rules and Limitations prescribed in the Case of a Bill.

Section. 8.

Clause 1: The Congress shall have Power To lay and collect Taxes, Duties, Imposts and Excises, to pay the Debts and provide for the common Defence and general Welfare of the United States; but all Duties, Imposts and Excises shall be uniform throughout the United States;

Clause 2: To borrow Money on the credit of the United States;

Clause 3: To regulate Commerce with foreign Nations, and among the several States, and with the Indian Tribes;

Clause 4: To establish an uniform Rule of Naturalization, and uniform Laws on the subject of Bankruptcies throughout the United States;

Clause 5: To coin Money, regulate the Value thereof, and of foreign Coin, and fix the Standard of Weights and Measures;

Clause 6: To provide for the Punishment of counterfeiting the Securities and current Coin of the United States;

Clause 7: To establish Post Offices and post Roads;

Clause 8: To promote the Progress of Science and useful Arts, by securing for limited Times to Authors and Inventors the exclusive Right to their respective Writings and Discoveries;

Clause 9: To constitute Tribunals inferior to the supreme Court;

Clause 10: To define and punish Piracies and Felonies committed on the high Seas, and Offences against the Law of Nations;

Clause 11: To declare War, grant Letters of Marque and Reprisal, and make Rules concerning Captures on Land and Water;

Clause 12: To raise and support Armies, but no Appropriation of Money to that Use shall be for a longer Term than two Years;

Clause 13: To provide and maintain a Navy;

Clause 14: To make Rules for the Government and Regulation of the land and naval Forces;

Clause 15: To provide for calling forth the Militia to execute the Laws of the Union, suppress Insurrections and repel Invasions;

Clause 16: To provide for organizing, arming, and disciplining, the Militia, and for governing such Part of them as may be employed in the Service of the United States, reserving to the States respectively, the Appointment of the Officers, and the Authority of training the Militia according to the discipline prescribed by Congress;

Clause 17: To exercise exclusive Legislation in all Cases whatsoever, over such District (not exceeding ten Miles square) as may, byCession of particular States, and the Acceptance of Congress, become the Seat of the Government of the United States, and to exercise like Authority over all Places purchased by the Consent of the Legislature of the State in which the Same shall be, for the Erection of Forts, Magazines, Arsenals, dock-Yards, and other needful Buildings;—And

Clause 18: To make all Laws which shall be necessary and proper for carrying into Execution the foregoing Powers, and all other Powers vested by this Constitution in the Government of the United States, or in any Department or Officer thereof.

Section. 9.

Clause 1: The Migration or Importation of such Persons as any of the States now existing shall think proper to admit, shall not be prohibited by the Congress prior to the Year one thousand eight hundred and eight, but a Tax or duty may be imposed on such Importation, not exceeding ten dollars for each Person.

Clause 2: The Privilege of the Writ of Habeas Corpus shall not be suspended, unless when in Cases of Rebellion or Invasion the public Safety may require it.

Clause 3: No Bill of Attainder or ex post facto Law shall be passed.

Clause 4: No Capitation, or other direct, Tax shall be laid, unless in Proportion to the Census or Enumeration herein before directed to be taken.

Clause 5: No Tax or Duty shall be laid on Articles exported from any State.

Clause 6: No Preference shall be given by any Regulation of Commerce or Revenue to the Ports of one State over those of another: nor shall Vessels bound to, or from, one State, be obliged to enter, clear, or pay Duties in another.

Clause 7: No Money shall be drawn from the Treasury, but in Consequence of Appropriations made by Law; and a regular Statement and Account of the Receipts and Expenditures of all public Money shall be published from time to time.

Clause 8: No Title of Nobility shall be granted by the United States: And no Person holding any Office of Profit or Trust under them, shall, without the Consent of the Congress, accept of any present, Emolument, Office, or Title, of any kind whatever, from any King, Prince, or foreign State.

Section. 10.

Clause 1: No State shall enter into any Treaty, Alliance, or Confederation; grant Letters of Marque and Reprisal; coin Money; emit Bills of Credit; make any Thing but gold and silver Coin a Tender in Payment of Debts; pass any Bill of Attainder, ex post facto Law, or Law impairing the Obligation of Contracts, or grant any Title of Nobility.

Clause 2: No State shall, without the Consent of the Congress, lay any Imposts or Duties on Imports or Exports, except what may be absolutely necessary for executing its inspection Laws: and the net Produce of all Duties and Imposts, laid by any State on Imports or Exports, shall be for the Use of the Treasury of the United States; and all such Laws shall be subject to the Revision and Controul of the Congress.

Clause 3: No State shall, without the Consent of Congress, lay any Duty of Tonnage, keep Troops, or Ships of War in time of Peace, enter into any Agreement or Compact with another State, or with a foreign Power, or engage in War, unless actually invaded, or in such imminent Danger as will not admit of delay.

Article. II.

Section. 1.

Clause 1: The executive Power shall be vested in a President of the United States of America. He shall hold his Office during the Term of four Years, and, together with the Vice President, chosen for the same Term, be elected, as follows

Clause 2: Each State shall appoint, in such Manner as the Legislature thereof may direct, a Number of Electors, equal to the whole Number of Senators and Representatives to which the State may be entitled in the Congress: but no Senator or Representative, or Person holding an Office of Trust or Profit under the United States, shall be appointed an Elector.

Clause 3: The Electors shall meet in their respective States, and vote by Ballot for two Persons, of whom one at least shall not be an Inhabitant of the same State with themselves. And they shall make a List of all the Persons voted for, and of the Number of Votes for each; which List they shall sign and certify, and transmit sealed to the Seat of the Government of the United States, directed to the President of the Senate. The President of the Senate shall, in the Presence of the Senate and House of Representatives, open all the Certificates, and the Votes shall then be counted. The Person having the greatest Number of Votes shall be the President, if such Number be a Majority of the whole Number of Electors appointed; and if there be more than one who have such Majority, and have an equal Number of Votes, then the House of Representatives shall immediately chuse by Ballot one of them for President; and if no Person have a Majority, then from the five highest on the List the said House shall in like Manner chuse the President. But in chusing the President, the Votes shall be taken by States, the Representation from each State having one Vote; A quorum for this Purpose shall consist of a Member or Members from two thirds of the States, and a Majority of all the States shall be necessary to a Choice. In every Case, after the Choice of the President, the Person having the greatest Number of Votes of the Electors shall be the Vice President. But if there should remain two or more who have equal Votes, the Senate shall chuse from them by Ballot the Vice President. *(See Note 8)*

Clause 4: The Congress may determine the Time of chusing the Electors, and the Day on which they shall give their Votes; which Day shall be the same throughout the United States.

Clause 5: No Person except a natural born Citizen, or a Citizen of the United States, at the time of the Adoption of this Constitution, shall be eligible to the Office of President; neither shall any Person be eligible to that Office who shall not have attained to the Age of thirty five Years, and been fourteen Years a Resident within the United States.

Clause 6: In Case of the Removal of the President from Office, or of his Death, Resignation, or Inability to discharge the Powers and Duties of the said Office, (See Note 9) the Same shall devolve on the Vice President, and the Congress may by Law provide for the Case of Removal, Death, Resignation or Inability, both of the President and Vice President, declaring what Officer shall then act as President, and such Officer shall act accordingly, until the Disability be removed, or a President shall be elected.

Clause 7: The President shall, at stated Times, receive for his Services, a Compensation, which shall neither be encreased nor diminished during the Period for which he shall have been elected, and he shall not receive within that Period any other Emolument from the United States, or any of them.

Clause 8: Before he enter on the Execution of his Office, he shall take the following Oath or Affirmation:--"I do solemnly swear (or affirm) that I will faithfully execute the Office of President of the United States, and will to the best of my Ability, preserve, protect and defend the Constitution of the United States."

Section. 2.

Clause 1: The President shall be Commander in Chief of the Army and Navy of the United States, and of the Militia of the several States, when called into the actual Service of the United States; he may require the Opinion, in writing, of the principal Officer in each of the executive Departments, upon any Subject relating to the Duties of their respective Offices, and he shall have Power to grant Reprieves and Pardons for Offences against the United States, except in Cases of Impeachment.

Clause 2: He shall have Power, by and with the Advice and Consent of the Senate, to make Treaties, provided two thirds of the Senators present concur; and he shall nominate, and by and with the Advice and Consent of the Senate, shall appoint Ambassadors, other public Ministers and Consuls, Judges of the supreme Court, and all other Officers of the United States, whose Appointments are not herein otherwise provided for, and which shall be established by Law: but the Congress may by Law vest the Appointment of such inferior Officers, as they think proper, in the President alone, in the Courts of Law, or in the Heads of Departments.

Clause 3: The President shall have Power to fill up all Vacancies that may happen during the Recess of the Senate, by granting Commissions which shall expire at the End of their next Session.

Section. 3.

He shall from time to time give to the Congress Information of the State of the Union, and recommend to their Consideration such Measures as he shall judge necessary and expedient; he may, on extraordinary Occasions, convene both Houses, or either of them, and in Case of Disagreement between them, with Respect to the Time of Adjournment, he may adjourn them to such Time as he shall think proper; he shall receive Ambassadors and other public Ministers; he shall take Care that the Laws be faithfully executed, and shall Commission all the Officers of the United States.

Section. 4.

The President, Vice President and all civil Officers of the United States, shall be removed from Office on Impeachment for, and Conviction of, Treason, Bribery, or other high Crimes and Misdemeanors.

Article. III.
Section. 1.

The judicial Power of the United States, shall be vested in one supreme Court, and in such inferior Courts as the Congress may from time to time ordain and establish. The Judges, both of the supreme and inferior Courts, shall hold their Offices during good Behaviour, and shall, at stated Times, receive for their Services, a Compensation, which shall not be diminished during their Continuance in Office.

Section. 2.

Clause 1: The judicial Power shall extend to all Cases, in Law and Equity, arising under this Constitution, the Laws of the United States, and Treaties made, or which shall be made, under their Authority;—to all Cases affecting Ambassadors, other public Ministers and Consuls;—to all Cases of admiralty and maritime Jurisdiction;—to Controversies to which the United States shall be a Party;—to Controversies between two or more States;—between a State and Citizens of another State; —between Citizens of different States, —between Citizens of the same State claiming Lands under Grants of different States, and between a State, or the Citizens thereof, and foreign States, Citizens or Subjects.

Clause 2: In all Cases affecting Ambassadors, other public Ministers and Consuls, and those in which a State shall be Party, the supreme Court shall have original Jurisdiction. In all the other Cases before mentioned, the supreme Court shall have appellate Jurisdiction, both as to Law and Fact, with such Exceptions, and under such Regulations as the Congress shall make.

Clause 3: The Trial of all Crimes, except in Cases of Impeachment, shall be by Jury; and such Trial shall be held in the State where the said Crimes shall have been committed; but when not committed within any State, the Trial shall be at such Place or Places as the Congress may by Law have directed.

Section. 3.

Clause 1: Treason against the United States, shall consist only in levying War against them, or in adhering to their Enemies, giving them Aid and Comfort. No Person shall be convicted of Treason unless on the Testimony of two Witnesses to the same overt Act, or on Confession in open Court.

Clause 2: The Congress shall have Power to declare the Punishment of Treason, but no Attainder of Treason shall work Corruption of Blood, or Forfeiture except during the Life of the Person attainted.

Article. IV.

Section. 1.

Full Faith and Credit shall be given in each State to the public Acts, Records, and judicial Proceedings of every other State. And the Congress may by general Laws prescribe the Manner in which such Acts, Records and Proceedings shall be proved, and the Effect thereof.

Section. 2.

Clause 1: The Citizens of each State shall be entitled to all Privileges and Immunities of Citizens in the several States.

Clause 2: A Person charged in any State with Treason, Felony, or other Crime, who shall flee from Justice, and be found in another State, shall on Demand of the executive Authority of the State from which he fled, be delivered up, to be removed to the State having Jurisdiction of the Crime.

Clause 3: No Person held to Service or Labour in one State, under the Laws thereof, escaping into another, shall, in Consequence of any Law or Regulation therein, be discharged from such Service or Labour, but shall be delivered up on Claim of the Party to whom such Service or Labour may be due.

Section. 3.

Clause 1: New States may be admitted by the Congress into this Union; but no new State shall be formed or erected within the Jurisdiction of any other State; nor any State be formed by the Junction of two or more States, or Parts of States, without the Consent of the Legislatures of the States concerned as well as of the Congress.

Clause 2: The Congress shall have Power to dispose of and make all needful Rules and Regulations respecting the Territory or other Property belonging to the United States; and nothing in this Constitution shall be so construed as to Prejudice any Claims of the United States, or of any particular State.

Section. 4.

The United States shall guarantee to every State in this Union a Republican Form of Government, and shall protect each of them against Invasion; and on Application of the Legislature, or of the Executive (when the Legislature cannot be convened) against domestic Violence.

Article. V.

The Congress, whenever two thirds of both Houses shall deem it necessary, shall propose Amendments to this Constitution, or, on the Application of the Legislatures of two thirds of the several States, shall call a Convention for proposing Amendments, which, in either Case, shall be valid to all Intents and Purposes, as Part of this Constitution, when ratified by the Legislatures of three fourths of the several States, or by Conventions in three fourths thereof, as the one or the other Mode of Ratification may be proposed by the Congress; Provided that no Amendment which may be made prior to the Year One thousand eight hundred and eight shall in any Manner affect the first and fourth Clauses in the Ninth Section of the first Article; and that no State, without its Consent, shall be deprived of its equal Suffrage in the Senate.

Article. VI.

Clause 1: All Debts contracted and Engagements entered into, before the Adoption of this Constitution, shall be as valid against the United States under this Constitution, as under the Confederation.

Clause 2: This Constitution, and the Laws of the United States which shall be made in Pursuance thereof; and all Treaties made, or which shall be made, under the Authority of the United States, shall be the supreme Law of the Land; and the Judges in every State shall be bound thereby, any Thing in the Constitution or Laws of any State to the Contrary notwithstanding.

Clause 3: The Senators and Representatives before mentioned, and the Members of the several State Legislatures, and all executive and judicial Officers, both of the United States and of the several States, shall be bound by Oath or Affirmation, to support this Constitution; but no religious Test shall ever be required as a Qualification to any Office or public Trust under the United States.

Article. VII.

The Ratification of the Conventions of nine States, shall be sufficient for the Establishment of this Constitution between the States so ratifying the Same.

Done in Convention by the Unanimous Consent of the States present the Seventeenth Day of September in the Year of our Lord one thousand seven hundred and Eighty seven and of the Independence of the United States of America the Twelfth. In witness whereof We have hereunto subscribed our Names,

GO WASHINGTON--Presidt. and deputy from Virginia
[Signed also by the deputies of twelve States.]

Amendments to the Constitution

ARTICLES IN ADDITION TO, AND AMENDMENTS OF, THE CONSTITUTION OF THE UNITED STATES OF AMERICA, PROPOSED BY CONGRESS, AND RATIFIED BY THE LEGISLATURES OF THE SEVERAL STATES, PURSUANT TO THE FIFTH ARTICLE OF THE ORIGINAL CONSTITUTION

Article [I.]

Congress shall make no law respecting an establishment of religion, or prohibiting the free exercise thereof; or abridging the freedom of speech, or of the press; or the right of the people peaceably to assemble, and to petition the Government for a redress of grievances.

Article [II.]

A well regulated Militia, being necessary to the security of a free State, the right of the people to keep and bear Arms, shall not be infringed.

Article [III.]

No Soldier shall, in time of peace be quartered in any house, without the consent of the Owner, nor in time of war, but in a manner to be prescribed by law.

Article [IV.]

The right of the people to be secure in their persons, houses, papers, and effects, against unreasonable searches and seizures, shall not be violated, and no Warrants shall issue, but upon probable cause, supported by Oath or affirmation, and particularly describing the place to be searched, and the persons or things to be seized.

Article [V.]

No person shall be held to answer for a capital, or otherwise infamous crime, unless on a presentment or indictment of a Grand Jury, except in cases arising in the land or naval forces, or in the Militia, when in actual service in time of War or public danger; nor shall any person be subject for the same offence to be twice put in jeopardy of life or limb; nor shall be compelled in any criminal case to be a witness against himself, nor be deprived of life, liberty, or property, without due process of law; nor shall private property be taken for public use, without just compensation.

Article [VI.]

In all criminal prosecutions, the accused shall enjoy the right to a speedy and public trial, by an impartial jury of the State and district wherein the crime shall have been committed, which district shall have been previously ascertained by law, and to be informed of the nature and cause of the accusation; to be confronted with the witnesses against him; to have compulsory process for obtaining witnesses in his favor, and to have the Assistance of Counsel for his defence.

Article [VII.]

In Suits at common law, where the value in controversy shall exceed twenty dollars, the right of trial by jury shall be preserved, and no fact tried by a jury, shall be otherwise re-examined in any Court of the United States, than according to the rules of the common law.

Article [VIII.]

Excessive bail shall not be required, nor excessive fines imposed, nor cruel and unusual punishments inflicted.

Article [IX.]

The enumeration in the Constitution, of certain rights, shall not be construed to deny or disparage others retained by the people.

Article [X.]

The powers not delegated to the United States by the Constitution, nor prohibited by it to the States, are reserved to the States respectively, or to the people.

Article [XI.]

The Judicial power of the United States shall not be construed to extend to any suit in law or equity, commenced or prosecuted against one of the United States by Citizens of another State, or by Citizens or Subjects of any Foreign State.

Proposal and Ratification

The Eleventh Amendment to the Constitution of the United States was proposed to the legislatures of the several States by the Third Congress, on the 4th of March 1794; and was declared in a message from the President to Congress, dated the 8th of January, 1798, to have been ratified by the legislatures of three-fourths of the States. The dates of ratification were: New York, March 27, 1794; Rhode Island, March 31, 1794; Connecticut,, May 8, 1794; New Hampshire, June 16, 1794; Massachusetts, June 26, 1794; Vermont, between October 9, 1794, and November 9, 1794; Virginia, November 18, 1794; Georgia, November 29, 1794; Kentucky, December 7, 1794; Maryland, December 26, 1794; Delaware, January 23, 1795; North Carolina, February 7, 1795.

Ratification was completed on February 7, 1795.

The amendment was subsequently ratified by South Carolina on December 4, 1797. New Jersey and Pennsylvania did not take action on the amendment.

Article [XII.]

The Electors shall meet in their respective states, and vote by ballot for President and Vice-President, one of whom, at least, shall not be an inhabitant of the same state with themselves; they shall name in their ballots the person voted for as President, and in distinct ballots the person voted for as Vice-President, and they shall make distinct lists of all persons voted for as President, and of all persons voted for as Vice-President, and of the number of votes for each, which lists they shall sign and certify, and transmit sealed to the seat of the government of the United States, directed to the President of the Senate;--The President of the Senate shall, in the presence of the Senate and House of Representatives, open all the certificates and the votes shall then be counted;—The person having the greatest number of votes for President, shall be the President, if such number be a majority of the whole number of Electors appointed; and if no person have such majority, then from the persons having the highest numbers not exceeding three on the list of those voted for as President, the House of Representatives shall choose immediately, by ballot, the President. But in choosing the President, the votes shall be taken by states, the representation from each state having one vote; a quorum for this purpose shall consist of a member or members from two-thirds of the states, and a majority of all the states shall be necessary to a choice. And if the House of Representatives shall not choose a President whenever the right of choice shall devolve upon them, before the fourth day of March next following, then the Vice-President shall act as President, as in the case of the death or other constitutional disability of the President. *(See Note 14)*--The person having the greatest number of votes as Vice-President, shall be the Vice-President, if such number be a majority of the whole number of Electors appointed, and if no person have a majority, then from the two highest numbers on the list, the Senate shall choose the Vice-President; a quorum for the purpose shall consist of two-thirds of the whole number of Senators, and a majority of the whole number shall be necessary to a choice. But no person constitutionally ineligible to the office of President shall be eligible to that of Vice-President of the United States.

Proposal and Ratification

The Twelfth Amendment to the Constitution of the United States was proposed to the legislatures of the several States by the Eighth Congress, on the 9th of December, 1803, in lieu of the original third paragraph of the first section of the second article; and was declared in a proclamation of the Secretary of State, dated the 25th of September, 1804, to have been ratified by the legislatures of 13, of the 17, States. The dates of ratification were: North Carolina, December 21, 1803; Maryland, December 24, 1803; Kentucky, December

27, 1803; Ohio, December 30, 1803; Pennsylvania, January 5, 1804; Vermont, January 30, 1804; Virginia, February 3, 1804; New York, February 10, 1804; New Jersey, February 22, 1804; Rhode Island, March 12, 1804; South Carolina,, May 15, 1804; Georgia,, May 19, 1804; New Hampshire, June 15, 1804.

Ratification was completed on June 15, 1804.

The amendment was subsequently ratified by Tennessee, July 27, 1804.

The amendment was rejected by Delaware, January 18, 1804; Massachusetts, February 3, 1804; Connecticut, at its session begun, May 10, 1804.

Article [XIII.]

Section. 1.

Neither slavery nor involuntary servitude, except as a punishment for crime whereof the party shall have been duly convicted, shall exist within the United States, or any place subject to their jurisdiction.

Section. 2.

Congress shall have power to enforce this article by appropriate legislation.

Proposal and Ratification

The Thirteenth Amendment to the Constitution of the United States was proposed to the legislatures of the several States by the Thirty-eighth Congress, on the 31st day of January, 1865, and was declared, in a proclamation of the Secretary of State, dated the 18th of December, 1865, to have been ratified by the legislatures of twenty-seven of the thirty-six States. The dates of ratification were: Illinois, February 1, 1865; Rhode Island, February 2, 1865; Michigan, February 2, 1865; Maryland, February 3, 1865; New York, February 3, 1865; Pennsylvania, February 3, 1865; West Virginia, February 3, 1865; Missouri, February 6, 1865; Maine, February 7, 1865; Kansas, February 7, 1865; Massachusetts, February 7, 1865; Virginia, February 9, 1865; Ohio, February 10, 1865; Indiana, February 13, 1865; Nevada, February 16, 1865; Louisiana, February 17, 1865; Minnesota, February 23, 1865; Wisconsin, February 24, 1865; Vermont, March 9, 1865; Tennessee, April 7, 1865; Arkansas, April 14, 1865; Connecticut,, May 4, 1865; New Hampshire, July 1, 1865; South Carolina, November 13, 1865; Alabama, December 2, 1865; North Carolina, December 4, 1865; Georgia, December 6, 1865.

Ratification was completed on December 6, 1865.

The amendment was subsequently ratified by Oregon, December 8, 1865;

California, December 19, 1865; Florida, December 28, 1865, (Florida again ratified on June 9, 1868, upon its adoption of a new constitution); Iowa, January 15, 1866; New Jersey, January 23, 1866, (after having rejected the amendment on March 16, 1865); Texas, February 18, 1870; Delaware, February 12, 1901, (after having rejected the amendment on February 8, 1865); Kentucky, March 18, 1976, (after having rejected it on February 24, 1865).

The amendment was rejected (and not subsequently ratified) by Mississippi, December 4, 1865.

Article [XIV.]

Section. 1.

All persons born or naturalized in the United States, and subject to the jurisdiction thereof, are citizens of the United States and of the State wherein they reside. No State shall make or enforce any law which shall abridge the privileges or immunities of citizens of the United States; nor shall any State deprive any person of life, liberty, or property, without due process of law; nor deny to any person within its jurisdiction the equal protection of the laws.

Section. 2.

Representatives shall be apportioned among the several States according to their respective numbers, counting the whole number of persons in each State, excluding Indians not taxed. But when the right to vote at any election for the choice of electors for President and Vice President of the United States, Representatives in Congress, the Executive and Judicial officers of a State, or the members of the Legislature thereof, is denied to any of the male inhabitants of such State, being twenty-one years of age,*(See Note 15)* and citizens of the United States, or in any way abridged, except for participation in rebellion, or other crime, the basis of representation therein shall be reduced in the proportion which the number of such male citizens shall bear to the whole number of male citizens twenty-one years of age in such State.

Section. 3.

No person shall be a Senator or Representative in Congress, or elector of President and Vice President, or hold any office, civil or military, under the United States, or under any State, who, having previously taken an oath, as a member of Congress, or as an officer of the United States, or as a member of any State legislature, or as an executive or judicial officer of any State, to support the Constitution of the United States, shall have engaged in insurrection or rebellion against the same, or given aid or comfort to the enemies thereof. But Congress may by a vote of two-thirds of each House, remove such disability.

Section. 4.

The validity of the public debt of the United States, authorized by law, including debts incurred for payment of pensions and bounties for services in suppressing insurrection or rebellion, shall not be questioned. But neither the United States nor any State shall assume or pay any debt or obligation incurred in aid of insurrection or rebellion against the United States, or any claim for the loss or emancipation of any slave; but all such debts, obligations and claims shall be held illegal and void.

Section. 5.

The Congress shall have power to enforce, by appropriate legislation, the provisions of this article.

Proposal and Ratification

The Fourteenth Amendment to the Constitution of the United States was proposed to the legislatures of the several States by the Thirty-ninth Congress, on the 13th of June, 1866. It was declared, in a certificate of the Secretary of State dated July 28, 1868, to have been ratified by the legislatures of 28, of the 37, States. The dates of ratification were: Connecticut, June 25, 1866; New Hampshire, July 6, 1866; Tennessee, July 19, 1866; New Jersey, September 11, 1866, (subsequently the legislature rescinded its ratification, and on March 24, 1868, readopted its resolution of rescission over the Governor's veto, and on Nov. 12, 1980, expressed support for the amendment); Oregon, September 19, 1866, (and rescinded its ratification on October 15, 1868); Vermont, October 30, 1866; Ohio, January 4, 1867, (and rescinded its ratification on January 15, 1868); New York, January 10, 1867; Kansas, January 11, 1867; Illinois, January 15, 1867; West Virginia, January 16, 1867; Michigan, January 16, 1867; Minnesota, January 16, 1867; Maine, January 19, 1867; Nevada, January 22, 1867; Indiana, January 23, 1867; Missouri, January 25, 1867; Rhode Island, February 7, 1867; Wisconsin, February 7, 1867; Pennsylvania, February 12, 1867; Massachusetts, March 20, 1867; Nebraska, June 15, 1867; Iowa, March

16, 1868; Arkansas, April 6, 1868; Florida, June 9, 1868; North Carolina, July 4, 1868, (after having rejected it on December 14, 1866); Louisiana, July 9, 1868, (after having rejected it on February 6, 1867); South Carolina, July 9, 1868, (after having rejected it on December 20, 1866).

Ratification was completed on July 9, 1868.

The amendment was subsequently ratified by Alabama, July 13, 1868; Georgia, July 21, 1868, (after having rejected it on November 9, 1866); Virginia, October 8, 1869, (after having rejected it on January 9, 1867); Mississippi, January 17, 1870; Texas, February 18, 1870, (after having rejected it on October 27, 1866); Delaware, February 12, 1901, (after having rejected it on February 8, 1867); Maryland, April 4, 1959, (after having rejected it on March 23, 1867); California,, May 6, 1959; Kentucky, March 18, 1976, (after having rejected it on January 8, 1867).

Article [XV.]

Section. 1.

The right of citizens of the United States to vote shall not be denied or abridged by the United States or by any State on account of race, color, or previous condition of servitude.

Section. 2.

The Congress shall have power to enforce this article by appropriate legislation.

Proposal and Ratification

The Fifteenth Amendment to the Constitution of the United States was proposed to the legislatures of the several States by the Fortieth Congress, on the 26th of February, 1869, and was declared, in a proclamation of the Secretary of State, dated March 30, 1870, to have been ratified by the legislatures of twenty-nine of the thirty-seven States. The dates of ratification were: Nevada, March 1, 1869; West Virginia, March 3, 1869; Illinois, March 5, 1869; Louisiana, March 5, 1869; North Carolina, March 5, 1869; Michigan, March 8, 1869; Wisconsin, March 9, 1869; Maine, March 11, 1869; Massachusetts, March 12, 1869; Arkansas, March 15, 1869; South Carolina, March 15, 1869; Pennsylvania, March 25, 1869; New York, April 14, 1869, (and the legislature of the same State passed a resolution January 5, 1870, to withdraw its consent to it, which action it rescinded on March 30, 1970); Indiana,, May 14, 1869; Connecticut,, May 19, 1869; Florida, June 14, 1869; New Hampshire,

July 1, 1869; Virginia, October 8, 1869; Vermont, October 20, 1869; Missouri, January 7, 1870; Minnesota, January 13, 1870; Mississippi, January 17, 1870; Rhode Island, January 18, 1870; Kansas, January 19, 1870; Ohio, January 27, 1870, (after having rejected it on April 30, 1869); Georgia, February 2, 1870; Iowa, February 3, 1870.

Ratification was completed on February 3, 1870, unless the withdrawal of ratification by New York was effective; in which event ratification was completed on February 17, 1870, when Nebraska ratified.

The amendment was subsequently ratified by Texas, February 18, 1870; New Jersey, February 15, 1871, (after having rejected it on February 7, 1870); Delaware, February 12, 1901, (after having rejected it on March 18, 1869); Oregon, February 24, 1959; California, April 3, 1962, (after having rejected it on January 28, 1870); Kentucky, March 18, 1976, (after having rejected it on March 12, 1869).

The amendment was approved by the Governor of Maryland,, May 7, 1973; Maryland having previously rejected it on February 26, 1870.

The amendment was rejected (and not subsequently ratified) by Tennessee, November 16, 1869.

Article [XVI.]

The Congress shall have power to lay and collect taxes on incomes, from whatever source derived, without apportionment among the several States, and without regard to any census or enumeration.

Proposal and Ratification

The Sixteenth Amendment to the Constitution of the United States was proposed to the legislatures of the several States by the Sixty-first Congress on the 12th of July, 1909, and was declared, in a proclamation of the Secretary of State, dated the 25th of February, 1913, to have been ratified by 36, of the 48, States. The dates of ratification were: Alabama, August 10, 1909; Kentucky, February 8, 1910; South Carolina, February 19, 1910; Illinois, March 1, 1910; Mississippi, March 7, 1910; Oklahoma, March 10, 1910; Maryland, April 8, 1910; Georgia, August 3, 1910; Texas, August 16, 1910; Ohio, January 19, 1911; Idaho, January 20, 1911; Oregon, January 23, 1911; Washington, January 26, 1911; Montana, January 30, 1911; Indiana, January 30, 1911; California, January 31, 1911; Nevada, January 31, 1911; South Dakota, February 3, 1911; Nebraska, February 9, 1911; North Carolina, February 11, 1911; Colorado, February 15, 1911; North Dakota, February 17, 1911; Kansas, February 18, 1911; Michigan, February 23, 1911; Iowa, February 24, 1911; Missouri, March 16, 1911; Maine, March 31, 1911; Tennessee, April 7, 1911; Arkansas, April 22,

1911, (after having rejected it earlier); Wisconsin,, May 26, 1911; New York, July 12, 1911; Arizona, April 6, 1912; Minnesota, June 11, 1912; Louisiana, June 28, 1912; West Virginia, January 31, 1913; New Mexico, February 3, 1913.

Ratification was completed on February 3, 1913.

The amendment was subsequently ratified by Massachusetts, March 4, 1913; New Hampshire, March 7, 1913, (after having rejected it on March 2, 1911).

The amendment was rejected (and not subsequently ratified) by Connecticut, Rhode Island, and Utah.

Article [XVII.]

The Senate of the United States shall be composed of two Senators from each State, elected by the people thereof, for six years; and each Senator shall have one vote. The electors in each State shall have the qualifications requisite for electors of the most numerous branch of the State legislatures.

When vacancies happen in the representation of any State in the Senate, the executive authority of such State shall issue writs of election to fill such vacancies: Provided, That the legislature of any State may empower the executive thereof to make temporary appointments until the people fill the vacancies by election as the legislature may direct.

This amendment shall not be so construed as to affect the election or term of any Senator chosen before it becomes valid as part of the Constitution.

Proposal and Ratification

The Seventeenth Amendment to the Constitution of the United States was proposed to the legislatures of the several States by the Sixty-second Congress on the 13th of May, 1912, and was declared, in a proclamation of the Secretary of State, dated the 31st of May, 1913, to have been ratified by the legislatures of 36, of the 48, States. The dates of ratification were: Massachusetts,, May 22, 1912; Arizona, June 3, 1912; Minnesota, June 10, 1912; New York, January 15, 1913; Kansas, January 17, 1913; Oregon, January 23, 1913; North Carolina, January 25, 1913; California, January 28, 1913; Michigan, January 28, 1913; Iowa, January 30, 1913; Montana, January 30, 1913; Idaho, January 31, 1913; West Virginia, February 4, 1913; Colorado, February 5, 1913; Nevada, February 6, 1913; Texas, February 7, 1913; Washington, February 7,

1913; Wyoming, February 8, 1913; Arkansas, February 11, 1913; Maine, February 11, 1913; Illinois, February 13, 1913; North Dakota, February 14, 1913; Wisconsin, February 18, 1913; Indiana, February 19, 1913; New Hampshire, February 19, 1913; Vermont, February 19, 1913; South Dakota, February 19, 1913; Oklahoma, February 24, 1913; Ohio, February 25, 1913; Missouri, March 7, 1913; New Mexico, March 13, 1913; Nebraska, March 14, 1913; New Jersey, March 17, 1913; Tennessee, April 1, 1913; Pennsylvania, April 2, 1913; Connecticut, April 8, 1913.

Ratification was completed on April 8, 1913.

The amendment was subsequently ratified by Louisiana, June 11, 1914.

The amendment was rejected by Utah (and not subsequently ratified) on February 26, 1913.

Article [XVIII.]

Section. 1.

After one year from the ratification of this article the manufacture, sale, or transportation of intoxicating liquors within, the importation thereof into, or the exportation thereof from the United States and all territory subject to the jurisdiction thereof for beverage purposes is hereby prohibited.

Section. 2.

The Congress and the several States shall have concurrent power to enforce this article by appropriate legislation.

Section. 3.

This article shall be inoperative unless it shall have been ratified as an amendment to the Constitution by the legislatures of the several States, as provided in the Constitution, within seven years from the date of the submission hereof to the States by the Congress.

Proposal and Ratification

The Eighteenth Amendment to the Constitution of the United States was proposed to the legislatures of the several States by the Sixty-fifth Congress, on the 18th of December, 1917, and was declared, in a proclamation of the Secretary of State, dated the 29th of January, 1919, to have been ratified by the legislatures of 36, of the 48, States. The dates of ratification were: Mississippi, January 8, 1918; Virginia, January 11, 1918; Kentucky, January 14, 1918; North Dakota, January 25, 1918; South Carolina, January 29, 1918; Maryland, February 13, 1918; Montana, February 19, 1918; Texas, March 4, 1918; Delaware, March 18, 1918; South Dakota, March 20, 1918; Massachusetts, April 2, 1918; Arizona,, May 24, 1918; Georgia, June 26, 1918; Louisiana, August 3, 1918; Florida, December 3, 1918; Michigan, January 2, 1919; Ohio, January 7, 1919; Oklahoma, January 7, 1919; Idaho, January 8, 1919; Maine, January 8, 1919; West Virginia, January 9, 1919; California, January 13, 1919; Tennessee, January 13, 1919; Washington, January 13, 1919; Arkansas, January 14, 1919; Kansas, January 14, 1919; Alabama, January 15, 1919; Colorado, January 15, 1919; Iowa, January 15, 1919; New Hampshire, January 15, 1919; Oregon, January 15, 1919; Nebraska, January 16, 1919; North Carolina, January 16, 1919; Utah, January 16, 1919; Missouri, January 16, 1919; Wyoming, January 16, 1919.

Ratification was completed on January 16, 1919. See Dillon v. Gloss, 256, U.S. 368, 376, (1921).

The amendment was subsequently ratified by Minnesota on January 17, 1919; Wisconsin, January 17, 1919; New Mexico, January 20, 1919; Nevada, January 21, 1919; New York, January 29, 1919; Vermont, January 29, 1919; Pennsylvania, February 25, 1919; Connecticut,, May 6, 1919; and New Jersey, March 9, 1922.

The amendment was rejected (and not subsequently ratified) by Rhode Island.

Article [XIX.]

The right of citizens of the United States to vote shall not be denied or abridged by the United States or by any State on account of sex.

Congress shall have power to enforce this article by appropriate legislation.

Proposal and Ratification

The Nineteenth Amendment to the Constitution of the United States was proposed to the legislatures of the several States by the Sixty-sixth Congress, on the 4th of June, 1919, and was declared, in a proclamation of the Secretary of State, dated the 26th of August, 1920, to have been ratified by the legislatures of 36, of the 48, States. The dates of ratification were: Illinois, June 10, 1919, (and that State readopted its resolution of ratification June 17, 1919); Michigan, June 10, 1919; Wisconsin, June 10, 1919; Kansas, June 16, 1919; New York, June 16, 1919; Ohio, June 16, 1919; Pennsylvania, June 24, 1919; Massachusetts, June 25, 1919; Texas, June 28, 1919; Iowa, July 2, 1919;

Missouri, July 3, 1919; Arkansas, July 28, 1919; Montana, August 2, 1919; Nebraska, August 2, 1919; Minnesota, September 8, 1919; New Hampshire, September 10, 1919; Utah, October 2, 1919; California, November 1, 1919; Maine, November 5, 1919; North Dakota, December 1, 1919; South Dakota, December 4, 1919; Colorado, December 15, 1919; Kentucky, January 6, 1920; Rhode Island, January 6, 1920; Oregon, January 13, 1920; Indiana, January 16, 1920; Wyoming, January 27, 1920; Nevada, February 7, 1920; New Jersey, February 9, 1920; Idaho, February 11, 1920; Arizona, February 12, 1920; New Mexico, February 21, 1920; Oklahoma, February 28, 1920; West Virginia, March 10, 1920; Washington, March 22, 1920; Tennessee, August 18, 1920.

Ratification was completed on August 18, 1920.

The amendment was subsequently ratified by Connecticut on September 14, 1920, (and that State reaffirmed on September 21, 1920); Vermont, February 8, 1921; Delaware, March 6, 1923, (after having rejected it on June 2, 1920); Maryland, March 29, 1941, (after having rejected it on February 24, 1920, ratification certified on February 25, 1958); Virginia, February 21, 1952, (after having rejected it on February 12, 1920); Alabama, September 8, 1953, (after having rejected it on September 22, 1919); Florida,, May 13, 1969; South Carolina, July 1, 1969, (after having rejected it on January 28, 1920, ratification certified on August 22, 1973); Georgia, February 20, 1970, (after having rejected it on July 24, 1919); Louisiana, June 11, 1970, (after having rejected it on July 1, 1920); North Carolina,, May 6, 1971; Mississippi, March 22, 1984, (after having rejected it on March 29, 1920).

Article [XX.]

Section. 1.

The terms of the President and Vice President shall end at noon on the 20th day of January, and the terms of Senators and Representatives at noon on the 3d day of January, of the years in which such terms would have ended if this article had not been ratified; and the terms of their successors shall then begin.

Section. 2.

The Congress shall assemble at least once in every year, and such meeting shall begin at noon on the 3d day of January, unless they shall by law appoint a different day.

Section. 3.

If, at the time fixed for the beginning of the term of the President, the President elect shall have died, the Vice President elect shall become President. If a President shall not have been chosen before the time fixed for the beginning of his term, or if the President elect shall have failed to qualify, then the Vice President elect shall act as President until a President shall have qualified; and the Congress may by law provide for the case wherein neither a President elect nor a Vice President elect shall have qualified, declaring who shall then act as President, or the manner in which one who is to act shall be selected, and such person shall act accordingly until a President or Vice President shall have qualified.

Section. 4.

The Congress may by law provide for the case of the death of any of the persons from whom the House of Representatives may choose a President whenever the right of choice shall have devolved upon them, and for the case of the death of any of the persons from whom the Senate may choose a Vice President whenever the right of choice shall have devolved upon them.

Section. 5.

Sections 1, and 2, shall take effect on the 15th day of October following the ratification of this article.

Section. 6.

This article shall be inoperative unless it shall have been ratified as an amendment to the Constitution by the legislatures of three-fourths of the several States within seven years from the date of its submission.

Proposal and Ratification

The Twentieth Amendment to the Constitution was proposed to the legislatures of the several states by the Seventy-Second Congress, on the 2d day of March, 1932, and was declared, in a proclamation by the Secretary of State, dated on the 6th day of February, 1933, to have been ratified by the legislatures of 36, of the 48, States. The dates of ratification were: Virginia, March 4, 1932; New York, March 11, 1932; Mississippi, March 16, 1932; Arkansas, March 17, 1932; Kentucky, March 17, 1932; New Jersey, March 21, 1932; South

Carolina, March 25, 1932; Michigan, March 31, 1932; Maine, April 1, 1932; Rhode Island, April 14, 1932; Illinois, April 21, 1932; Louisiana, June 22, 1932; West Virginia, July 30, 1932; Pennsylvania, August 11, 1932; Indiana, August 15, 1932; Texas, September 7, 1932; Alabama, September 13, 1932; California, January 4, 1933; North Carolina, January 5, 1933; North Dakota, January 9, 1933; Minnesota, January 12, 1933; Arizona, January 13, 1933; Montana, January 13, 1933; Nebraska, January 13, 1933; Oklahoma, January 13, 1933; Kansas, January 16, 1933; Oregon, January 16, 1933; Delaware, January 19, 1933; Washington, January 19, 1933; Wyoming, January 19, 1933; Iowa, January 20, 1933; South Dakota, January 20, 1933; Tennessee, January 20, 1933; Idaho, January 21, 1933; New Mexico, January 21, 1933; Georgia, January 23, 1933; Missouri, January 23, 1933; Ohio, January 23, 1933; Utah, January 23, 1933.

Ratification was completed on January 23, 1933.

The amendment was subsequently ratified by Massachusetts on January 24, 1933; Wisconsin, January 24, 1933; Colorado, January 24, 1933; Nevada, January 26, 1933; Connecticut, January 27, 1933; New Hampshire, January 31, 1933; Vermont, February 2, 1933; Maryland, March 24, 1933; Florida, April 26, 1933.

Article [XXI.]

Section. 1.

The eighteenth article of amendment to the Constitution of the United States is hereby repealed.

Section. 2.

The transportation or importation into any State, Territory, or possession of the United States for delivery or use therein of intoxicating liquors, in violation of the laws thereof, is hereby prohibited.

Section. 3.

This article shall be inoperative unless it shall have been ratified as an amendment to the Constitution by conventions in the several States, as provided in the Constitution, within seven years from the date of the submission hereof to the States by the Congress.

Proposal and Ratification

The Twenty-First amendment to the Constitution was proposed to the several states by the Seventy-Second Congress, on the 20th day of February, 1933, and was declared, in a proclamation by the Secretary of State, dated on the 5th day of December, 1933, to have been ratified by 36, of the 48, States. The dates of ratification were: Michigan, April 10, 1933; Wisconsin, April 25, 1933; Rhode Island,, May 8, 1933; Wyoming,, May 25, 1933; New Jersey, June 1, 1933; Delaware, June 24, 1933; Indiana, June 26, 1933; Massachusetts, June 26, 1933; New York, June 27, 1933; Illinois, July 10, 1933; Iowa, July 10, 1933; Connecticut, July 11, 1933; New Hampshire, July 11, 1933; California, July 24, 1933; West Virginia, July 25, 1933; Arkansas, August 1, 1933; Oregon, August 7, 1933; Alabama, August 8, 1933; Tennessee, August 11, 1933; Missouri, August 29, 1933; Arizona, September 5, 1933; Nevada, September 5, 1933; Vermont, September 23, 1933; Colorado, September 26, 1933; Washington, October 3, 1933; Minnesota, October 10, 1933; Idaho October 17, 1933; Maryland October 18, 1933; Virginia, October 25, 1933; New Mexico, November 2, 1933; Florida, November 14, 1933; Texas, November 24, 1933; Kentucky, November 27, 1933; Ohio, December 5, 1933; Pennsylvania, December 5, 1933; Utah, December 5, 1933; Maine December 6, 1933; Montana, August 6, 1934.

Ratification was completed on December 5, 1933.

Article [XXII.]

Section. 1.

No person shall be elected to the office of the President more than twice, and no person who has held the office of President, or acted as President, for more than two years of a term to which some other person was elected President shall be elected to the office of the President more than once. But this article shall not apply to any person holding the office of President when this article was proposed by the Congress, and shall not prevent any person who may be holding the office of President, or acting as President, during the term within which this article becomes operative from holding the office of President or acting as President during the remainder of such term.

Section. 2.

This article shall be inoperative unless it shall have been ratified as an amendment to the Constitution by the legislatures of three-fourths of the several states within seven years from the date of its submission to the states by the Congress.

Proposal and Ratification

The Twenty-Second Amendment to the Constitution was proposed to the states by Congress on March 21, 1947. The dates of ratification were: Maine,, March 31, 1947, Michigan, March 31, 1947, Iowa, April 1, 1947, Kansas, April 1, 1947, New Hampshire, April 1, 1947, Delaware, April 2, 1947, Illinois, April 3, 1947, Oregon, April 3, 1947, Colorado, April 12, 1947, California, April 15, 1947, New Jersey, April 15, 1947, Vermont, April 15, 1947, Ohio, April 16, 1947, Wisconsin, April 16, 1947, Pennsylvania, April 29, 1947, Connecticut, May 21, 1947, Missouri, May 22, 1947, Nebraska, May 23, 1947, Virginia, January 28, 1948, Mississippi, February 12, 1948, New York, March 9, 1948, South Dakota, January 21, 1949, North Dakota, February 25, 1949, Louisiana, May 17, 1950, Montana, January 25, 1951, Indiana, January 29, 1951, Idaho, January 30, 1951, New Mexico, February 12, 1951, Wyoming, February 12, 1951, Arkansas, February 15, 1951, Georgia, February 17, 1951, Tennessee, February 20, 1951, Texas, February 22, 1951, Nevada, February 26, 1951, Utah, February 26, 1951, Minnesota, February 27, 1951, * North Carolina, February 28, 1951, South Carolina, March 13, 1951, Maryland, March 14, 1951, Florida, April 16, 1951, Alabama, May 4, 1951

Ratification was completed on February 27, 1951.

Article [XXIII.]

Section. 1.

The District constituting the seat of government of the United States shall appoint in such manner as the Congress may direct:

A number of electors of President and Vice President equal to the whole number of Senators and Representatives in Congress to which the District would be entitled if it were a state, but in no event more than the least populous state; they shall be in addition to those appointed by the states, but they shall be considered, for the purposes of the election of President and Vice President, to be electors appointed by a state; and they shall meet in the District and perform such duties as provided by the twelfth article of amendment.

Section. 2.

The Congress shall have power to enforce this article by appropriate legislation.

Proposal and Ratification

The Twenty-Third Amendment to the Constitution was proposed to the states by Congress on June 17, 1960. The dates of ratification were: Hawaii, June 23, 1960, Massachusetts, August 22, 1960, New Jersey, December 19, 1960, New York, January 17, 1961, California, January 19, 1961, Oregon, January 27, 1961, Maryland, January 30, 1961, Idaho, January 31, 1961, Maine, January 31, 1961, Minnesota, January 31, 1961, New Mexico, February 1, 1961, Nevada, February 2, 1961, Montana, February 6, 1961, South Dakota, February 6, 1961, Colorado, February 8, 1961, Washington, February 9, 1961, West Virginia, February 9, 1961, Alaska, February 10, 1961, Wyoming, February 13, 1961, Delaware, February 20, 1961, Utah, February 21, 1961, Wisconsin, February 21, 1961, Pennsylvania, February 28, 1961, Indiana, March 3, 1961, North Dakota, March 3, 1961, Tennessee, March 6, 1961, Michigan, March 8, 1961, Connecticut, March 9, 1961, Arizona, March 10, 1961, Illinois, March 14, 1961, Nebraska, March 15, 1961, Vermont, March 15, 1961, Iowa, March 16, 1961, Missouri, March 20, 1961, Oklahoma, March 21, 1961, Rhode Island, March 22, 1961, Kansas, March 29, 1961, Ohio, March 29, 1961, New Hampshire, March 30, 1961.

Ratification was completed on March 29, 1961.

Article [XXIV.]

Section. 1.

The right of citizens of the United States to vote in any primary or other election for President or Vice President, for electors for President or Vice President, or for Senator or Representative in Congress, shall not be denied or abridged by the United States or any state by reason of failure to pay any poll tax or other tax.

Section. 2.

The Congress shall have power to enforce this article by appropriate legislation.

Proposal and Ratification

The Twenty-Fourth Amendment to the Constitution was proposed to the states by Congress on August 27, 1962. The dates of ratification were: Illinois, November 14, 1962, New Jersey, December 3, 1962, Oregon, January 25, 1963, Montana, January 28, 1963, West Virginia, February 1, 1963, New York, February 4, 1963, Maryland, February 6, 1963, California, February 7,

1963, Alaska, February 11, 1963, Rhode Island, February 14, 1963, Indiana, February 19, 1963, Utah, February 20, 1963, Michigan, February 20, 1963, Colorado, February 21, 1963, Ohio, February 27, 1963, Minnesota, February 27, 1963, New Mexico, March 5, 1963, Hawaii, March 6, 1963, North Dakota, March 7, 1963, Idaho, March 8, 1963, Washington, March 14, 1963, Vermont, March 15, 1963, Nevada, March 19, 1963, Connecticut, March 20, 1963, Tennessee, March 21, 1963, Pennsylvania, March 25, 1963, Wisconsin, March 26, 1963, Kansas, March 28, 1963, Massachusetts, March 28, 1963, Nebraska, April 4, 1963, Florida, April 18, 1963, Iowa, April 24, 1963, Delaware, May 1, 1963, Missouri, May 13, 1963, New Hampshire, June 12, 1963, Kentucky, June 27, 1963, Maine, January 16, 1964, South Dakota, January 23, 1964, Virginia, February 25, 1977, North Carolina, May 3, 1989.

Ratification was completed on January 23, 1964.

Article [XXV.]

Section. 1.

In case of the removal of the President from office or of his death or resignation, the Vice President shall become President.

Section. 2.

Whenever there is a vacancy in the office of the Vice President, the President shall nominate a Vice President who shall take office upon confirmation by a majority vote of both Houses of Congress.

Section. 3.

Whenever the President transmits to the President pro tempore of the Senate and the Speaker of the House of Representatives his written declaration that he is unable to discharge the powers and duties of his office, and until he transmits to them a written declaration to the contrary, such powers and duties shall be discharged by the Vice President as Acting President.

Section. 4.

Whenever the Vice President and a majority of either the principal officers of the executive departments or of such other body as Congress may by law provide, transmit to the President pro tempore of the Senate and the Speaker of the House of Representatives their written declaration that the President is unable to discharge the powers and duties of his office, the Vice President shall immediately assume the powers and duties of the office as Acting President.

Thereafter, when the President transmits to the President pro tempore of the Senate and the Speaker of the House of Representatives his written declaration that no inability exists, he shall resume the powers and duties of his office unless the Vice President and a majority of either the principal officers of the executive department or of such other body as Congress may by law provide, transmit within four days to the President pro tempore of the Senate and the Speaker of the House of Representatives their written declaration that the President is unable to discharge the powers and duties of his office. Thereupon Congress shall decide the issue, assembling within forty-eight hours for that purpose if not in session. If the Congress, within twenty-one days after receipt of the latter written declaration, or, if Congress is not in session, within twenty-one days after Congress is required to assemble, determines by two-thirds vote of both Houses that the President is unable to discharge the powers and duties of his office, the Vice President shall continue to discharge the same as Acting President; otherwise, the President shall resume the powers and duties of his office.

Proposal and Ratification

The Twenty-Fifth Amendment to the Constitution was proposed to the states by Congress on July 6, 1965. The dates of ratification were: Nebraska, July 12, 1965, Wisconsin, July 13, 1965, Oklahoma, July 16, 1965, Massachusetts, August 9, 1965, Pennsylvania, August 18, 1965, Kentucky, September 15, 1965, Arizona, September 22, 1965, Michigan, October 5, 1965, Indiana, October 20, 1965, California, October 21, 1965, Arkansas, November 4, 1965, New Jersey, November 29, 1965, Delaware, December 7, 1965, Utah, January 17, 1966, West Virginia, January 20, 1966, Maine, January 24, 1966, Rhode Island, January 28, 1966, Colorado, February 3, 1966, New Mexico, February 3, 1966, Kansas, February 8, 1966, Vermont, February 10, 1966, Alaska, February 18, 1966, Idaho, March 2, 1966, Hawaii, March 3, 1966, Virginia, March 8, 1966, Mississippi, March 10, 1966, New York, March 14, 1966, Maryland, March 23, 1966, Missouri, March 30, 1966, New Hampshire, June 13, 1966, Louisiana, July 5, 1966, Tennessee, January 12, 1967, Wyoming, January 25, 1967, Washington, January 26, 1967, Iowa, January 26, 1967, Oregon, February 2, 1967, Minnesota, February 10, 1967, Nevada, February 10, 1967, Connecticut, February 14, 1967, Montana, February 15, 1967, South Dakota, March 6, 1967, Ohio, March 7, 1967, Alabama, March 14, 1967, North Carolina, March 22,

1967, Illinois, March 22, 1967, Texas, April 25, 1967, Florida, May 25, 1967. Ratification was completed on February 10, 1967.

Article [XXVI.]

Section. 1.

The right of citizens of the United States, who are 18, years of age or older, to vote, shall not be denied or abridged by the United States or any state on account of age.

Section. 2.

The Congress shall have the power to enforce this article by appropriate legislation.

Proposal and Ratification

The Twenty-Sixth Amendment to the Constitution was proposed to the states by Congress on March 23, 1971. The dates of ratification were: Connecticut, March 23, 1971, Delaware, March 23, 1971, Minnesota, March 23, 1971, Tennessee, March 23, 1971, Washington, March 23, 1971, Hawaii, March 24, 1971, Massachusetts, March 24, 1971, Montana, March 29, 1971, Arkansas, March 30, 1971, Idaho, March 30, 1971, Iowa, March 30, 1971, Nebraska, April 2, 1971, New Jersey, April 3, 1971, Kansas, April 7, 1971, Michigan, April 7, 1971, Alaska, April 8, 1971, Maryland, April 8, 1971, Indiana, April 8, 1971, Maine, April 9, 1971, Vermont, April 16, 1971, Louisiana, April 17, 1971, California, April 19, 1971, Colorado, April 27, 1971, Pennsylvania, April 27, 1971, Texas, April 27, 1971, South Carolina, April 28, 1971, West Virginia, April 28, 1971, New Hampshire, May 13, 1971, Arizona, May 14, 1971, Rhode Island, May 27, 1971, New York, June 2, 1971, Oregon, June 4, 1971, Missouri, June 14, 1971, Wisconsin, June 22, 1971, Illinois, June 29, 1971, Alabama, June 30, 1971, Ohio, June 30, 1971, North Carolina, July 1, 1971, Oklahoma, July 1, 1971, Virginia, July 8, 1971, Wyoming, July 8, 1971, Georgia, October 4, 1971. Ratification was completed on July 1, 1971.

Article [XXVII.]

No law varying the compensation for the services of the Senators and Representatives shall take effect until an election of Representatives shall have intervened.

Proposal and Ratification

The Twenty-Seventh Amendment to the Constitution was proposed to the states by Congress September 25, 1789. The dates of ratification were: Maryland, December 19, 1789, North Carolina, December 22, 1789, South Carolina, January 19, 1790, Delaware, January 28, 1790, Vermont, November 3, 1791, Virginia, December 15, 1791, Ohio, May 6, 1873, Wyoming, March 6, 1978, Maine, April 27, 1983, Colorado, April 22, 1984, South Dakota, February 21, 1985, New Hampshire, March 7, 1985, Arizona, April 3, 1985, Tennessee, May 23, 1985, Oklahoma, July 10, 1985, New Mexico, February 14, 1986, Indiana, February 24, 1986, Utah, February 25, 1986, Arkansas, March 6, 1987, Montana, March 17, 1987, Connecticut, May 13, 1987, Wisconsin, July 15, 1987, Georgia, February 2, 1988, West Virginia, March 10, 1988, Louisiana, July 7, 1988, Iowa, February 9, 1989, Idaho, March 23, 1989, Nevada, April 26, 1989, Alaska, May 6, 1989, Oregon, May 19, 1989, Minnesota, May 22, 1989, Texas, May 25, 1989, Kansas, April 5, 1990, Florida, May 31, 1990, North Dakota, March 25, 1991, Alabama, May 5, 1992, Missouri, May 5, 1992, Michigan, May 7, 1992, New Jersey, May 7, 1992, Illinois, May 12, 1992, California June 26, 1992.

Ratification was completed on May 7, 1992.

Notes

Introduction

1. Leick, Gwendolyn, *The Babylonians: An Introduction* (New York: Routledge, 2003), p. 54.

2. Gilson, Etienne, "Introduction," *City of God* (New York: Image Books, 1958), p. 17-18.

3. *Ibid.*, pp. 22-27.

4. Bill Gertz, *Breakdown: The Failure of American Intelligence to Defeat Global Terror* (New York: Penguin, 2002).

Chapter 1: The Rise of Empires on a Foundation of Justice

1. This is the description of Marduk on Hammurabi's monolith. It appears that Marduk, who was the Lord of Babylon after the time of Hammurabi, was attributed more exalted status in time. The *Enuma Elish*, probably written about the twelfth century B.C., is a fully developed creation story. Seven cuneiform clay tablets containing this Babylonian creation myth were found in the ruins of the library of Assyrian emperor Ashubanipal (667-626 B.C.) in Ninevah in the mid-nineteenth century. Marduk, a supernatural being, had parents who were also gods. In the sixth tablet, he created human beings to do menial tasks for the gods.

2. Anderson, Bernhard, *Understanding the Old Testament* (New Jersey: Prentice-Hall, 1966), p. 28.

3. Leick, Gwendolyn, *The Babylonians* (New York: Routledge, 2003), pp. 75-83.

4. Ibid., pp. 34-41.

5. Trevor, Albert A., *History of Ancient Civilization* (New York: Harcourt, Brace, 1936), p. 36.

6. Leick, *op. cit.,* p. 40.

7. Trevor, *op. cit.,* p. 102.

8. *Genesis* 11: 5-6.

9. Livius, Titus, *The History of Rome, Vol. I* (New York: E.P. Dutton, 1912) http://etext.lib.virginia.edu.

10. http://dsc.discovery.com/news/briefs/20030512/rome.html.

11. Livius, Titus, *The History of Rome, Vol. I* (New York: E.P. Dutton, 1912), 1.57-1.60.

12. A chronological list of events of the Roman Republic and Roman Empire is at http://www.roman-empire.net/republic/rep-index.html.

13. Gibbon, *The Decline and Fall of the Roman Empire*, ed. D. M. Low (New York: Harcourt, Brace and Company, 1960), p. 21.

14. Cicero, *De Oratore*, Loeb Classical Library No. 348 (Cambridge, MA: Harvard University Press), I.44.

15. See, "Roman Law" in *Funk and Wagnalls New Encyclopedia*, v. 22, pp. 365-366.

16. Gibbon, *op.cit.* pp. 20-21.

Chapter 2: Maintaining the Empires of Babylon and Rome

1. Gwendolyn Leick, *The Babylonians: An Introduction* (New York: Routledge, 2003) contains a concise summary of the history and life of Babylon from its ancient roots to its disappearance into the sands.

2. W.W. Davies, *The Codes of Hammurabi and Moses* (Cincinnati: Jennings and Graham, 1905), pp. 7-15. Bernhard W. Anderson, *Understanding the Old Testament* (New Jersey: Prentice Hall, 1966), pp. 96-97.

3. Bernhard W. Anderson, *Understanding the Old Testament* (New Jersey: Prentice Hall, 1966), pp. 357-427.

4. Ali Sina, Faith Freedom International, http://rationalthinking.humani sts.net/origin_of_god.htm).

5. Berhard W. Anderson, *op. cit.*, cites a late Babylonian tax receipt of Murashu and Sons which shows that Jews of Babylon had controlling interest in the business, p. 376.

6. http://encarta.msn.com/encyclopedia_1741502785/Roman_Empire. html#s49.

7. Gibbon, *op. cit.*, pp. 56 ff.

8. Charles Norris Cochrane, *Christianity and Classical Culture* (New York: Oxford University Press, 1980), p. 153.

9. Gibbon, *op. cit.*, pp. 250 ff.

10. Funk and Wagnall's, *New Standard Encyclopedia* (New York: 1931), Vol. XXI, p. 266.

11. Cited by Cochrane, *op. cit.*, p. 155.

12. Gibbon, *op. cit.*, p. 423.

Chapter 3: Thoughts After the Roman Empire: Love, Power, and Justice

1. Leonel L. Mitchell, *The Meaning of Ritual* (New York: Paulist Press, 1977), pp. 11-13. This was based on research by Johanenes Maringer, *The Gods of Prehistoric Man* (New York: A. A. Knopf, 1960).

2. Arnold van Gennep, *The Rites of Passage* (Chicago: University of Chicago Press, 1960); Victor Turner, *Dramas, Fields, Metaphors* (Ithaca: Cornell University Press, 1974), pp. 231-233, and *The Ritual Process* (Chicgo: Aldine, 1969) pp. 94-95.

3. Gordon L. Anderson, "Rites of Passage for World Peace," *Peace Research*, August, 1982.

4. Robert E. Goodin, "Rites of Rulers," *The British Journal of Sociology*, September 1978, pp. 281-289.

5. Cited in W. T. Jones, *Masters of Political Thought*, vol. II (Boston: Houghton Mifflin, 1949), pp. 34-35.

6. Nicolo Machiavelli, *Discourses*, I, 11-14. See Jones, *op. cit*, pp. 22-52.

7. Thomas Hobbes, *Leviathan,* ed. Michael Oakeshott (New York: Collier Books, 1962), Part I, chapters 10-13.

8. John Locke, *Of Civil Government,* in Jones, *op. cit.,* pp. 164-165.

9. John Locke, *Of Civil Government,* VI, in Jones, *op. cit.,* pp. 159-161.

10. Montesquieu, *Spirit of the Laws,* I, 2., in Jones, *op. cit.,* p. 227.

11. *Ibid.,* in Jones, *op. cit.,* p. 245-247.

12. Paul Tillich, *Love, Power, and Justice* (New York: Oxford University Press, 1980, first edition 1954), p. 77.

13. Reinhold Niebuhr, *Moral Man and Immoral Society* (New York: Scribner's, 1960), p. 200.

14. *Ibid., p. 9.*

15. Reinhold Niebuhr, *Faith and Politics,* ed. Ronald H. Stone (New York: George Braziller, 1968), p. 103.

16. Reinhold Niebuhr, *The Nature and Destiny of Man* (New York: Scribner's, 1964), vol. II, p. 246.

Chapter 4: God, Religion, and the State

1. William G. McLoughlin, *Isaac Backus and the American Pietistic Tradition* (Boston: Little, Brown, 1967), p. 127.

2. "Epigenesis" refers to a form of integration by layering over previous layers with a new layer. It is typically used in reference to rock layers in geology, or in genetics. However, it has been used in the theory of political integra-

tion, and it is in this sense the term is used. With reference to the concept of God, the more recent conception includes or covers the more limited conceptions in the previous layer of history. See: Amitai Etzioni, "The Epigenesis of Political Communities at the International Level," in James N. Rosenau, ed., International Politics and Foreign Policy (New York: The Free Press, 1969), pp. 346ff.

3. Bernhard W. Anderson, *Understanding the Old Testament,* pp. 28-29.

4. Bernhard W. Anderson, *Understanding the Old Testament,* p. 40. Anderson refers to a hypothesis developed by Karl Budde, *The Religion of Israel in Exile* (New York:1899), and defended by H.H. Rowley, From *Joseph to Joshua.* This interpretation was criticized by T. J. Meek, *Hebrew Origins,* and Martin Buber, *The Prophetic Faith.*

5. W. W. Davies, *The Codes of Hammurabi and Moses* (New York: Eaton and Mains, 1905), pp. 7-9.

6. Sigmund Mowinckel, "Psalms at the Enthronement Festival of Yahweh," *The Psalms in Israel's Worship* (Nashville: Abingdon, 1979), chapter 5. Anderson refers to the Psalms as "the hymnbook of the Second Temple," *op. cit.,* p. 465.

7. Matthew 6:9.

8. John 1:1.

9. "For God so loved the world, that he gave his only begotten Son, that whosoever believeth in him should not perish, but have everlasting life" (John 3:16).

10. Augustine, *The City of God,* p. 116.

11. For example, Luke 1:32, "He shall be great, and shall be called the Son of the Highest: and the Lord God shall give unto him the throne of his father David."

12. Matthew 1:1-16.

13. For example, Richard Leigh, Henry Lincoln, and Michael Baigent, *Holy Blood, Holy Grail* (New York: Dell, 1983); or Jean-Yves Leloup, ed., *The Gospel of Mary Magdalene* (Rochester, VT: Inner Traditions, 2002).

14. Luke 3:23-38.

15. Owen Chadwick, *The Reformation* (New York: Penguin Books, 1977), pp. 190-191.

16. Conrad Cherry, ed., *God's New Israel: Religious Interpretations of American Destiny* (New York: Prentice Hall, 1971).

17. John Cotton, *An Exposition of the Thirteenth Chapter of the Revelation* (London, 1656), p. 72. Cited by H. Richard Niebuhr, The Kingdom of God in America (New York: Harper and Row, 1959), p. 76.

18. Roger Williams, *The Bloudy Tenant,* pp. 219 f. Cited by Niebuhr, *ibid.,* p. 77.

19. For example, in 1670, the Aberdeen Lodge had thirty-nine "ac-

cepted" members while only ten remained "operative" masons, http://www.mystae.com/restricted/streams/masons/mhistory.html.

20. Sidney Hayden, *Washington and his Masonic Compeers* (New York: Masonic Publishing, 1866), p. 236.

21. See, Melvin M. Johnson, *The Beginnings of Freemasonry in America* (New York: George H. Doran, 1924) and Kendrick, Lamberton, and Sachse, *Bi-Centenary of the Birth of the Right Worshipful Past Grand Master, Brother Benjamin Franklin* (Lancaster, PA: New Era Printing, 1906).

22. Alfred Owen Aldridge, *Benjamin Franklin and Nature's God* (Durham, NC: Duke University Press, 1967), p. 145.

23. Sidney E. Mead, *The Lively Experiment: The Shaping of Christianity in America* (New York: Harper and Row, 1976), p. 41.

24. Bernard Fay, *Revolution and Freemasonry, 1680-1800*, p. 231. The text can be found on the following website: http://odur.let.rug.nl/~usa/D/1751-1775/7yearswar/albany.htm.

25. The earliest recorded sermon for Masons in Christ Church was "Brotherly Love Recommended," delivered by Rev. Charles Brockwell, on Dec. 27, 1749.

26. Cushing Strout, *The New Heavens and the New Earth* (New York: Harper and Row, 1974), p. 59.

27. Bernard Fay, *Revolution and Freemasonry, 1680-1800*, and Madison C. Peters, *Masons as Makers of America* (Brooklyn, New York: The Patriotic League, 1917).

28. Alan Heimert, *Religion and the American Mind: From the Great Awakening to the Revolution* (Cambridge, MA: Harvard University Press, 1968).

29. For example, Norman Cousins wrote, "No man's words had a greater impact on the people of the American colonies in arousing them to the call of national independence," *In God We Trust: The Religious Beliefs and Ideas of the Founding Fathers* (New York: Harper Bros., 1958), p. 390.

30. Alan Heimert, *op. cit.*

31. As late as July 21, 1775, after the delegates from several colonies had met in Philadelphia on May 10, Benjamin Franklin was still trying to organize a "Federation of Colonies." This is the date on the draft for the Articles of Confederation he submitted.

32. Robert T. Handy, *A History of the Churches in the United States and Canada,* (New York: Oxford University Press, 1976).

33. Jonathan Edwards referred to America as a "city upon a hill," reviving the Puritan notion that the Kingdom of God could be planted in America and spread as an example to England and the rest of the world, *Thoughts Concerning the Present Revival of Religion,* 1742. Printed in *The Works of President Edwards,* 4 vols. (New York: 1868), 314-315.

34. H. Richard Niebuhr, *The Kingdom of God in America* (New York:

Harper & Row, 1959), p. 103.

35. Edmund Burke's two speeches were titled, *American Taxation* (1774) and *Conciliation with America* (1775).

36. Sidney E. Mead, *The Lively Experiment: The Shaping of Christianity in America* (New York: Harper and Row, 1976), pp. 40-41.

37. Eugen Lennhoff, *The Freemasons* (New York: Oxford University Press, 1934), p. 76.

38. Catherine L. Albanese, *Sons of the Fathers: The Civil Religion of the American Revolution* (Philadelphia: Temple University Press, 1977).

Chapter 5: The Formation of the United States

1. Agreed to by Congress November 15, 1777. In force after ratification by Maryland, March 1, 1781 This was text was obtained from The Avalon Project at Yale Law School, http://www.yale.edu/lawweb/avalon/artconf.htm.

2. Peter Marshall and David Manuel, *The Light and the Glory* (Grand Rapids, MI: Baker Book House, 1977), p. 340.

3. W. B. Allen, ed., *George Washington: A Collection,* Indianapolis: Liberty Classics, 1988), pp. 359-364.

4. *Ibid.,* pp. 365-369.

5. Major William Jackson from South Carolina was the official Secretary of the Convention, but his notes were not as good as those of several of the delegates. Madison's notes are most often cited. See Catherine Drinker Bowen, *Miracle at Philadelphia* (Boston: Little, Brown, 1986), pp. 30-31.

6. Allen, *op. cit.,* p. 369.

7. Cited by Norman Cousins, *In God We Trust: The Religious Beliefs and Ideas of the Founding Fathers* (New York: Harper Bros., 1958), pp. 17-18.

8. *Ibid.* pp. 18-19. Franklin went on to tell Stiles that he thought Jesus' moral teachings were very good, but that many dogmas based on them, or claims to Jesus' divinity seemed dubious. A bit more of Franklin's view can be gleaned from his review of Thomas Paine's *Age of Reason* in 1785. He recommended that Paine burn the manuscript because, while it defended general religion, it undermined particular religion, which was necessary for childrearing and maintenance of public order. He concluded warning, "If men are so wicked with religion, what would they be if without it?"

9. Thomas Jefferson, "Letter to James Madison, December 20, 1787," in *The Papers of Thomas Jefferson,* ed. Julian P. Boyd (Princeton: Princeton University Press, 1958), Vol. 12, p. 442.

10. Edward Banfield, ed. *Civility and Citizenship* (New York: Paragon House, 1992), p. x.

11. *Ibid.,* xi.

12. Aristotle, *The Politics,* Book VI, Chapter 4, translated by Carnes Lord (Chicago: University of Chicago Press, 1984), pp. 186-188.

13. Thomas Jefferson, "Letter to James Madison, December 20, 1787," in *The Papers of Thomas Jefferson,* ed. Julian P. Boyd (Princeton: Princeton University Press, 1958), Vol. 12, p. 442.

Chapter 6: Checks and Balances on Political Power

1. Greg Palast, *The Best Democracy Money Can Buy* (New York: Penguin Putnam, 2003).

2. Charles H. Sheldon, *The Supreme Court: Politicians in Robes* (London: Glencoe Press, 1970), p. xxi.

3. Robert Bork, *The Tempting of America* (New York: The Free Press, 1990), p. 114.

4. *Ibid.,* p. 115.

5. Kaus, Mickey. "A World Without Roe?" *Newsweek* (14 Sept. 1987), p. 33. Cited by David W. Croft, "Does the Supreme Court Abuse Its Power?" (http://www.alumni.caltech.edu/~croft/archives/academic/court.html).

6. The *Miranda* decision held that suspects had to be informed of their rights before questioning or their statements were inadmissible. It was designed to prevent coerced testimony or testimony given under duress from being used as evidence to convict a suspect. The legislation (18 U.S.C Sec. 3501) would have made voluntary statements admissible even if the suspect had not been "Mirandized."

7. http://supct.law.cornell.edu/supct/html/99-5525.ZD.html.

8. From the statement by James Madison, June 26, 1787: "In order to judge of the form to be given to this institution, it will be proper to take a view of the ends to be served by it. These were first to protect the people agst. their rulers: secondly to protect the people agst. the transient impressions into which they themselves might be led. A people deliberating in a temperate moment, and with the experience of other nations before them, on the plan of Govt. most likely to secure their happiness, would first be aware, that those chargd. with the public happiness, might betray their trust. An obvious precaution agst. this danger wd. be to divide the trust between different bodies of men, who might watch & check each other." *The Debates in the Federal Convention of 1787 reported by James Madison: June 26,* http://www.yale.edu/lawweb/avalon/debates/626.htm.

9. Alexander M. Bickel, *The Least Dangerous Branch: The Supreme Court at the Bar of Politics* (New Haven: Yale University Press, 1986), xi.

10. *The Debates in the Federal Convention of 1787 reported by James Madison: June 26, op. cit.*

11. Cited from the website of the National Taxpayers Union: http://www.ntu.org/main/press.php?PressID=343.

12. It was ratified two centuries later see, http://caselaw.lp.findlaw.com/data/constitution/amendment27/.

13. Sean M. Theriault, *Paying an Electoral Price for Supporting a Congressional Pay Raise,* http://www.la.utexas.edu/~seant/salary.doc.

14. http://www.safehaven.com/showarticle.cfm?id=608&pv=1.

15. Katherine M. Skiba, *Milwaukee Journal Sentinel,* May 27, 2001. http://www.jsonline.com/news/nat/may01/spend27052601.asp.

16. U.S. Bureau of the Census, *Statistical Abstract of the United States, 1999 Edition,* (Washington, DC: GPO, 1999), Table # 567.

17. Michael Voslensky, *Nomenklatura: The Soviet Ruling Class, An Insider's Report,* trans. Eric Mosbacher (New York: Doubleday, 1984).

18. Public Law 108-7, 108th Congress, http://frwebgate.access.gpo.gov/cgi-bin/useftp.cgi?IPaddress=162.140.64.21&filename=publ007.108&directory=/diskb/wais/data/108_cong_public_laws.

19. Congressional Record: January 22, 2004 (Senate), [Page S129-S157].

20. Energy Committee Chairman Sen. Pete Domenici (R-N.M.) said that the bill's opponents have made future blackouts, like the kind the Northeast suffered over the summer of 2003, more likely. "The blackouts in America will remain alive and possible because we will have thrown out the window the reliability standards that are in this bill because some want to make the case on an issue like MTBE or the like," said Domenici. "If you like blackouts, then you vote to kill this bill," *CNN Money* Online Magazine, http://money.cnn.com/2003/11/21/news/economy/energybill/.

21. *Public Citizen,* http://www.citizen.org/cmep/energy_enviro_nuclear/electricity/energybill/2003/articles.cfm?ID=10726.

22. Gordon L. Anderson, "Outsourcing America," *The World and I,* January, 2004, pp. 38-43.

23. John Fitzgerald Molloy, *The Fraternity: Lawyers and Judges in Collusion* (St. Paul: Paragon House, 2004).

24. *Ibid.,* Chapter 12.

Chapter 7: Regulating Financial Power

1. Thom Hartman, "America's First Globalization Protest: The Boston Tea Party," (http://www.crforum.com/teaparty.shtml).

2. Several citations are documented by Thom Hartmann in "America's First Anti-Globalization Protest," http://www.crforum.com/teaparty.shtml, and "Jefferson's Dream," http://www.crforum.com/jefferson.shtml.

3. Thomas Jefferson, "To James Madison, Paris Dec. 20. 1787" in Merrill

D. Peterson, ed., *The Portable Thomas Jefferson* (New York: Penguin, 1975), p. 429.

4. Thomas Jefferson, "Letter to James Madison, 20 December, 1787," in *The Papers of Thomas Jefferson,* ed. Julian P. Boyd (Princeton: Princeton University Press, 1958), Vol. 12, p. 442.

5. Marvin Meyers, ed., *The Mind of the Founder: Sources of the Political Thought of James Madison* (Hanover, NH: University Press of New England, 1981), pp. 159-160.

6. James Madison, *National Gazette* article on 3 March 1792. Cited by Thom Hartman in "Jefferson's Dream," *op. cit.*

7. Robert L. Hetzel, *The Relevance of Adam Smith* (http://www.rich.frb.org/pubs/ relevance/). A quote from Smith, The pretence that corporations are necessary to the better government of the trade is without foundation.' http://www.newint.org/issue347/history.htm

8. "The Founding of the Fed," Federal Reserve Bank of New York website (http://www.ny.frb.org/aboutthefed/history_article.html)

9. Meyers, *op. cit.,* pp. 389-90.

10. "Thomas Jefferson to George Logan, 1816," *The Writings of Thomas Jefferson,* Paul Leicester Ford, ed., 10 Vols., (New York, 1892-99), vol 10, p. 69.

11. Thom Hartmann, *Unequal Protection: The Rise of Corporate Dominance and the Theft of Human Rights* (New York: Rodale, 2002), p. 75.

12. *Ibid.,* p. 83.

13. *Ibid.,* pp. 84-87.

14. "The Founding of the Fed," *op. cit.*

15. Italics mine.

16. Richard L. Grossman and Frank T. Adams, *Taking Care of Business: Citizenship and the Charter of Incorporation* (Cambridge, MA: Charter, Ink., 1993). Cited by David T. Radcliffe (http://www.ratical.org/corporations/TCoBeij.html).

17. Two discussions of this topic are referred to the reader: Thom Hartmann, "End Corporate Personhood," *Unequal Protection: The Rise of Corporate Dominance and the Theft of Human Rights* (New York: Rodale, 2002), pp. 251-257, and Marjorie Kelly, "Corporations Are Not Persons," *The Divine Right of Capital: Dethroning the Corporate Aristocracy* (San Francisco: Berrett-Koehler, 2001), pp. 159 ff.

18. "Anti-trust Law," in *West's Encyclopedia of American Law* (http://iris.nyit.edu/~shartman/mba0101/trust.htm).

19. Ron Chernow, House *of Morgan: An American Banking Dynasty and the Rise of Modern Finance* (New York: Grove Press, 2001).

20. For example, "How the Federal Reserve Caused the Depression" (http://www.perfecteconomy.com/principal---federal-reserve-system.html);   or, "Secrets of the Federal Reserve" (http://www.apfn.org/apfn/reserve.htm).

21. See Lawrence J. Broz, *The International Origins of the Federal Reserve System* (Ithaca, New York: Cornell University Press, 1997).

22. Silvano A. Wueschner, *Charting Twentieth-Century Monetary Policy: Herbert Hoover and Benjamin Strong, 1917-1927* (Westport, CT: Greenwood Press, 1999).

23. For example, Milton Friedman and Anna Schwartz, *A Monetary History of the United States, 1867-1960* (New Jersey: Princeton University Press, 1963); Alan Meltzer, *A History of the Federal Reserve, Vol. 1: 1913-1951* (Chicago: University of Chicago Press, 2003); Elmus Wicker, *The Banking Panics of the Great Depression* (New York: Cambridge University Press, 1996).

24. This is from the 2003 Minnesota Legislative Review prepared by the Minnesota Legislative evaluation assembly: "A case in point: The State Department omnibus bill had a line, of which many legislators were unaware, providing payment of $369,000 of taxpayers' money to pay the lawyers of the four plaintiffs who brought action before the Supreme Court appointed Panel which determined the new congressional and legislative districts of 2002. This was for time allegedly spent by the lawyers in preparing redistricting proposals to present to the Panel, though some of the proposals they presented had been drawn by regular legislative and gubernatorial employees who had been routinely and fully paid for their time and effort out of funds duly appropriated for this purpose in the 2001 and 2002 budgets.

These lawyers, and the factions they represented, like the previous legislature itself, did not try to agree on a plan they wanted the Panel to proclaim. None of their proposals were adopted by the Panel. However, they *could* agree on two things: 1) to get their fellow lawyers to petition the Panel to order taxpayer-paid compensation for themselves, and 2) how to divide the booty. A cuddly arrangement; only it reeks! The four plaintiffs the Panel ordered paid are the state Republican party, the state DFL party, then-Senator Moe and the five then-DFL Congressmen, and Jesse Ventura. The Secretary of State would not pay, since no money was appropriated, so unnamed legislators slipped into a conference committee omnibus bill the $369,000 appropriation."

25. See, Roger Meiners and Ryan Amacher, eds., *Federal Support of Higher Education* (New York: Paragon House, 1987).

26. Adam Smith was critical of the influences of concentrated and large corporations as interfering with the free market. In the passage below, he could be describing the bankers' rationale for asking American politicians to repeal the Glass-Steagall Act of 1933:

> Merchants and master manufacturers are...the two classes of people who commonly employ the largest capital, and who by their wealth draw to themselves the greatest share of the public

consideration. As during their whole lives they are engaged in plans and projects, they have frequently more acuteness of understanding than the greater part of country gentlemen. As their thoughts, however, are commonly exercised rather about the interest of their own particular branch of business, than about that of the society, their judgment, even when given with the greatest candour (which it has not been upon every occasion) is much more to be depended upon with regard to the former of those two objects than with regard to the latter. Their superiority over the country gentleman is not so much in their knowledge of the public interest, as in their having a better knowledge of their own interest than he has of his. It is by this superior knowledge of their own interest that they have frequently imposed upon his generosity, and persuaded him to give up both his own interest and that of the public, from a very simple but honest conviction that their interest, and not his, was the interest of the public. The interest of the dealers, however, in any particular branch of trade or manufactures, is always in some respects different from, and even opposite to, that of the public. To widen the market and to narrow the competition, is always the interest of the dealers. To widen the market may frequently be agreeable enough to the interest of the public; but to narrow the competition must always be against it, and can serve only to enable the dealers, by raising their profits above what they naturally would be, to levy, for their own benefit, an absurd tax upon the rest of their fellow-citizens. The proposal of any new law or regulation of commerce which comes from this order ought always to be listened to with great precaution, and ought never to be adopted till after having been long and carefully examined, not only with the most scrupulous, but with the most suspicious attention. It comes from an order of men whose interest is never exactly the same with that of the public, who have generally an interest to deceive and even to oppress the public, and who accordingly have, upon many occasions, both deceived and oppressed it.

Adam Smith, *The Wealth of Nations,* Book I, (Everyman's Library, Sixth Printing, 1991), pp. 87-88, 231-232. Cited by Anup Shah, "The Rise of Corporations," (http://www.globalissues.org/TradeRelated/Corporations/Rise.asp).

Chapter 8: Universal Education

1. Dr. Benjamin Rush, From *A Plan for the Establishment of Public Schools and the Diffusion of Knowledge in Pennsylvania; to Which Are Added, Thoughts upon the Mode of Education Proper in a Republic.* Addressed to the Legislature and Citizens of the State. (Philadelphia: Thomas Dobson, 1786). http://www.schoolchoices.org/roo/rush.htm.

2. H. Shelton Smith, Robert T. Handy, and Lefferts A. Loetscher, *American Christianity: An Historical Interpretation with Representative Documents*, Vol. II, pp. 255 ff.

3. http://www.hermes-press.com/education_index.htm#newlaw.

4. George Counts most significant writings include *The Principles of Education* (1924) with J. Crosby Chapman and "Dare the School Build a New Social Order?" (1932).

5. Charlotte Thomson Iserbyt, *The Deliberate Dumbing Down of America* (Bath, ME: 3D Research Co., 2000).

6. http://www.law.umkc.edu/faculty/projects/ftrials/scopes/evolut.htm.

7. Geoffrey Partington, "Families and Education: Reform from Above or Below?" in Ralph Segalman, ed., *Reclaiming the Family* (St. Paul: Paragon House, 1998), p. 135.

8. Milton Friedman, "Public Schools: Make Them Private," *Washington Post*, Feb. 19, 1995. Reprinted at http://www.cato.org/pubs/briefs/bp-023.html.

9. E. D. Hirsch, Jr., *Cultural Literacy: What Every American Needs to Know* (New York: Vintage, 1988).

10. E. D. Hirsch, Jr., *The Schools We Need and Why We Don't Have Them* (New York: Anchor, 1999).

Chapter 9: Social Welfare

1. See Harold Jones, *Personal Character and National Destiny* (St. Paul, Paragon House, 2002).

2. See R. H. Tawney, *Religion and the Rise of Capitalism* (New York, Harcourt, Brace and World, 1926).

3. Matthew 26:11.

4. H. Shelton Smith, Robert T. Handy, and Lefferts A. Loetscher, *American Christianity: An Historical Interpretation with Representative Documents* (New York: Charles Scribner's Sons), Vol. 1, pp. 539-542.

5. David J. Rothman, *The Discovery of the Asylum: Social Order and Disorder in the New Republic* (Boston: Little, Brown, 1971).

6. Alfred North Whitehead, *Essays in Science and Philosophy* (NY, 1947), p. 153.

7. H. Shelton Smith, Robert T. Handy, and Lefferts A. Loetscher, *op. cit.,*

vol. 2, pp. 10-19.

8. Emery B. Gibbs, "The Anti-Masonic Movement," in *Proceedings of the Grand Lodge of Massachusetts, 1917* (Cambridge: Caustic-Claflin, 1918) p. 497.

9. Lenhoff, *op. cit.*, p. 135.

10. Ingolf Vogeler, *Reconstruction: 1860-1880,* http://www.uwec.edu/geography/Ivogeler/w188/south/reconst.htm, compiled from Eric Foner, *Reconstruction: America's Unfinished Revolution, 1963-1877* (New York: Harper and Rows, 1980; W.E.B. Du Bois, *Black Reconstruction in America, 1860-1880* (New York: Atheneum, 1983); and, Charles Joyner, *Down by the Riverside: A South Carolina Slave Community* (Chicago: University of Chicago, 1984).

11. Robert T. Handy, ed., *The Social Gospel in America: Gladden, Ely and Rauschenbusch* (New York: Oxford University Press, 1966), p. 7.

12. *Ibid.,* p. 179.

13. See, for example, http://www.usatoday.com/money/industries/health/2003-01-08-workers-strikes_x.htm. This article states that 2003 health insurance premiums rose 15 percent over 2002, a rate more than 10 percent higher than inflation.

14. Guenter B. Risse, *Mending Bodies, Saving Souls: A History of Hospitals* (New York: Oxford University Press, 1999).

15. Dr. Tom Saving, Social Security Trustee, Department of Economics, Texas A&M University and National Center for Policy Analysis. Presentation posted at http://www.ncpa.org/prs/tst/andyrettenmaier.pdf.

Chapter 10: The United States and the World

1. William B. Allen, ed., *George Washington: A Collection* (Indianapolis, IN: Liberty Fund, 1988), pp. 522ff.

2. http://www.econlib.org/library/Taussig/tsgEnc1.html.

3. Alfred T. Mahan, "The United States Looking Outward," *Atlantic Monthly,* LXVI (December, 1890), 816-24.

4. http://students.northseattle.edu/~mnutti/seas/amfilcubwar.html

5. http://alohaquest.com/arbitration/

6. Jonathan Zasloff, "Law and the Shaping of American Foreign Policy: The Twenty Years' Crisis" Los Angeles, CA: UCLA School of Law Research Paper No. 3-06, 2003. http://ssrn.com/abstract=395962.

7. *Ibid.,* pp. 7-8.

8. Carnegie sold his steel empire to financiers pulled together by J. P. Morgan for $250 million. The deal was secretly pulled together by Charles M. Schwab, http://en.wikipedia.org/wiki/Andrew_Carnegie.

9. Elias B. Sanford, *Federal Council of Churches of Christ in America* (New

York: Revell Press, 1909), pp. 140-141.

10. Charles S. MacFarland, ed., *Church Unity at Work* (New York: Federal Council of Churches, 1913), pp. 198-202.

11. Samuel McCrea Cavert, ed., *Twenty Years of Church Federation* (New York: Federal Council of Churches, 1929, p. 89.

12. Reinhold Niebuhr, "Religion's Limitations," *The World Tomorrow,* March 1920, p. 78.

13. Robert Moats Miller, *American Protestantism and Social Issues, 1919-1939* (Chapel Hill, NC: University of North Carolina Press, 1958), pp. 330ff.

14. MacFarland, *op. cit.,* p. 163.

15. Ron Chernow, *The House of Morgan* (New York: Grove Press, 2001), p. 203.

16. *Ibid.,* p. 283.

1.7 *Ibid.,* p, 236.

18. *Ibid.,* p. 310.

19. Paul Kennedy, *The Rise and Fall of the Great Powers* (New York: Vintage Books, 1989), p. 328.

20. *Ibid.,* p. 330.

21. J. M. Keynes, *The Economic Consequences of Peace,* pp. 211. Cited by E. H. Carr, *The Conditions of Peace* (New York: MacMillan, 1942), p. 60.

22. Zasloff, *op. cit.,* pp. 21ff.

23. Cited by Zasloff, *op. cit.,* p. 27.

24. Kennedy, *op. cit.,* p. 328.

25. Hans J. Morgenthau, *Politics Among Nations* (New York: Alfred A. Knopf, 1948).

26. Otto Frederick Nolde, *Free and Equal: Human Rights in Ecumenical Perspective* (Geneva: World Council of Churches, 1968), pp. 20-21. See also, James T. Shotwell, *Autobiography* (Indianapolis: Bobbs-Merrill, 1961).

27. For a good overview see Patrick Hayden, *The Philosophy of Human Rights* (St. Paul: Paragon House, 2001).

28. William I. Robison, *A Theory of Global Capitalism: Production, Class and State in a Transnational World* (Baltimore: Johns Hopkins University Press, 2004).

29. James R. Mancham, *War on America Seen from the Indian Ocean* (St. Paul: Paragon House, 2002).

Selected Bibliography

Albanese, Catherine L., *Sons of the Fathers: The Civil Religion of the American Revolution* (Philadelphia: Temple University Press, 1977).

Aldridge, Alfred Owen, *Benjamin Franklin and Nature's God* (Durham, NC: Duke University Press, 1967).

Allen, W. B., ed., *George Washington: A Collection* (Indianapolis: Liberty Classics, 1988).

Anderson, Bernhard, *Understanding the Old Testament* (New Jersey: Prentice-Hall, 1966).

Aristotle, *The Politics,* ed. T.A. Sinclair (Middlesex, UK: Penguin Books, 1962).

Augustine, *City of God* (New York: Image Books, 1958).

Banfield, Edward, ed., *Civility and Citizenship* (New York: Paragon House, 1992).

Bickel, Alexander M., *The Least Dangerous Branch: The Supreme Court at the Bar of Politics* (New Haven: Yale University Press, 1986).

Boardman, John, Jasper Griffin, and Oswyn Murray, *The Oxford History of the Roman World* (New York: Oxford University Press, 1986).

Bork, Robert H., *The Tempting of America: The Political Seduction of the Law* (New York: The Free Press, 1990).

Boyd, Julian P., ed., *The Papers of Thomas Jefferson,* (Princeton, NJ: Princeton University Press, 1958).

Broz, Lawrence J., *The International Origins of the Federal Reserve System* (Ithaca, NY: Cornell University Press, 1997).

Carr, E. H., *The Conditions of Peace* (New York: MacMillan, 1942).

Cavert, Samuel McCrea, ed., *Twenty Years of Church Federation* (New York: Federal Council of Churches, 1929).

Cicero, *De Oratore,* Loeb Classical Library No. 348 (Cambridge, MA: Harvard University Press).

Chadwick, Owen, *The Reformation* (New York: Penguin Books, 1977).

Chernow, Ron, *House of Morgan: An American Banking Dynasty and the Rise of Modern Finance* (New York: Grove Press, 2001).

Cherry, Conrad, ed., *God's New Israel: Religious Interpretations of American Destiny* (New York: Prentice Hall, 1971).

Cochrane, Charles Norris, *Christianity and Classical Culture* (New York: Oxford University Press, 1980).

Cousins, Norman, *In God We Trust: The Religious Beliefs and Ideas of the Founding Fathers* (New York: Harper Bros., 1958).

Davies, W. W., *The Codes of Hammurabi and Moses* (Cincinnati: Jennings and Graham, 1905).

Du Bois, W. E. B., *Black Reconstruction in America, 1860-1880* (New York: Atheneum, 1983).

Fay, Bernard, *Revolution and Freemasonry, 1680-1800* (Boston: Little, Brown, 1935).

Foner, Eric, *Reconstruction: America's Unfinished Revolution, 1963-1877* (New York: Harper and Row, 1988).

Friedman, Milton, and Schwartz, Anna, *A Monetary History of the United States, 1867-1960* (Princeton, NJ: Princeton University Press, 1963).

Gertz, Bill, *Breakdown: The Failure of American Intelligence to Defeat Global Terror* (New York: Penguin, 2002).

Gibbon, Edward, *The Decline and Fall of the Roman Empire* (NY; Harcourt, Brace, 1960).

Goodin, Robert E., "Rites of Rulers," *The British Journal of Sociology,* September 1978.

Handy, Robert T., *A History of the Churches in the United States and Canada,* (New York: Oxford University Press, 1976).

Handy, Robert T., ed., *The Social Gospel in America: Gladden, Ely and Rauschenbusch* (New York: Oxford University Press, 1966).

Hartmann, Thom, *Unequal Protection: The Rise of Corporate Dominance and the Theft of Human Rights* (Rodale Press, 2002).

Heimert, Alan, *Religion and the American Mind: From the Great Awakening to the Revolution* (Cambridge, MA: Harvard University Press, 1968).

Hirsch, E. D., Jr., *Cultural Literacy: What Every American Needs to Know* (New York: Vintage, 1988).

Hirsch, E. D., Jr., *The Schools We Need and Why We Don't Have Them* (New York: Anchor, 1999).

Hobbes, Thomas, *Leviathan* (New York: Collier, 1962).

Jones, Harold, *Personal Character and National Destiny,* St. Paul, Paragon House, 2002.

Jones, W. T., *Masters of Political Thought,* (Boston: Houghton Mifflin, 1949).

Kennedy, Paul, *The Rise and Fall of the Great Powers* (New York: Vintage Books, 1989).

Leick, Gwendolyn, *The Babylonians: An Introduction* (New York: Routledge, 2003).

Lennhoff, Eugen, *The Freemasons* (New York: Oxford University Press, 1934).

Livius, Titus, *Early History of Rome* (New York: Penguin, 1991).

Locke, John, *Of Civil Government* (New York: Prometheus, 1986).

Marshall, Peter, and Manuel, David, *The Light and the Glory* (Grand Rapids, MI: Baker Book House, 1977).

Mead, Sidney E., *The Lively Experiment: The Shaping of Christianity in America* (New York: Harper and Row, 1976).

MacFarland, Charles S., ed., *Church Unity at Work* (New York: Federal Council of Churches, 1913).

Machiavelli, Nicolo, *Discourses* (New York, Penguin, 1984).

Mahan, Alfred T., "The United States Looking Outward," *Atlantic Monthly*, LXVI (December, 1890).

Mancham, James R., *War on America Seen from the Indian Ocean* (St. Paul, MN: Paragon House, 2002).

McLoughlin, William G., *Isaac Backus and the American Pietistic Tradition* (Boston: Little, Brown, 1967).

Meltzer, Alan, *A History of the Federal Reserve, Vol. 1: 1913-1951* (Chicago: University of Chicago Press, 2003).

Meyers, Marvin, ed., *The Mind of the Founder: Sources of the Political Thought of James Madison* (Hanover, NH: University Press of New England, 1981).

Miller, Robert Moats, *American Protestantism and Social Issues, 1919-1939* (Chapel Hill, NC: University of North Carolina Press, 1958).

Mitchell, Leonel L., *The Meaning of Ritual* (New York: Paulist Press, 1977).

Molloy, John Fitzgerald, *The Fraternity: Lawyers and Judges in Collusion* (St. Paul: Paragon House, 2004).

Montesquieu, *Spirit of the Laws* (Cambridge, UK: Cambridge University Press, 1989).

Mowinckel, Sigmund, "Psalms at the Enthronement Festival of Yahweh," *The Psalms in Israel's Worship* (Nashville: Abingdon, 1979).

Niebuhr, H. Richard, *The Kingdom of God in America* (New York: Harper & Row, 1959).

Niebuhr, Reinhold, *Faith and Politics,* ed. Ronald H. Stone (New York: George Braziller, 1968).

Niebuhr, Reinhold, *Moral Man and Immoral Society* (New York: Scribner's, 1960).

Niebuhr, Reinhold, *The Nature and Destiny of Man* (New York: Scribner's, 1964).

Nolde, Otto Frederick, *Free and Equal: Human Rights in Ecumenical Perspective* (Geneva: World Council of Churches, 1968).

Palast, Greg, *The Best Democracy Money Can Buy* (New York: Penguin Putnam, 2003).

Richey, Russell E., and Jones, Donald G., eds., *American Civil Religion* (New York: Harper, 1974).

Risse, Guenter B., *Mending Bodies, Saving Souls: A History of Hospitals* (New York: Oxford University Press, 1999).

Rothman, David J., *The Discovery of the Asylum: Social Order and Disorder in the New Republic* (Boston: Little, Brown, 1971).

Sanford, Elias B., *Federal Council of Churches of Christ in America* (New York: Revell Press, 1909).

Sheldon, Charles H. *The Supreme Court: Politicians in Robes* (London: Glencoe Press, 1970).

Shotwell, James T., *Autobiography* (Indianapolis: Bobbs-Merrill, 1961).

Sontag, Frederick and Roth, John K., *The American Religious Experience: The Roots, Trends, and Future of Theology* (New York: Harper and Row, 1972).

Smith, Adam, *The Wealth of Nations* (New York: Bantam, 2003).

Tawney, R.H., *Religion and the Rise of Capitalism* (New York, Harcourt, Brace and World, 1926).

Tillich, Paul, *Love, Power, and Justice* (New York: Oxford University Press, 1980).

Trevor, Albert A., *History of Ancient Civilization* (New York: Harcourt, Brace, 1936).

Voslensky, Michael, *Nomenklatura: The Soviet Ruling Class, An Insider's Report*, trans. Eric Mosbacher (New York: Doubleday, 1984).

Wicker, Elmus, *The Banking Panics of the Great Depression* (New York: Cambridge University Press, 1996).

Wueschner, Silvano A., *Charting Twentieth-Century Monetary Policy: Herbert Hoover and Benjamin Strong, 1917-1927* (Westport, CT: Greenwood Press, 1999).

Zasloff, Jonathan, "Law and the Shaping of American Foreign Policy: The Twenty Years' Crisis" (Los Angeles, CA: UCLA School of Law Research Paper No. 3-06, 2003).

Index